THE RICHEST OF THE RICH

THE WEALTHIEST 250 PEOPLE IN
BRITAIN SINCE 1066

BY

PHILIP BERESFORD
&
WILLIAM D. RUBINSTEIN

PUBLISHED IN ASSOCIATION WITH THE
SOCIAL AFFAIRS UNIT

THE
SOCIAL
AFFAIRS
UNIT

HARRIMAN HOUSE LTD

3A Penns Road
Petersfield
Hampshire
GU32 2EW
GREAT BRITAIN

Tel: +44 (0)1730 233870
Fax: +44 (0)1730 233880
Email: enquiries@harriman-house.com
Website: www.harriman-house.com

First published in Great Britain in 2007
Copyright © Harriman House Ltd

The rights of Philip Beresford and William D. Rubinstein to be identified as Authors
has been asserted in accordance with the Copyright, Design and Patents Act 1988.

ISBN: 1-905641-54-0
ISBN 13: 978-1905641-54-3

Printed and bound by Biddles Ltd, King's Lynn, Norfolk

ABOUT THE AUTHORS

Philip Beresford compiles the annual Rich List for *The Sunday Times*. He was previously editor of *Management Today* and industrial editor of *The Sunday Times* before taking up wealth-tracking full time.

William D. Rubinstein is Professor of History at the University of Wales, Aberystwyth. He writes on a wide variety of topics, including elites and the wealthy in Britain and Australia.

CONTENTS

INTRODUCTION

Britain's richest person of the last Millennium is a Norman lord, who fought at the Battle of Hastings and was rewarded with lands and estates that in modern terms would be worth over £81bn. Surprisingly, in a savage period of British history where life was cheap even for the aristocracy, Alan Rufus actually managed to die a peaceful death with his fortune intact in 1093. Britain's all-time rich list is dominated by wealth from Norman times. Four of our top six – led by Rufus – came with the Norman Conquest, reflecting the rewards handed on by the Conqueror to his allies for their part in the 1066 invasion and the subsequent pacification of the North and Wales.

Alan Rufus heads *The Richest of the Rich*: a comprehensive study of Britain's 250 richest people in history, from the time of William the Conqueror to the present. To present a level playing field, we have take the individual's share of the net national income (NNI) when they died and expressed it in today's terms as a percentage of the £1,065bn gross domestic product.

As a result, the figures are huge. The total wealth of the 250 – all billionaires in today's money – is a staggering £2,279,104bn. The minimum figure required to enter the immortal rich list is over £2.5bn in today's terms. Alan Rufus is over four times richer than Lakshmi Mittal, the richest living person in the list with a £19bn fortune. In fact, so dominated is the list by early and medieval figures, that only eighteen of the current crop of British or British-based billionaires make it here, including the Duke of Westminster and Sir Richard Branson.

Nine of the seventeen current billionaires are non-British by birth. Some are tycoons who have made their fortunes abroad, such as Mittal or Roman Abramovich, the Russian-born owner of Chelsea Football Club. They find London a congenial place to live and work, not least because of the relaxed tax regime they enjoy which only taxes their income here and not their vast overseas wealth. This has become a source of great political controversy in recent times, though there is as yet no indication that the Labour government will abolish the tax regime for them. Then there are the foreign-born tycoons who have become British citizens or actually made their fortunes here, such as Iraqi-born Nadhmi Auchi or property tycoon Simon Halabi.

Finally, we have some traditional British fortunes in the shape of Earl Cadogan, whose ownership of 100 acres of booming Chelsea has pushed the family fortune to £2.61bn. Even much maligned British industry has thrown up James Ratcliffe, a self-made chemicals tycoon who is building a new ICI and a £3.3bn fortune to boot.

Yet the most striking impression made by the list is the extent to which it is dominated by wealthy persons from the Middle Ages and the early modern periods, how few of the wealthiest ever persons made their fortunes since the Industrial Revolution, let alone since the Second World War.

Right up to the early Middle Ages, the monarch in effect 'owned' the whole country and could give it away to favourites. In addition, the Jews who came with William the Conqueror as official moneylenders and tax collectors were legally the property of the king and all their revenues could be confiscated by him. Christians were not allowed to lend money at interest. This continue until the Jews were expelled in 1290. This development came as parliament was securing some rights and a nascent middle class was developing.

Indeed, London was a flourishing commercial centre by the time of the election of its first mayor in around 1193 (Ken Livingstone please note), and the City of London had a semi-independent status. In the first half of the thirteenth century, eight intermarried mercantile families produced some 45 alderman for the city. A long period of political battle with the monarchy ensued but after 1327, the City ceased to be subject to direct royal interference. The later rise of City guilds and merchant companies provided the economic muscle for the middle class to later challenge royal and aristocratic political privilege. It is no surprise that 79 of the top 250 richest Britons of all time are drawn from the financial and mercantile sectors, mainly from the late Middle Ages onwards.

Strong economic growth in the late thirteenth and early fourteenth centuries was interrupted by the Black Death, which began near the Caspian Sea in 1343, and reached England in mid 1348. It was particularly virulent in 1349, and up to 50% of the English population died as a result. Almost 1,000 villages were completely wiped out and the English economy did not fully recover until after 1400, which is why wealth figures for the 1350-1410 period are lower than for the previous era.

During the Wars of the Roses and the resulting turmoil that engulfed England in the fifteenth century, the monarchs enriched themselves and their relatives from office holding, taxes and other revenues, but were increasingly checked by parliament. Later Henry VIII was able to secure some valuable additional revenue from the dissolution of the Monasteries from 1518 to 1547. In 1518, there were over 600 religious establishments in England and Wales, supporting over 40,000 monks, nuns and lay people.

Their estimated income was £136,000 a year and they owned 2m acres, which was around 20% of the total cultivated land area. Over the next 25 years, the land of the churches, their buildings and property were sold off to great secular landowners such as the Russells (hence the Duke of Bedford now resides at Woburn Abbey).

Mercantile wealth was given a huge boost with the formation of joint stock companies chartered by parliament. These enjoyed a monopoly of trade with a particular area and were owned by their stockholders who bought and sold shares. The Russia Company was the first to be chartered in 1555, and it enjoyed a monopoly of the lucrative trade (in skins, tallows, minerals, etc.) with Russia, especially via the Baltic. Others followed: the Levant Company (1581), the East India Company (originally a Regulated Company, founded in 1600, but then chartered as a joint stock company in 1657), the Virginia Company (1606), the Hudson's Bay Company (1670) the Royal African Company (1672) and the South Sea Company (1710).

Many of the richest Elizabethan merchants were connected with one or another of these companies. During the Elizabethan period, there was enormous price inflation, with wheat prices quadrupling between 1540 and 1575. In general this actually helped the British economy and Britain's rise to world prominence. The scale of business fortunes also rose sharply at the time, with several in the £100,000 to £500,000 range by the time of James I.

The stage was thus set for the showdown between the increasingly confident and prosperous mercantile class and a monarchy bent on maintaining its political power. Victory for parliament in the Civil War marked the real end of the monarch's absolute economic as well as political power. In 1698, parliament voted William III a Civil List of around £700,000 a year, raised from the monarch's hereditary revenues to cover civil government, the royal household and the royal lifestyle.

In 1760, parliament's grip on the royal purse strings was tightened further when George III was guaranteed £800,000 a year in exchange for surrendering most of his hereditary revenues from the Crown Estate. In the late eighteenth century, much of the Civil List was actually used by the government for election expenses. By the time of Victoria, the private income of the monarchy outside the Crown Estate was quite small. In 1883, her private land yielded an income of only £5,561 according to Bateman in his book *The Great Landowners of Great Britain and Ireland* (1883). This important work, listing how much all large landowners owned based upon parliamentary returns, stated that the queen then owned 27,441 acres, mainly in Aberdeenshire, worth £5,561 p.a., a fraction of what a duke might own. Of course the queen and the royal family received a very large annual income from the Civil List, but this was voted to them by parliament.

But as royal wealth declined, so the start of the Industrial Revolution in the eighteenth century marked the rise of a new business and industrial class. Canals, textiles, iron, steel, and above all coal produced some huge fortunes which are well represented in the list of the 250 richest Britons of all time. There are 27 in various areas of industry and transport. Depressing though is the comparison with America. Whereas the 40 richest Americans of all time, produced by *Forbes* magazine in 1999, has four current billionaires led by Gates in the new technology sector of software and high technology, there are no past or current Britons in these sunrise industries. Sir Richard Branson is making a tilt in that direction but is not really there yet. For the sake of all our prosperity, let's hope he makes it.

For the past 350 years, wealth has had to have been earned (or inherited) by some more or less legitimate means. In the distant past, however, kings were free to hand out vast estates to their favourites and relatives. They often came to a violent end and indeed of the 250 in the list, 29 died a violent death. Of these: thirteen were executed, six died in battle, eight were murdered, one died of starvation while hidden in a priest hole, and another in an accident. The last to die violently was the Earl of Stafford, whose execution in 1641 came just before the Civil War. In addition, until the late eighteenth century high office holding (including the holding of bishoprics and other ecclesiastical offices) often led to the accumulation of vast wealth far in excess of the salaries of these offices, high as they were. Often this income generated on the side came from means which would now universally be termed corrupt. Such sources of wealth have largely vanished during the past two hundred years.

The list points to a virtual straight-line diminution in the relative size of the largest fortunes in British history between the Middle Ages and the present. This appears to be in direct contradiction to two of the best-known theories of income distribution, those of Karl Marx and Simon Kuznets. Marx, of course, argued that wealth would increasingly be concentrated in fewer and fewer hands. There is no evidence whatsoever from this list that Marx's views are true. Kuznets, a Nobel Prize winning American economist, in an influential paper written in 1955, put forward the view that income became more concentrated as a result of the industrial revolution, with its super-rich industrialists, and has become more widely distributed in the twentieth century. Again, there would appear to be no evidence from the statistics and approach used here to support the view: top wealth-holders created by the Industrial Revolution were simply not as rich, in relative terms, as those of pre-industrial times.

Another striking feature of this list is the "conservative" nature of top fortunes, with land-owning and inherited wealth forming the basis of a very large share of these fortunes into the twentieth century. We reckon that 146 of our 250 inherited their wealth, which is almost exactly inverse of the ratio in recent *Sunday Times* rich lists. Looking to the basis of the fortunes, land ownership and property provides the basis for 122 of the 250.

At all times, it was generally easy for very wealthy persons to acquire titles and to move into, marry into, or have their children marry into the old aristocracy. The British aristocracy has been unique in its remarkable ability to absorb "new money", which is one secret of why it has lasted so long. Though the ages, there have always been a trickle of very wealthy women, but the list is overwhelmingly male (244 out of 250). Fortunes earned in the Empire were significant, but not as important as some historians believe. Indeed, it appears that the only real overseas fortunes came from the East India Company officials as who simply looted the treasuries they controlled and repatriated their wealth back to Britain.

The idea of a North-South divide is nothing new as the list shows. Just as recent *Sunday Times* Rich Lists show, London and the South East remain the dominant bases for current fortunes; 136 of the 250 here either lived in London and the South East, made their money there or bought up estates in the area. Dare one suggest that the current fashion for well-heeled young bankers flush with City bonuses to buy up large Home Counties estates is merely history repeating itself – as ever.

We have not included any reigning monarchs in the list, although we have included their close relatives when their wealth warranted it. During the Middle Ages and down to Tudor times or later, the Sovereign could effectively dispose of much of the country, meeting resistance by removing heads. It makes little sense to ask what William the Conqueror was worth, therefore. From the seventeenth century, Sovereigns were doubtless always very wealthy, but necessarily received most of their immediate income from parliamentary grants. Today, the personal property of the queen is certainly much less than what the semi-public wealth actually is, which is often included in estimates of her personal fortune (such as the Royal Art Collection).

Writing this book raised two immediate questions: how does one choose the names, and how does one compare wealth many centuries ago with wealth in more recent times and today? Before the early nineteenth century, there is simply no easy way to draw up a comprehensive list of Britain's wealthiest persons. There were no official lists or comprehensive taxation records. In the Middle Ages, the cash economy was probably not universal and some forms of wealth included the personal service of knights and the like. For the period until the beginning of the nineteenth century, our list was compiled from a very wide variety of biographical sources, most of which are mentioned in the "Rules of Engagement" in the Appendices.

Given the lack of comprehensive sources which identify the very rich, it seems almost certain that we have missed some of the very wealthiest persons. On the other hand, it will be seen how widely we have trawled, and it seems unlikely to us that we have omitted anyone who was astronomically wealthy in the context of their time.

From the early nineteenth century (precisely, from 1809), much more accurate information exists about the names and wealth of the very rich. From then, the probate records provide comprehensive information about wealth at death, bearing in mind that during the nineteenth century the valuation figures excluded land (which we have added in to arrive at our figures for nineteenth century wealth holders), and that estate duty avoidance obviously diminishes the value of these figures during most of the twentieth century.

Comparing wealth hundreds of years ago with wealth in the recent past plainly raises many difficult questions. What we have done is to compare the wealth of every individual in our study with estimated Net National Income (NNI) at that time, derived from a variety of academic studies. NNI figures are estimates, and, especially for the very distant past, rough estimates, but they are accurate in a broad sense.

It should be noted that we are strictly speaking, comparing different things here – wealth and income – but we have assumed that there is a relatively fixed ratio between national income and national wealth (which is much more difficult to define or measure). One advantage of comparing individual wealth with NNI is that one can arrive at an approximate percentage of how much of the national "cake" Britain's richest men and women owned through the ages.

There are striking patterns here. Apart from comparing wealth to NNI, the only other plausible basis for long-term comparisons is to use an inflation-based index. This would probably lead to broadly similar conclusions, but would not necessarily catch the effects of the ever-increasing British national income on the relative wealth of the wealthiest. So read on.

THE RICH LIST

Alan Rufus

(d 1093)
Land
Wealth: £11,000
Net National Income: £150,000
% of NNI: 7.33%

£81.331 billion

Alan Rufus was a man born in the right time and place. The second of at least seven legitimate sons of Count Eudo, regent of Brittany from 1040 to 1047, and Orguen, or Agnes, his Angevin wife. Alan was called Rufus ('the Red') to distinguish him from a younger brother, Alan Niger ('the Black'). His father, Eudo, was a brother of the Breton duke Alan III; the mother of Eudo and Alan III was an aunt of William the Conqueror. He was probably recruited into the service of his second cousin William of Normandy before the 1066 invasion.

A Breton contingent, probably including Rufus and another of his brother's, Brien, played an important role at the Battle of Hastings and settled in England thereafter. After helping to defeat an attack on Exeter by the sons of Harold in 1069, Brien apparently returned to Brittany, leaving Rufus as indisputably the most senior of the Bretons in England. He then proved his loyalty to William between 1069 and 1072, by helping to crush a rebellion in the north of England. The brutal suppression of the rebellion, known as the Harrying of the North, led to the loss of 150,000 lives and the ensuing scorched earth policy reduced survivors to cannibalism.

Rufus already held a great deal of land in Cambridgeshire, Suffolk, and Norfolk and was rewarded with land in Yorkshire and Lincolnshire, extending to Northampton and

London. His position was then further enhanced by the fall of Ralph de Gael in 1075, much of whose forfeited land in East Anglia he acquired.

Rufus became Earl of Richmond and built Richmond Castle to police the remaining local populace. By 1086, he was one of the richest and most powerful men in England and remained close to William I, accompanying him to Normandy and Maine on several occasions after 1066. He died in 1093 and was succeeded by his brother, Alan Niger.

His huge land holdings gave him an annual income of around £1,100 a year, and a fortune at his death of around £11,000. That was around 7.33% of the net national income (NNI) of £150,000 at the time. If he had an equivalent percentage of today's NNI, Rufus would be worth the staggering sum of £81.3bn, making him easily the richest Briton of all time.

William Of Warenne

(d 1088)
Land
Wealth: £10,000
Net National Income: £150,000
% of NNI: 6.66%

£73.923 billion

Conspicuous loyalty to William the Conqueror made William of Warenne one of the richest men in one of the richest kingdoms in Europe. The younger son of Rudolf of Varenne in Normandy, Warenne entered ducal service under the then William of Normandy in the early 1050s as a very young man. He distinguished himself at the Battle of Mortemer in 1054, and was granted estates in upper Normandy, but it was the invasion of England in 1066 that set him on the path to huge wealth. He fought at the Battle of Hastings and was rewarded with lands which within twenty years extended into thirteen counties, most notably strategically important estates in Sussex centred around Lewes.

Through the early period of the Norman conquest, he showed his support for the Crown by playing a leading role in suppressing a revolt by the Earls of Hereford and Norfolk. Life became more difficult after William the Conqueror died and Warenne supported William Rufus in his claim to the throne against Robert Curthouse and Odo of Bayeux. Warenne was rewarded with the title Earl of Surrey in 1088, but did not live long to enjoy it. He was seriously wounded that same year in the Siege of Pevensey by an arrow in his leg and died at Lewes Priory, which he had founded.

His dynasty survived as the Earls of Surrey until 1347, and played an influential role in public life until their demise.

Figures on land values and national income at the time are sketchy but we estimate that Warenne's land holdings would have been worth around £10,000 of a £150,000 net national income figure of the day. In today's money, 6.6% of the British gross domestic product would be nearly £74bn, a colossal fortune indeed.

The Earl Of Arundel and Warenne

(c 1307-1376)
Land
Wealth: £150,000
Net National Income: £2.8m
% of NNI: 5.35%

£59.382 billion

Though his father was executed in 1326, it was not until 1330 that the Earl of Arundel succeeded to his title and later to the greater part of his estates. He proved to be one of Edward III's most loyal generals, taking part in virtually every important campaign on the Continent. War proved to be a profitable operation for Arundel, as K.B. McFarlane noted in *The Nobility of Later Medieval England*:

Edward III's companions had reason enough to be content with his policy of aggression. It is impossible to say how much Arundel had multiplied his capital by skillful investment, but its original source was almost certainly the war. He was not the only baron to turn moneylender.

Arundel's wealth was also increased substantially after 1353, when he succeeded, by right of his mother, to the earldom of Warenne (or Surrey), and by 1370, Edward III was more than £20,000 in his debt.

For all his warlike exploits on behalf of the king, Arundel died peacefully. A remarkable inventory of his assets was made including a huge hoard of gold, silver and bullion stored in the high tower at Arundel, worth around £30,000 at current values. A further £20,000 was stored in London for him by his agent, John Philpot, and another £10,000 on the family estate in the Welsh March. He was also owed some £4,500 in outstanding loans. But as the inventory did not run to his land holdings, his personal wardrobe, his jewels or the furnishing of his castles and homes, a wealth valuation of perhaps £150,000 is appropriate. That would have represented around 5.35% of the £2.8m national income figure at his death, which in today's terms would be over £59.3bn.

Robert Of Mortain

(c 1031-1090)
Land
Wealth: £8,000
Net National Income: £150,000
% of NNI: 5.33%

£59.155 billion

The half brother of William the Conqueror, Robert was created Count of Mortain in south-west Normandy around 1055. He later played a leading role in the 1066 invasion of England and its subsequent pacification until 1069, proving himself to be an effective military leader. Robert is depicted on the Bayeux Tapestry advising William on strategy after the landings. His reward was immense. Within twenty years of the Conquest, he had 800 manors all over Britain from Sussex to Yorkshire in the north and out to Cornwall in the west.

While his lands were valued at around £2,500 at prevailing prices, his total wealth is put at around £8,000, or over 5.3% of net national income (£59.1bn in today's GDP). However, Robert's wealth did not save him when William the Conqueror died. He rebelled against the Crown going to William Rufus and withstood the six-week siege at Pevensey (where William of Warenne was fatally wounded), but after his submission to William Rufus, he was pardoned and withdrew to Normandy where, surprisingly, he died peacefully in 1090.

The Earl Of Arundel and Surrey

(1346-1397)
Land
Wealth: £150,000
Net National Income: £3m
% of NNI: 5%

£55.498 billion

Succeeding his father to the title and huge family wealth in 1376, Arundel was appointed Admiral of the West in 1377, at the ripe old age of 31. His early naval exploits were not covered with glory. Though he saved Southampton from a French assault, he was driven off Harfleur and later defeated by a Spanish fleet. On land, he had equally little success: negligence on watch gave the French the chance to raise the Siege of St. Malo when they destroyed a mine. And he was equally sluggish in defending his tenants against French raids on the Sussex coast.

Fortunately, his military fortunes improved in the 1380s. In the spring of 1387, he prepared an expedition against the French, which defeated a large alliance of Flemish, French and Spanish ships off Margate. A hundred ships filled with wine were captured. Arundel's popularity at home soared when he refused to profit from the huge haul (he hardly needed the money), and as a results, wine was cheap in Britain for a year.

Immediately after that battle he sailed to Brest, revictualed the town, which was still held by the British, destroyed French forts, and returned to England in triumph plundering the French countryside and ships on the way. Back home, he entered into intrigue against Richard II, and became the king's fiercest enemy. A brief spell fighting the French again resulted in great pillaging around La Rochelle.

Through the early 1390s, an uneasy peace prevailed between Arundel and the king – though he was briefly imprisoned in the Tower for arriving late for the queen's funeral – but in 1397, Arundel moved to open rebellion against the Crown. The conspiracy was betrayed by his son-in-law, the Earl of Nottingham. Richard II then reneged on a deal to respect Arundel's safety if he surrendered, and had him arrested and sent to the Tower. Arundel was quickly tried and condemned for treason, but Richard commuted the terrible punishment for treason to a simple decapitation. The execution followed swiftly with Arundel exhorting the executioner to 'sharpen well his axe'. Bands of Cheshiremen had been gathered at the Tower Hill execution site to overawe any Londoners who might have been sympathetic to Arundel. Richard, fearful that he would become a martyr, ordered all traces of Arundel's burial to be removed.

Arundel's wealth would have been much the same as his father's at £150,000, but with a higher national income at his death, his share had fallen to perhaps 5%, making him worth over £55.4bn at today's prices.

Odo Of Bayeux

(c 1030-1097)
Land
Wealth: £7,500
Net National Income: £150,000
% of NNI: 5%

£55.498 billion

Half-brother to William the Conqueror, Odo was one of the most powerful men in Britain after the 1066 invasion. His wealth arose from his royal connection, and he was piling up his asset wealth even before the invasion. William made him Bishop of the immensely lucrative see of Bayeux while Odo was still a teenager. He played an active part in William's invasion and subsequent conquest of Britain and was generously rewarded with the earldom of Kent and vast English estates, which were worth over £3,000 a year by the 1080s.

Odo increased his wealth by settling land disputes for a price, and he acquired an unsavoury reputation for luxury, vice and cruelty but proved to be an efficient military commander, helping William to pacify the north of England.

In the twenty years after the Conquest, Odo also managed to increase the yield on his land holdings by around 40%, which would have increased his wealth substantially. We estimate that his total wealth would have been around £7,500, representing 5% of net national income. In today's terms, that would have been a chunky £55.4bn fortune, but it did not save Odo from an ignominious end.

His position depended on good relations with the king, yet in 1082, William decided to destroy his brother. Odo was arrested and imprisoned in Rouen. He was restored by

William Rufus, but made the mistake of joining the rebellion by the 'old guard' against the new king. Their defeat led to the confiscation of Odo's English lands. He spent his last years at Bayeux but died in Sicily in 1097, on his way to the First Crusade.

John Of Gaunt, The Duke Of Lancaster

(1340-1399)
Land
Wealth: £150,000
Net National Income: £3m
% of NNI: 5%

£55.498 billion

The greatest noble in late medieval England, John of Gaunt, the Duke of Lancaster, was the third son of Edward III. He married well and his wife, Blanche, bought with her a huge Lancaster inheritance. John was created Duke of Lancaster in 1362, at the age of 22. After Blanche's death, he married the daughter of the King of Castile in Spain.

Though not renowned as a military leader, John of Gaunt campaigned on the Continent for the king. He proved to be an effective diplomat and, in an increasingly troubled England in the late fourteenth century, a force for stability.

His wealth – put at around £150,000 – represented about 5% of national income (some £55.4bn in today's money). It also enabled him to keep about 200 retainers who dominated local commissions and local government, where they, too, were a force for peace and stability. Surprisingly for such a turbulent period, he died peacefully in 1399.

The Duke Of Lancaster

(1299-1361)
Land
Wealth: £100,000
Net National Income: £2.6m
% of NNI: 3.84%

£42.622 billion

Henry of Grossmont, later the first Duke of Lancaster, was Edward II's right-hand man in the opening phase of the Hundred Years' War, serving as soldier diplomat and administrator. He took part in fifteen expeditions against the Scots and on the Continent. When not fighting for the king, he was on crusades or headed diplomatic missions.

His wealth stemmed from the four earldoms and estates in 26 counties, inherited from his father, the Earl of Lancaster, which yielded an income of around £8,380 a year. His successful campaigns in France also resulted in huge hauls of booty and valuable estates. In one town, for example, he was granted the right to coinage, and in another area the monopoly over salt.

So important was Lancaster to the king that he was created a duke in 1351, only the second English duke after the Black Prince. He was granted Lancashire as a palatinate at a time when other similar 'franchises' were being curbed. His vast wealth was matched by huge spending on everything, ranging from buildings to charity work and retainers. Lancaster was not above ruthlessly increasing his wealth by force, seizing property he liked and removing any obstacles in his path.

But for all his wealth and power, he failed to produce a male heir to carry on his line. He died in 1361, and his wealth went to his surviving daughter, Blanche, who passed on the family wealth to her husband, John of Gaunt (q.v.), who also took the dukedom. Lancaster left a a sizeable fortune of around £100,000, representing over 3.8% of the net national income figure. In today's money that is an awesome £42.6bn.

Edward, The Black Prince

(1330-1376)
Land
Wealth: £85,000
Net National Income: £2.7m
% of NNI: 3.14%

£34.852 billion

The eldest son of Edward III, Edward, known as the Black Prince, was created Earl of Chester in 1333, Duke of Cornwall in 1337, and Prince of Wales in 1343. Together, these titles gave him an annual income of £8,600.

A brilliant commander in the Hundred Years' War, he distinguished himself at the Battle of Crecy in 1346, at the age of 16. Ten years later, he crushed the French at Poitiers, capturing their king in the process. Further wealth came when he was appointed Prince of Aquitaine in 1362, and through his marriage to the heiress Joan of Kent.

Though regarded as a charismatic and inspirational leader, the Black Prince died an invalid in England at the early age of 46. He had intervened in Spanish affairs, defeating a leading Spanish commander in 1367, and restoring the King of Castile to his throne, but caught an infection that progressively incapacitated him.

His £85,000 fortune at his death – over 3% of national income – would be worth at least £34.8bn today.

The Earl Of Warwick

(1382-1439)
Land
Wealth: £100,000
Net National Income: £3.3m
% of NNI: 3.03%

£33.631 billion

An outstanding soldier of his day, the Earl of Warwick came from a line which had dominated the West Midlands since 1268. He augmented his considerable family fortune by marrying two heiresses. His first wife, Elizabeth Berkeley, did not produce a male heir, so he remarried, this time to the widowed Isabel Despencer, and produced a son.

Warwick maintained a large retinue and a fine household, whilst also developing the local economy of Warwick and making the River Avon navigable. He fought in many campaigns from the age of 21 to within a couple of years of his death through ill-health in 1439.

His son, who inherited the title and lands, died before he could produce a male heir. The Beauchamp line died but the earldom passed to his brother-in-law, Richard Neville, who became the most famous Warwick of all. Known as 'Warwick the Kingmaker', he lived from 1428 until his death at the Battle of Barnet in 1471.

Warwick's inheritance, supplemented by the fortunes from his two wives, gave him an annual income of over £5,000 a year. In all, his asset wealth was in the order of £100,000, over 3% of the national income of the day. In today's money that would be £33.6bn.

The Earl Of Arundel

(1381-1415)
Land
Wealth: £80,000
Net National Income: £3m
% of NNI: 2.66%

£29.52 billion

At the age of 16, Arundel's father was executed by Richard II. He was deprived of his title and inheritance, and was to spend his early years as a virtual slave in the custody of the Duke of Exeter and later under Exeter's steward. Arundel effected his escape to the Continent, where he would have starved but for the help of relatives abroad. He allied himself to the future Henry IV and landed with him in England in 1399. When Henry overthrew Richard, Arundel had his revenge on the steward who had imprisoned him: Ignoring a royal command that the man should be imprisoned in the Tower, Arundel had him executed and carried the unfortunate's head on a pole in triumph through the streets of London.

Though his lands were restored by the new king, Arundel's Welsh estates particularly had been devastated by war. But he effected a good marriage to a daughter of the King of Portugal, which was important in cementing the close alliance of the two countries and Henry IV advanced Arundel the large sums necessary to bring his bride to Britain 'with magnificence and glory'. The marriage will also have helped bolster Arundel's finances.

By the time of his death from dysentery in 1415, after campaigning in France, the £150,000 fortune of his father had nearly been halved to around £80,000, or about 2.66% of national income (£29.5bn in today's terms).

Aaron Of Lincoln

(d 1186)
Finance
Wealth: £25,000
Net National Income: £1m
% of NNI: 2.5%

£27.749 billion

The leading banker in twelfth century Britain, Aaron was a prominent member of the Jewish community that had established itself in Britain during the second half of the century. There were tight restrictions on Jewish commercial and civil rights at the time, but Aaron proved to be simply indispensable to the Crown and the landed classes.

When he died, in the 1185/86 period, his property and outstanding loans owed to him went to the Crown. The debts owing were so great that a special government office, called Aaron's Exchequer, was established to chase them up. He had clients in 25 countries, including kings, archbishops, and nine Cistercian abbeys, who together owed him a total of 6,500 marks. The government office took twenty years to finish its work.

As well as lending money, Aaron helped arrange finance to build Lincoln Cathedral and two abbeys. He prospered because of the lack of liquidity in a land-based economy, which enabled interest rates of up to 60% to be charged.

His overall wealth would have been around £25,000 at the time of his death, some 2.5% of national income, or £27.7bn in today's money.

Archbishop Thomas Becket

(c 1120-1170)
Church
Wealth: £20,000
Net National Income: £900,000
% of NNI: 2.22%

£24.641 billion

There are few deaths in English history, apart from that of Diana, Princess of Wales, that are as well chronicled as that of Thomas Becket, the Archbishop of Canterbury in 1170. He was murdered in his own cathedral on the 29 December 1170 on the orders, however indirect, of King Henry II. There were five people in the cathedral as he was hacked to pieces by the king's men. Such was the flood of miracles that followed his assassination that he was canonised a saint just three years later and for three and a half centuries afterwards, until the time of the reformation, the tourist trade at Canterbury benefited as pilgrims flocked from all over the world to kneel at the shrine of St. Thomas.

The picture left with us is that of a saintly priest opposing a dangerous king. In fact, Thomas Becket was worldly-wise indeed. Prior to becoming the Archbishop of Canterbury, he had been the young king's confidante and the Chancellor of England. He was also a knight who fought a number of battles on the king's behalf, in France and elsewhere. But most of all he was the supreme money man of his time. Through his friendship with the king and during his period as Chancellor he amassed a fortune, requiring 52 clerks to run his affairs.

Becket also had a military entourage of 700 knights, the equivalent of a modern army division. When he went to visit Paris once, he took with him 250 servants and paid the equivalent of £20,000 for a plate of eels. Most of this arose from the custody he maintained over vacant bishoprics, manors and so on, all granted to him by the king. In 1164, the king accused him of having made £30,000 out of this, although this was probably an exaggeration.

We go for the lower figure of £20,000, representing 2.22% of net national income of £900,000. This makes him worth about £24.6bn in modern money.

Bishop Ranulf Flambard

(1060-1128)
Church
Wealth: £5,000
Net National Income: £250,000
% of NNI: 2%

£22.19 billion

This royal favourite of his time had an unusual end. He lived to be 68 years old, more than double the normal lifespan of the times, and died a natural death in his own bed. Those two facts aside, he is one of the most extraordinary though least known figures in English history. According to the historian, Southern:

The great line of administrators who fashioned and finally destroyed the medieval system of government in England begins with Flambard.

The son of a poor priest in Bayeux, Flambard attached himself to Odo of Bayeux (q.v.) and after the Conquest became chaplain to the Conqueror. But it was under William's successor, William Rufus, that he made his name and fortune.

From his position as the king's chaplain he enforced royal writs, usually relating to fines, penalties or confiscation. He became a leading legal expert and administrator, the de facto enforcer for at least three chancellors. Flambard's main task was simply to impose Norman rule by fining and penalising the conquered out of their lands. He was accused by one chronicler of going around measuring England with a rope so he could impose taxes. A self-made man, Flambard built his fortune by taking a cut on all of the exactions he made and used the money to buy lands and make loans.

When he fell out of royal favour on the death of William Rufus in 1100, he again used a rope, this time to escape from the Tower of London. He then married off his wife to a rich farmer and bought himself the Bishopric of Durham, with its vast revenues and power, for £1,000. His attempted seduction and rape of his wife's niece, Theodora, in 1114 led her to become one of England's most famous hermits, Christina of Markyate.

By the time Flambard died in 1128, he was worth £5,000. This represented about 2% of national income: in today's money that would be over £22bn.

The Duke Of Gloucester

(1335-1397)
Land
Wealth: £60,000
Net National Income: £3m
% of NNI: 2%

£22.19 billion

The Duke of Gloucester's life was one long intrigue which eventually proved fatal, against his nephew Richard II. The son of a he was born rich, married even richer and, given the nature of the times, was murdered by royal courtiers, who thought they had acted for the king until he caught and executed them.

To understand this Duke of Gloucester one has to know the Plantagenets. They were the royal house of England between 1154 and 1455, and descendants of the Empress Maud and her second husband, Geoffrey Plantagenet, Count of Anjou. One of the most important Plantagenets, and one of the founders of the family wealth was Thomas of Woodstock, the seventh son of Edward III, the 7th Plantagenet King. As the son of the king he had all sorts of minor wealth, but his father saw to it that in one step, that of marriage, he became one of the richest men in the Kingdom.

It was the Sovereign's prerogative in those days to dispose of estates and their female owners where there was no male heir. One of the greatest of all estates arising from the Conquest, next only to that of Odo of Bayeux, was that of Bohun. In 1374, when he was 20, Edward affianced his son to Elinor, one of two daughters of the last Bohun. By 1380, Thomas had charge of his wife's estates and also those of her sister. In 1377, he carried the sceptre at the coronation of his nephew,

Richard II, who eventually made him Duke of Gloucester. He spent most of the years between 1385 and 1388 either conspiring against the king or actually holding him de facto captive. But he paid the price. In 1397, he was personally arrested by his nephew at his Essex castle and transported to Calais where he was found dead some days later.

His huge lands and possessions were worth £60,000 at his death and came to 2.0% of net national income, which at the time was £3m. His nephew confiscated all his lands, but that merely meant that one Plantagenet took from another to redistribute to yet a third Plantagenet. All the lands were back in the hands of Gloucester's descendants within a few years.

Area breakdown of the 250 fortunes

Area	Number
South East and London	136
South West	26
Midlands	17
Yorkshire	15
North West	13
Ireland	9
Wales	9
North East	8
Overseas	6
Scotland	6
East Anglia	5

Sir Robert Knollys

(c 1317-1407)
Land
Wealth: £60,000
Net National Income: £3m
% of NNI: 2%

£22.19 billion

Born around 1317, probably in Cheshire, Knollys was the premier soldier of his age who achieved 'regal wealth' by the relatively simple means of murder, rape, extortion and finally pillage on a grand scale.

A contemporary of Edward III and John of Gaunt, he regularly fought with them in France, which was the main arena for his military operations. Writing of one of the campaigns, the *Dictionary of National Biography* reports:

The English supported themselves by plunder and the country people fled before them into the fortresses. Knollys, whose policy was to do as much damage as possible, did not attempt any sieges and contented himself with the exaction of heavy ransoms.

When Knollys' main fortress at Derval in Brittany was besieged he broke the terms of a surrender and his own hostages were executed by the French. He promptly retaliated by beheading his French prisoners and throwing their bodies over the wall of the city to the French who then lifted the siege.

He lent the equivalent of millions to the king, secured on royal plate and royal jewels, but he was also the persistent beneficiary of kingly rewards, including the manor of what is now St. Pancras in London, given to him by the City fathers in London after he saved them from a riot by beheading the ringleaders. His plunder from France enabled him to amass huge estates in Norfolk, Wiltshire, Kent and London.

He died, peacefully at home, worth £60,000 in 1407, when net national income was around £3m. In modern terms he was worth about £17.3bn. He had no heirs and his will, still extant, dispersed his fortune, which would be worth a staggering £22.1bn in today's money.

The Duke Of Sutherland

(1758-1833)
Land
Wealth: £7m
Net National Income: £362m
% of NNI: 1.93%

£21.421 billion

At the age of 32, the Duke of Sutherland was appointed British ambassador to France. It was 1790, and the young English aristocrat would have had a close view of the revolution until his departure in 1792. Indeed his wife, on returning to Britain, was brought before the revolutionary tribunal at Abbeville, and detained for a short time.

The experience must have been terrifying for an obviously aristocratic family. And few were more aristocratic or wealthy than Sutherland and his wife (they were married in 1785). She was the Countess of Sutherland in her own right and owned most of the far northern Scottish county. In 1803, he inherited from his maternal uncle, the last Duke of Bridgewater, the Bridgewater Canal and estates, and from his father, the Marquess of Stafford, estates in Yorkshire, Staffordshire Wolverhampton and Shropshire. With these land holdings, he was described by a contemporary chronicler as a 'leviathan of wealth'.

After 1807, Sutherland took little part in active politics and devoted himself to the patronage of art and his estates. His wealth came in useful, allowing him to build up a large art collection. He spent over £72,000 buying Stafford House in London and gave it to his son along with an additional £30,000 with which to complete the building work. Sutherand had previously given his son an estate worth £25,000 a year in rent.

Sutherland spent the early 1800s improving his Midland estates and it was not until 1812 that he turned his attention to Sutherland. A government-supported scheme to improve communications to the far North was backed by Sutherland and he matched the government spending pound for pound. In twenty years, he built 450 miles of roads and 134 bridges, but his name is forever linked to the Highland clearances. He did clear thousands of peasants from the interior of his estates, breaking up the clan system in the process. Tales of ruthless evictions abounded but contemporary chroniclers reckoned these were exaggerated. Certainly, he reduced rents, improved conditions locally and brought many thousands of acres under cultivation.

A liberal in politics (despite having witnessed the French Revolution), Sutherland supported the 1832 Reform Bill, and invested heavily in railways and canals. He was actually raised to the dukedom early in 1833, just months before his death in Sutherland.

His personal wealth was valued at over £1m at the Prerogative Court of Canterbury, with smaller amounts being assessed at York and Scotland. In all, with the family estates, he was easily worth £7m and possibly as much as £10m. At the lower figure, his wealth would have been around 1.9% of national income, or £21.4bn in today's money.

Sir John Spencer

(d 1610)
Merchant
Wealth: £500,000
Net National Income: £26m
% of NNI: 1.92%

£21.311 billion

Sir John Spencer was a London merchant who amassed so much money that he outshone the aristocracy with its inherited wealth. Spencer, the son of a country squire from Waldingfield in Suffolk, moved to London and started out in the cloth trade, joining the Clothmakers' Company. By 1570, his trade with Spain, potentially an aggressor against England, was so enormous that the State papers record the matter. But he was also the largest London trader with Turkey and Venice and was later accused of monopolising the trade with Tripoli.

He was so rich that pirates in Dunkirk came all the way to Canonbury in London to kidnap him for ransom, but they failed. He was friendly with Elizabeth I, who visited him at Canonbury, possibly because he provided foreign intelligence for her spy master, Walshingham, or lent her money, or both. His daughter married Lord Compton, later the Earl of Northampton, having been smuggled out of her father's house in a laundry basket by her fiancé.

A miser, Sir John 'Rich' Spencer died leaving between £500,000 and £800,000 in 1610, none of it for charitable purposes. At the time, net national income was £26m and his wealth was 1.92% of that figure. In modern times he would have been worth £21.3bn.

James Craggs

(c 1657-1721)
Finance
Wealth: £1.5m
Net National Income: £80m
% of NNI: 1.88%

£20.804 billion

The importance of good political connections in building a fortune is evident in the life of James Craggs. In his case it was his close working relationship with the Duke of Marlborough which made him enormously wealthy in the late seventeenth and early eighteenth century.

Born in County Durham in around 1657, Craggs went to the local free grammar school. At 21, he and his father sold off the family property and Craggs travelled to London to make his fortune. Like other bright and ambitious men of the day, he saw that cosying up to the aristocracy was the way to advancement. After serving the Duke of York and the Earl of Peterborough, he became steward to the latter's son-in-law, the Duke of Norfolk, in 1684, aged around 27. He made a good marriage that year to the daughter of a corn chandler. Crucially she was reputedly a maidservant to Lady Marlborough and it was his connection with the Marlboroughs which saw Craggs prosper.

It may have been his financial acumen which saw Craggs recommended to Lady Marlborough in the first instance: by the 1690s he was acting as the Earl of Marlborough's private secretary while branching out into army clothing contracts and financial brokerage, paying particular attention to the East India Company. Corruption, the necessary bedfellow of so many self-made fortunes of the day was never far away though. Craggs' refusal to submit his clothing accounts to the parliamentary commissioners of public accounts saw him committed to the Tower on 7 March 1695 for obstructing their inquiries. While in the Tower it was revealed that Craggs had received the largest single payment disbursed by the governor of the East India Company, Sir Thomas Cooke, part of it for his own use in the campaign to maintain the company's monopoly. But none of this did lasting damage to Craggs, who had been quickly released from the Tower.

In 1700, he was appointed secretary to the commission for stating the debts due to the army, but also continued his involvement in the East India Company. He served as a director of the old company in 1700-01 and 1702-5, and having been involved in the negotiations between the old and new East India companies, in 1702-4 he was manager of the united company.

The accession of Queen Anne to the throne in 1702 increased Craggs's prospects of official employment, associated as he was with the Marlboroughs. The Duchess was the new queen's closet confidante at the time. Craggs was elected as MP for Grampound, a seat presumably made available to him because of his close links with Marlborough and Lord Godolphin, the Lord High Treasurer and a financial wizard in his own right. Marlborough was keen to accommodate Craggs with an office, writing in August 1702 that he should be kept in good humour 'for I shall be able to make more use of him, than of any ten others'.

In December 1702, Craggs was appointed as secretary to the master-general of the ordnance, Marlborough, adding the position of clerk of the deliveries on 18 June 1703. He retained the latter until March 1711, and his secretaryship until Marlborough's dismissal at the end of that year. In parliament, Craggs supported the ministry, being sure to attend regularly, but his real importance as a politician lay in his access to Marlborough and the way in which the Duke used him as an intermediary with other political groups.

With the disintegration of the predominantly Whig ministry led by Lord Godolphin in the summer of 1710, Craggs was employed as a go-between to the new ministers. In the parliamentary attack on Marlborough which followed the Duke's dismissal at the end of 1711, Craggs defended his mentor, particularly over his claims to be captain general for life. With Marlborough in exile from the end of 1712, Craggs continued to participate in the Whig opposition to the Tory ministry. However, he lost his seat at the 1713 election. With the accession of George I, Craggs was soon re-instated as clerk of deliveries of the ordnance, being promoted in 1715 to joint postmaster general. However, he failed to regain a seat in the Commons.

As a leading proprietor of South Sea stock, he was an obvious candidate to join with the Chancellor of the Exchequer, John Aislabie, in negotiating the scheme whereby the government's debt was to be converted into South Sea stock in 1719. When the share price of the company's stock began to fall dramatically in the autumn of 1720, he was at the centre of attempts to remedy the situation, hosting a series of discussions between the company, the government and the Bank of England.

However, as a close associate of the company's chief cashier, Robert Knight, Craggs was deeply implicated when the South Sea Bubble burst. In January 1721, the Commons inquiry into the company's finances reported that he had received £30,000 worth of stock for which he had not paid. The death of his son on 16 February 1721 seemed to destroy him and he died on 16 March of apoplexy, although there were reports that it was suicide.

Craggs' death provided a convenient scapegoat for the ministry and he was found to have encouraged the South Sea scheme for his own profit. The bulk of his property lay in the Lewisham and Greenwich area and his estate was forced to pay £68,920 in compensation: a relatively insignificant amount considering that his entire estate was valued at £1.5bn, or £14,000 per annum. In today's money that would be a hefty £20.8bn fortune.

Lakshmi Mittal

(dob 02/09/1950)
Steel

Wealth: £19.25 billion

Lakshmi Mittal stunned the world's steel industry in early 2006 with an audacious takeover bid for Arcelor, the second biggest steel maker in the world after Mittal Steel. By June 2006, after an acrimonious bid battle, he finally secured the Luxembourg and French based operation for £17.8bn. Arcelor Mittal, as the new venture is called, is the world leader producing 115m tonnes of steel, around 10% of the market. It was a bold move and Mittal says that cost savings are on track and the merger was going 'beautifully' as the two companies had complimentary skills.

Mittal, whose wealth has grown by acquiring and turning round ailing, formerly state-owned mills around the world, knows all there is to know about steel and wants to end the fragmentation of the industry and its constant boom-bust cycles. Though he likes to describe himself as a son of the desert from Rajasthan, he learnt about business and steel industry in Calcutta. His father, Mohan, had moved to the city after Partition and built up a steel operation, while young Lakshmi excelled at university, topping his class in business and accountancy.

After working in the family business, Mittal moved to Indonesia in 1976, reckoning that at the time 'Indian conditions were very suffocating for growth and development'. With backing from his father, he founded a steel plant and by the mid 1980s was a serious player in the world's steel community. In 1995, he separated his own steel operation from the family's Indian businesses, and went his own way. Mittal settled in London, where he loves to live, though retains his Indian passport.

The family's stake in Mittal Steel prior to the completion of the merger in early 2007 was worth nearly £17bn as the shares had risen sharply. The family will emerge with around 43.4% of the new entity. From 1998 to 2005, the Mittals received £1.57bn in dividends from its steel operations, including a bumper £1.38bn in 2004. Some £434m of this has been reinvested elsewhere, leaving £1.13bn in family hands. The Mittals will receive at least £413m in dividends from the new group in 2007.

A separate investment portfolio is now worth around £570m, while Mittal also has a small Indonesian steel business, which is not part of the main group, worth nearly £146m. Among his British investments, Mittal has a 4.3% stake worth £10m in the quoted RAB Capital hedge fund via his private vehicle Karrick Trust.

While Mittal has a £9m pile in London's exclusive Bishop's Avenue, he also set a world record for a private home when he paid a reputed £70m to Bernie Ecclestone, the Formula One supremo, for a house in Kensington Palace Gardens. In June 2004, he also splashed out £30m for his daughter's wedding.

The separate investments and other assets together add around £2bn. In all, we estimate that the Mittal family is now worth in the region of £19.25bn.

Robert Spencer

(d 1627)
Land
Wealth: £500,000
Net National Income: £29m
% of NNI: 1.72%

£19.091 billion

Robert Spencer, the first Baron Spencer of Wormleighton, was an ancestor of the present Earl Spencer, Sir Winston Churchill, and the present Duke of Marlborough. He was born wealthy, though no one seems sure of the date, the son of Sir John Spencer, a landowner in Northampton. His father claimed an ancestry going back to Robert Despencer, steward to the Conqueror, whose descendants were the favourites of Edward II.

Spencer, who was created a baron in 1603, improved vastly on his inheritance by buying all the land around Althorp and Wormleighton in Northampton, leasing other lands and converting most of the acreage into pasture for sheep, just as the wool trade boomed.

His capacity to raise credit was considerable and with his strong family connections with London, he was almost certainly able to lend his money effectively and to speculate successfully in the City. His relatives include the Earl of Dorset, the Earl of Derby and Viscount Brackley, who were all immensely rich, and he was also connected to the Plantagenet.

He invested in the purchase of huge tracts of land in Virginia in what is now the USA, and by the time James I came to the throne in 1603, Robert Spencer was reputed to be the richest man in England.

His son married the daughter of the Earl of Southampton and was created Earl of Sunderland in 1643, allegedly by bribing the king.

Spencer died in 1627, and his estate is estimated to have been worth £500,000 at a time when net national income was £29m. In modern money he would have been worth about £19bn.

The Duke Of Buckingham

(c 1457-1483)
Land
Wealth: £60,000
Net National Income: £3.6m
% of NNI: 1.66%

£18.425 billion

This violent Plantagenet deposed a king, his nephew, Edward V and had the king and the king's brother, the Duke of York, murdered in the Tower of London. At the heart of his approach to power was wealth, particularly the greatest fortune in England at that time, the Bohun inheritance of land handed down in that family from the time of the Conquest.

Such was Buckingham's importance as a prince of royal blood that he was allowed to assume the full rights of his title and become a Knight of the Garter at the age of just 16. He soon applied to his nephew for the Bohun lands, which carried with them an income of £1,000 a year, as well as knights and soldiers. He got his inheritance and became 'head of the wealthiest and most long established of the English magnate families'.

Having placed Richard on the throne in June 1483, he then demanded the rest of his inheritance, the suzerainty of Wales and of the Marcher lands, each of which brought more acres and more revenues. By July 1483, he had the land. Then for no reason known to historians, he rebelled against Richard with fatal consequences.

As was usual at the time, upon his execution his lands, the Bohun lands, were confiscated to await a new distribution within the Plantagenet family.

When the axe fell he was only 26 but worth £60,000 at a time when net national income was £3.6m and he accounted for 1.66% of that, making him worth about £18.4bn in current money.

John Holland, The Duke Of Exeter

(1352-1400)
Land
Wealth: £50,000
Net National Income: £3m
% of NNI: 1.66%

£18.420 billion

John Holland, later the Duke of Exeter, married one of John of Gaunt's daughters, receiving considerable grants of land from the king at the time.

Holland, a staunch and loyal follower of Richard II, proved to be a fine soldier and later an admiral. After returning from Spain in 1387, where he commanded the English army, he was created Earl of Huntingdon and given an immense grant of land. As a valued adviser to Richard, Huntingdon had honours heaped on him in quick succession: constable of Conway Castle, governor of Carlisle and in 1397, the dukedom of Exeter.

When Henry IV challenged Richard for the throne, Exeter acted as his chief spokesman. After Richard was overthrown in 1399, his power base collapsed and he was forced to give up the dukedom and lands granted at the time. In January 1400, he entered into a conspiracy against Henry IV. It was crushed and he was captured by the Countess of Hereford. She had him beheaded in the presence of the Earl of Arundel, whose father's death Exeter had helped bring about. His head was displayed until Henry IV ordered that it be buried with his body.

Holland's estates were forfeited, but his son, who had a distinguished military career, particularly at Agincourt, won back his lands and titles, culminating in the restoration of the dukedom in 1443. He was also granted lands in Normandy and held office, such as the appointment as the king's lieutenant in Aquitaine at around £1,000 a year.

Holland's wealth (and his son's) was around £50,000 at prevailing prices, the equivalent of around £18.4bn in today's money.

Robert Of Belleme, Earl Of Shrewsbury

(c 1052-1130)
Land
Wealth: £10,000
Net National Income: £600,000
% of NNI: 1.6%

£17.759 billion

The Norman Conquest was a violent, rapacious land grab, illegal even by the simple and crude laws of the time. The beneficiaries were William's followers, chief amongst them Roger of Montgomery, the first Earl of Shrewsbury. Before Roger died, his eldest son, Robert, had acquired, probably by force of arms, extensive lands in Normandy and Maine in France. When Robert's younger brother was killed in a Viking raid on Anglesea, four years after their father died, Robert inherited the Earldom and even more land in Normandy as well as land in Sussex. Later he bought the fief of Tickhill in the English Midlands and acquired the county of Ponthieu by marriage.

Within his realms Robert was notorious for his cruelty, even in a time of cruelty. A violent family – even his mother Mabel met her death at the hands of a murderer. Because he controlled the key strategic landholdings in Normandy and in England, and was immensely rich, he was probably the mightiest Baron of his time, someone the king had to take very seriously. Robert supported Robert Curthose, an opponent of Henry I who became king in 1100. Curthose rebelled and was defeated in 1106, but Robert maintained his opposition to Henry. In 1112, Henry had him arrested and thrown in jail where he died around 1130.

At the time of his death, Robert was worth about £10,000 at a time when net national income was £600,000. He would have been worth £17.7bn in modern money.

The twelve rich list members who died in prison or as a result of long imprisonment

Rich list member	Wealth
Robert of Belleme, Earl of Shrewsbury (1052-c1130)	£17.759bn
The Earl of Cornwall (1209-72)	£14.370bn
Sir Theodore Janssen (c 1658-1748)	£13.874bn
Lord Cromwell (c 1394-1456)	£12.980bn
The Earl of Northumberland (1564-1632)	£12.875bn
Archbishop George Neville (c 1432-1476)	£7.880bn
Sir John Moleyns (d 1361)	£6.104bn
Viscount Lovell (1454-c1487)	£5.993bn
Sir Henry Garraway (1575-1646)	£3.774bn
Henry Despencer (c 1341-1406)	£3.662bn
Giles Strangways (1615-1675)	£3.107bn
Sir Richard Gurney (1577-1647)	£3.107bn

Hugh Despencer The Younger

(d 1326)
Land
Wealth: £80,000
Net National Income: £5m
% of NNI: 1.6%

£17.759 billion

Why become a dictator, especially the dictator of a very reluctant country called England? Hugh Despencer, known as "the Younger", had a simple answer: 'To make myself rich.' He achieved his aim, and is one of the very few people in history to have been allowed, for the record, to say exactly why he did it. You make yourself powerful so that you can make yourself rich. This despite the fact that he was very wealthy to start with.

King Edward I had used his privileges over his female relatives and married Despencer the Younger to his granddaughter, an heiress to part of the great Clare fortune. When his brother-in-law, the Duke of Gloucester, was killed at Bannockburn, Despencer acquired, via his wife, one third of the Clare inheritance. But that was not enough. For four years, from 1322 to 1326, Despenser the Elder, the cat's paw of his son (as was the king), ran a dictatorship in England.

The elder Despenser, the Earl of Winchester, was rich anyhow, very rich, and his son, by the abuse of law and the use of blackmail and extortion as sanctioned by law, had also made himself very rich. But not rich enough, since there were parts of the kingdom of England still not within his ownership, or alternatively within his control, by 1321. In that year, the Marcher Lords attacked Despencer and defeated him in what is known as the Despencer War.

The Marchers wasted Despencer's land and forced the king to exile him briefly, but the next year they were beaten and Despencer assumed total dominance over the king, a dominance that some historians suggest was homosexual in character.

The four years of the dictatorship were appalling, even by the standards of the time. Despenser grabbed lands everywhere, forcing unfavourable exchanges even on the king's brother. A widow, Mary de St. Pol, the Countess of Pembroke, was forced to hand over £20,000 – the equivalent of over £3bn – and vast quantities of livestock, in return for a twentieth of their value. By 1326, Despencer personally owned Chepstow, Usk, Tonbridge Castle, Gower and vast tracts of England.

Secure in Edward II's favour, Despencer imprisoned and tortured his opponents, and manipulated the legal system to enrich himself further, with the full cooperation of the royal judiciary. He was blatantly corrupt but untouchable and his regime was a reign of terror according to the historian Fryde.

But in 1326, the Marchers rebelled again, Despencer's army was defeated at Hereford and he was executed, slowly and with enormous cruelty before what was left of his forces. His father met the same fate. The following year Edward II was deposed, incarcerated in Berkeley Castle and murdered there. The English don't like dictatorships much.

Despencer the Younger's income at the time of his death was £7,514 a year, with movables worth £3,136 on his English estates and with £5,880 on deposit with Italian bankers. His lands were worth about £65,000. This gave him a total value of £80,000, 1.6% of a net national income of £5m, making him worth £17.7bn in modern money.

Cardinal Henry Beaufort

(1375-1447)
The Rich Cardinal
Wealth: £50,000
Net National Income: £3.3m
% of NNI: 1.52%

£16.968 billion

Being the second of four illegitimate children of a powerful duke – namely John of Gaunt, Duke of Lancaster – was no hindrance to Henry Beaufort's advance up the Catholic Church in feudal England. Raised in the ducal household, Beaufort was marked out for a clerical career from an early age. He resided at Peterhouse, Cambridge, in 1388-9 and at Queen's College, Oxford, from 1390 to around 1393. Studying theology he was ordained deacon on 7 April 1397, aged around 22.

His aristocratic roots helped him gather church and other appointments and in 1396, he was provided by papal bull to the deanery of Wells, while the University of Oxford made him its chancellor in April 1397, still just 22. His father even managed to legitimize his birth. John of Gaunt, now at the height of his influence with Richard II, married Beaufort's mother in 1396, and their issue, the Beauforts, were legitimized by papal bull and royal charter in 1396-7.

In 1399, he was installed as Bishop of Lincoln aged just 24. Bishop Beaufort played no part in the deposition of Richard II by his half-brother Henry Bolingbroke, who became Henry IV. During the early years of Henry's reign, he eschewed politics and lived mainly in his extensive diocese. In late 1402, he was sent to Brittany to conduct the new queen, Joan of Navarre, to England where, on her arrival, he officiated at the royal marriage.

Finally, on 28 February 1403, Beaufort was appointed Chancellor of England, where he successfully defended the Crown's interests against a critical House of Commons, eventually securing a substantial grant of taxation. His elevation to the rich see of Winchester in November 1404 was the reward for his political service to the Crown. He resigned the Chancellorship on 2 March 1405, though remained an active member of the council for another year.

For the next six years, Beaufort played a crucial role in government, securing English land and alliances in France, but he also established good relations with the Prince of Wales, the future Henry V. Initially, this was to cost him dear. From 1411 to Henry IV's death in 1413, Beaufort was in disgrace for siding with the Prince of Wales against the king. But when Henry V acceded to the throne in 1413, Beaufort helped raise the money for the campaign that led to the British triumph at Agincourt in 1415. Indeed his palace at Wolvesey became the king's headquarters in the weeks preceding the Agincourt expedition.

After the victory, Beaufort's role grew both in complex negotiations and in helping to finance further expeditions to France. In 1417, taxation was insufficient to underwrite a large army and loans were secured. Beaufort became a leading lender to the government, advancing £14,000. At this point, his relations with Henry V took a turn for the worse. Ostensibly taking a pilgrimage, Beaufort went to Italy where he threw his weight behind a candidate for the papacy who would back England against France. Beaufort's own name was put forward at one stage but the winner was Odo Colonna, who was elected as Martin V with English support. Beaufort was appointed a Cardinal as a reward and was allowed to keep the wealthy see of Winchester too.

Henry V was furious as he feared Beaufort might work with the new Pope to expand the power of the Church in England at the Crown's expense. Beaufort was forbidden from accepting the Pope's offer on pain of losing the see of Winchester and all his wealth. Confined to his diocese and excluded from politics, Beaufort more than once contemplated resigning his see and making his way to Rome. In the end, he reined in his resentment and remained in England.

It was Henry's insatiable need for money that led to Beaufort's partial rehabilitation. Henry turned to the Bishop for a loan of £17,666. With only £5,693 of his previous loan repaid, it meant that some £26,000 of his wealth was now in the king's hands. Although the repayment of the whole loan was secured on the customs of Southampton and he had the gold crown in pledge, it could take ten years to discharge the loan in full.

Henry V's death in 1422 meant the throne passed to his infant son, while power rested with Henry V's two brothers: the dukes of Bedford and Gloucester. Beaufort sided with Bedford and provided funds for his campaigning in France, while earning the undying enmity of Gloucester. By 1425, the hatred almost turned into open warfare when forces loyal to Gloucester and Beaufort confronted each other. A truce was brokered by Bedford but at the cost of Beaufort having his political power clipped. Bedford endeavoured to sweeten the pill by procuring from Pope Martin V the cardinalate that Beaufort had been forced to waive in 1419. Beaufort also secured repayment of all he had loaned the Crown, and his withdrawal from English politics once again foreshadowed a new area of activity. For the Pope made him leader of a crusade against the Hussites of Bohemia and gave him power in Germany to mobilize an effective army.

As ever, finding the money and manpower for the army was difficult and Beaufort went to England in search of support. By 1429, he had raised some forces but before they could be sent to Germany, a crisis erupted in France and Beaufort's men were sent there to help. Naturally, the Pope was outraged and all hope for Beaufort to have a career in papal service ended there and then.

Fortunately, he had earned Bedford's undying gratitude and despite opposition from Gloucester was rehabilitated. Again his wealth was put to good use financing a 7,000 strong army for campaigning in France. The young Henry VI was also coming of age and Beaufort attended his coronations in both London and Paris, where he actually crowned the new king in 1431. But Gloucester had not finished. As Beaufort had his treasure secretly shipped from England, Gloucester got wind of what was happening and seized it at the port of Sandwich. Beaufort also faced treason charges but he was able to use all his statecraft and guile to have the charges dropped and his fortune restored. His ability to make further loans helped Beaufort's uncanny ability to survive and bounce back.

But for as long as the war with France continued, the Council could not easily dispense with his wealth and abilities, and by 1433, his financial support was again urgently required by Bedford to send further reinforcements to France. Indeed, in May 1433, Bedford decided he must return to England, displace Gloucester as vice-regent, re-organise English finances, and revive support for the war. Under Bedford's protection Beaufort therefore returned to the Council and to his role as financier of the English Crown.

Bedford's death in 1435 removed Beaufort's protection at court but Gloucester was inhibited from attacking the cardinal for financial reasons. He loaned £18,666 to finance armies in France, while by 1436, the young Henry VI was beginning to exercise some measure of royal authority, and this afforded Beaufort a degree of security. Beaufort was now convinced of the necessity for a settlement with France that could guarantee the retention of Normandy and led peace talks which came to naught.

The young king was by now showering land in Dorset and Wales on Beaufort despite Gloucester's opposition. But Beaufort was now ageing and attended council less frequently after 1440. His one shot at securing a legacy failed when his nephew, John Beaufort, Earl of Somerset, led an army to France in 1443 financed by £22,666 from Beaufort. In the event, Somerset failed to bring the French to battle and, having achieved nothing of military significance, returned in disgrace. It was an ignominious conclusion to the Cardinal's political career and he retired and died in 1447.

Henry Beaufort's wealth was notorious and he was known as the Rich Cardinal. The source of his wealth remains as unclear as it was to his contemporaries, but the revenues of his see, the perquisites of office and influence, the export of wool, and his elder brother's legacy are all possible sources. At the height of his career, his fortune was around £50,000, or £16.9bn in today's money.

The Duke Of Suffolk

(1396-1450)
Land
Wealth: £50,000
Net National Income: £3.3m
% of NNI: 1.51%

£16.747 billion

Like much of the aristocracy in medieval times, William de la Pole started out relatively poor – a younger son – but got his first leg up the ladder of wealth when both his father and brother died in 1415, and he became the Earl of Suffolk.

With a reputation as a poet and as the very embodiment of chivalry he went to war in France in 1417. Under Henry V he quickly obtained high military rank, as Admiral of Normandy, Commander of the Forces and eventually a Knight of the Garter.

Back home in England, after being defeated in 1433, he became the key figure in the Palace as its steward. By 1440, he had become effectively the leader of the government. Henry VI had succeeded the hero of Agincourt, Henry V, seven years after the latter's death, in 1429. In the interval the Duke of Bedford had ruled as Regent with Suffolk as his deputy. By 1445, Suffolk had acquired a huge collection of royal favours, each bringing revenues and assets with them. He was granted the whole county of Pembroke in 1447, made chief steward of the Duchy of Lancaster, Great Chamberlain, Admiral of England and warden of the Cinque ports.

According to historians Suffolk, the one-time poet, enjoyed the profits of extortion, coercion and manipulation of justice and totally dominated the government. In 1450, he was impeached for treason, having lost the war in France and with it Normandy. He had been taken prisoner in France and ransomed, apparently with his own money, to the tune of £20,000.

Suffolk was murdered on his way to exile, leaving a fortune, minus the ransom, which still stood at £50,000, the equivalent of 1.5% of net national income of £3.3m at the time. In modern money that would be £16.7bn.

The Duke Of Chandos

(1673-1744)
Speculation
Wealth: £1.2m
Net National Income: £80m
% of NNI: 1.5%

£16.649 billion

The South Sea Bubble, a vast and purely speculative rise in shares in the South Sea Company in 1720, made James Brydges, Duke of Chandos, the first non-landed millionaire in British history. That was in August 1720. By the end of September he was writing to his banker, Cantillon, asking for a loan of £30-40,000, the equivalent of £3-4m nowadays.

But James Brydges had started out life neither rich nor a Duke, even if his father was a Lord. No more than a country squire, Lord Chandos had very briefly been an ambassador in Constantinople where he had married a merchant's daughter. Their son is described by his biographers C.H. and Muriel Baker as:

having the characteristics of the country landowner, the counting house and the banker blended.

James Brydges came to London in 1701, with few connections and no employment. His first job was as a clerk on the Admiralty Council. In 1705, he was made paymaster of the foreign forces. According to the Bakers:

Mr Brydges entered the paymasters office a relatively poor man, just under 30, and closed its doors behind him eight years later, one of the richest men in England.

He did this by imposing heavy commissions on his foreign contractors, by taking bribes from food and equipment suppliers and by using the funds paid by parliament to make private investments. This was what a paymaster was expected to do in those days, but it still had to be done in secrecy and with subterfuge, and many anxious years were spent covering one's tracks.

The Duke of Marlborough had helped obtain the job for Chandos. Ironically, Marlborough's own ancestor, John, first Duke of Marlborough, had failed to cover his tracks, and only escaped the auditor general by jumping in a boat at Portsmouth, when the general and his posse were detained at Horndean.

Chandos was made a Duke in 1719, for no clear reason – other than perhaps having paid the king a bribe. Chandos was badly damaged by the bursting of the bubble in 1720, but he still managed to go on buying old masters, including Michelangelos, until he died in 1744. He was Handel's patron and one of only two men in England with a private orchestra. His son was later Master of the Horse to the Prince of Wales and the Grand Master of the Freemasons.

In today's money, Chandos would easily be worth £16.6bn.

Sir James Lowther

(1673-1755)
Land
Wealth: £2m
Net National Income: £135m
% of NNI: 1.48%

£16.427 billion

The Lonsdale estates in Cumbria are partly traceable to Sir James Lowther, who was reckoned to be the richest commoner of his time. He was regularly appointed an MP and held positions in the Ordnance Office between 1696 and 1708, until he came into his inheritance in 1706. This happened on the death of his father, who had disinherited Lowther's elder brother, a notorious spendthrift and rake.

An industrious man who never married, Sir James made the business and expansion of his inheritance his life's work. In this he was very successful. He was parsimonious to a degree but invested heavily in new technology to mine the rich seams of coal on his property. From the age of 50 he had severe gout, and had his leg amputated at the age of 77, but went on putting bills before parliament to open roads and turnpikes until he died at the age 82.

At the time of his death he was said to have an income of £25,000 a year, from coal mining, landed property, investments on government bonds and mortgage holdings. He left his estate to his cousin, also Sir James, and it was worth about £2m when he received it in 1756. In today's money, that would be worth just over £16.4bn.

The 1st Earl Of Cork

(1566-1643)
Land
Wealth: £500,000
Net National Income: £35m
% of NNI: 1.42%

£15.761 billion

Richard Boyle, later the 1st Earl of Cork and known as the 'Great Earl', came from Canterbury, Kent. He landed in Ireland with just £27, 3s, in his pocket in the wake of the conquest and occupation of the country under Elizabeth I in 1588. Using counterfeit letters, Boyle obtained introductions to high figures in the occupation government. He became an escheator to the Escheator General and used this post to make a modest profit. Knowing that land was the only way to wealth and success he married an heiress in Limerick and came into a landed estate worth £500.

In 1592, he did a stint in jail on charges of theft. The complainants went to Elizabeth herself and at his trial before Star Chamber her intervention saved Cork and his accusers were suspended from office in Ireland. Subsequently, he went back to Ireland and bought the estates of Sir Walter Raleigh there for a very small sum. He became the virtual governor of Munster, where he installed members of the occupation army on lands taken from the Irish and then started industrialising the province.

By 1629, he was a Lord but in 1633, the Earl of Stafford was appointed Lord Deputy in Ireland and soon fined the overmighty Cork £15,000, and then started new agitation against him. Stafford should have remembered what happened to Cork's previous accusers. Events went against him and he was beheaded, with Cork attending the execution. The Irish rebelled on a grand scale in 1641, and Cork defended the English interest successfully in Munster.

When he died he was worth £500,000 when British net national income was £35m. He had a 1.42% slice of it and that would make him worth, in modern money, £15.7bn. He was almost certainly the richest man ever to live in Ireland.

The 1st Earl Of Warwick

(1428-1471)
Land
Wealth: £50,000
Net National Income: £3.5m
% of NNI: 1.42%

£15.761 billion

The chroniclers describe him as:

The most ambitious and daring of politicians, strategists and pirates, but one whose disastrous over-caution as a tactician lost him all his battles.

Known as "the Kingmaker", Richard Nevill was no commoner, but a man of royal and aristocratic descent, being at once Earl of Warwick and Earl of Salisbury when being Earl meant owning the place named in your title.

His manner of adding to the Nevill estates in the north of England and the Warwick estates he acquired by marriage was to use his ascendancy in the court, in effect in the government, to acquire the lands of others and where that did not work to indulge in night-time raids and assassinations of followers of the Lancastrian cause in the civil War of the Roses. He also helped to unseat Henry VI in 1460, had him placed in the Tower of London where he was murdered, and replaced him with Edward IV.

At home Warwick kept a splendid household, retinue, fleet of ships, and train of artillery. King Edward gave him many confiscated estates and offices of profit such as Great Chamberlain and Admiral of England, as well as Steward of the Duchy of Lancaster. Despite the king's generosity, Warwick rebelled and tried to replace Edward. He was defeated and killed at the Battle of Barnet in 1471.

He died leaving estates worth £50,000, about 1.42% of net national income, which would make him worth £15.7bn in modern money.

William Pulteney, Earl Of Bath

(1684-1764)
Land
Wealth: £2m
Net National Income: £150m
% of NNI 1.33%

£14.896 billion

A leading politician and later satirical journalist, William Pulteney came from a well-to-do London family. His father was an army colonel and his grandfather, a substantial London landowner and MP for Westminster. A bright lad, Pulteney was educated at Westminster School and at Christ Church, Oxford, where he was a noted classical scholar, being chosen to deliver the congratulatory speech to Queen Anne on her visit in 1702. He was also a noted sportsman, excelling particularly at horse riding and fencing.

After Oxford and the obligatory Grand Tour of Europe, Pulteney rushed home to take his seat in the Commons, having won a seat as MP for Hedon, Yorkshire in the 1705 general election, at the age of 21. He owed this seat to the patronage of Henry Guy, former secretary to the Treasury, who was a close friend of the family. Pulteney had keen political skills and he was soon regarded as a rising star of the Whigs. In 1708, he fell in with Robert Walpole, another rising Whig, with whom Pulteney was associated for most of his political career, first as an ally and later as a deadly enemy.

The death of Henry Guy in February 1711, left Pulteney independently rich. Guy left him an estate at Stoke Newington, Middlesex, another at Muswell Hill, and money and other property, eventually realising some £20,000, which was to be invested in land. Guy also left Pulteney his property at Hedon, which included the town hall.

Despite a new Tory administration, Pulteney continued to support the Whigs and Walpole. In January 1712, he defended first Walpole and then John Churchill, Duke of Marlborough, against charges of corruption relating to government army contracts. Pulteney kept in close touch with Walpole when the latter was imprisoned in the Tower, and so angered the Tories with his attacks that he was nearly locked up as well. In 1713, Pulteney began his second career as a political satirist with a work that was included in a book by Walpole.

When George I came to power in 1714, Pulteney's reward for supporting the Whigs was his appointment as secretary-at-state for war. Soon after, he married a considerable heiress whose father was a rich businessman. Her dowry was some £6,000. Pulteney used his position to help his new father-in-law to become deputy commissary-general of the army in 1716, MP for Steyning in 1722, and commissary-general in 1724.

The new couple set up house in Arlington Street, Piccadilly. Pulteney's wife was acknowledged as very good-looking though with a reputation of having been free with her favours in the past. This was later to be used to punishing effect by satirists intent on attacking her husband. She appears in one print with her bare backside being used as a desk by a secretary and later she was branded 'Mrs Pony' and 'Bath's ennobled Doxy'. Like Pulteney she was also good with money and managed her own separate fortune.

The death of his father in 1715, saw Pulteney inherit a life interest in the London estates settled by the will of his grandfather. This property primarily comprised part of Cleveland Row opposite St James's Palace, together with a large part of the western side of Soho and two pieces of undeveloped land on the northern side of Piccadilly. Pulteney immediately began to plan developments and improvements across the whole estate.

The development in Soho is today represented by the area bounded by Wardour Street and Carnaby Street, with Great Pulteney Street at its heart. In Piccadilly the eastern portion extends from Piccadilly Circus to Sackville Street, and the western area covers Bolton Street to Down Street. It was on this portion that Pulteney built his London home after his elevation to the peerage as Bath.

Despite the odd hiccup, Pulteney's support for Walpole continued up until 1720. Walpole was returned to favour at the Treasury and promised office to a number of his Whig supporters. Pulteney was not among them and all he was offered was a peerage, which he refused with some anger. It was reckoned that Walpole hoped to sideline Pulteney as a serious rival with the peerage. Certainly Pulteney had profited handsomely from investing in the South Sea Company, as he had sold out before the 'bubble' burst and enhanced his reputation for understanding public finance. Further, from the resultant profits he purchased the Bathwick estate, comprising 600 acres of agricultural and nursery-garden land on the east side of the River Avon opposite Bath. He also used his own and his wife's money to purchase the Wrington estate, of about 4,000 acres, in north Somerset.

In spite of his increasing attacks on Walpole, Pulteney was still prospering: the Pulteney estates in London were converted from a lease from the Crown into a freehold. Politically, top government posts still eluded him though he was rewarded with minor office. Pulteney grew increasingly angry with Walpole, even accusing him of corruption.

In 1726, this opposition took a new turn and opened a new chapter in Pulteney's career. He helped launch *The Craftsman*, the *Private Eye* of its day, initially as a single-sheet publication which later developed as a newspaper with a circulation of 13,000 at its peak in 1731. Pulteney, a friend of Jonathan Swift and Alexander Pope, was a star contributor. The death of George I in 1727 provided no hope for Pulteney who stepped up his savage attacks on Walpole. The government struck back. In November 1729, Richard Franklin, the publisher of *The Craftsman*, was prosecuted by the government, but a sympathetic jury acquitted him. This popular verdict prompted Pulteney to celebrate in print himself with the ballad 'The Honest Jury', and he even fought a duel with a political opponent in 1731.

For the next eleven years, Pulteney harried Walpole's administration in print and in parliament to no avail. When Walpole fell in 1742, it seemed as if Pulteney's hour had come. But he declined major office and simply took a seat in Cabinet and was re-admitted to the privy council. He then accepted a peerage and became Lord Bath, which did not go down well with his critics and satirists. In 1746, Pulteney came tantalisingly close to power and was asked to form a government, but two days later, unable to form an administration, he declined. Leaving government, he sat in the Lords until his death in 1764. He left a London estate, and others in Bathwick, Wrington, Burrington and Ubley, in Somerset, and property in Shropshire, Monmouthshire, Staffordshire, and Northamptonshire.

His personal estate in the form of cash and investments was estimated variously at between £600,000 and £1.2m at the time. He was certainly one of the richest men in Britain at his death. In all, with his vast land holdings, Pulteney was easily worth £2m. In today's money that would be nearly £14.9bn.

Richard, The Earl Of Cornwall

(1209-1272)
Land
Wealth £50,000
Net National Income: £3.7m
% of NNI: 1.35%

£14.37 billion

Richard, Earl of Cornwall started almost at the top and stayed there. He was the second son of King John (1199-1216) and the younger brother of Henry III. But he made himself a very rich man, rich enough to buy a crown, though it was not the one he desired (the Crown of England).

Described by some as a kind of vice king, he carried out all sorts of tasks for his brother and is credited with being one of the great stabilising influences in the kingdom at a time of great turbulence. He made three very successful marriages, each with great dowries, and was offered the Crown of Sicily by the Pope, but first he had to conquer the place. In relation to the offer of Sicily to this crown-hungry man, he is said to have remarked:

You might as well say; I will sell or give you the moon. Go up and take it.

His pragmatism was also evident in his quarrels with his brother the king, of which it was said that Richard never quarrelled with Henry without coming away a richer man. He re-minted the coinage starting in 1247, from which he made £20,000. He lent £40,000 to the Crown and he controlled Cornwall and its lucrative tin mines. He bought the Crown of Germany by buying the votes of three of the electors for £28,000.

He had land at Wallingford, Berkhampstead and Eye. He

received from the Pope the income from all those who got out of their vows to go on a crusade by paying a fee, in return for siding with the Pope over who got the surplus from the revenues of the English Church. He was crowned King of the Romans, which made him Holy Roman Emperor designate, but the Imperial Crown never came to him.

He died of a stroke in 1272 and at the time was said to be worth £50,000, about 1.35% of net national income at the time. In modern money he would have been worth about £14.3bn.

Sir Theodore Janssen

(c 1658-1748)
Finance
Wealth: £1m
Net National Income: £80m
% of NNI: 1.25%

£13.874 billion

His father, a Frenchman, the youngest son of Baron de Herz, was beheaded by the Duke of Parma for rebellion in the Netherlands. But before he lost his head, his father gave his son Theodore £20,000 and sent him to England, where he prospered as both financier and MP for Yarmouth. King William knighted him and Queen Anne made him a baronet at the request of the future King George I.

Janssen lost out when the company of which he was a director, the South Sea Company, exploded in a speculative bubble burst in the autumn of 1720. At one stage he was just behind the Duke of Chandos in having made almost a million in the speculative upsurge. He lost £50,000 in the crash and was fined half his £500,000 fortune by Walpole the Prime Minister, as well as being sacked as MP and imprisoned by the Sergeant at Arms for his role in the affair.

Nonetheless, he died very rich and all three of his sons inherited the baronetcy and prospered. In 1720, he was worth around £1m, only the second person to make such a sum. This was about 1.25% of net national income at the time. He would have been worth £13.8bn in modern money.

Sir John Pulteney

(c 1290-1349)
Merchant
Wealth: £50,000
Net National Income: £4m
% of NNI: 1.25%

£13.873 billion

Sir John Pulteney was born the son of gentry from Sussex and Leicestershire. What was unusual about him was that he went into trade, almost unheard of for aristocrats of the day. Apprenticed to a London draper, probably around 1305 or 1310, by 1330 he was rich enough to negotiate on behalf of the king and the City with the great Flemish traders.

He eventually became mayor of London on three occasions and was knighted in the company of the Black Prince by the king. Apart from the wealth he amassed in the City, Pulteney also inherited sizeable lands in Leicestershire and Northamptonshire. He owned 23 manors in five counties and land in Middlesex, Kent, Cambridgeshire, Warwick, Suffolk and London at the time of his death. He owned three beautiful houses, at Pevsner, Coldharbour and Pulteney Inn and later the London house of the Black Prince and of the Duke of Exeter. He is said to have been the greatest citizen landlord of rural acres in the fourteenth century.

At the time of his death Pulteney had given away a lot of his wealth to charity but is still thought to have been worth about £50,000, which was 1.25% of net national income at the time. In modern money he would have been worth £13.8bn.

John Churchill, 1st Duke Of Marlborough

(1650-1722)
Soldier and land
Wealth: £1m
NNI: £82m
% of NNI: 1.22%

£13.644 billion

Born in Devon to an impoverished royalist cavalry captain during the English Civil War, the young John Churchill was educated by a clergyman and his unemployed father. His father's prospects looked up with the restoration of the monarchy in 1660. After a spell in Dublin, his father, Winston, became Sir Winston Churchill and they moved back to London.

The young John Churchill had the good fortune to become a page of honour to the Duke of York, who went on to obtain for the seventeen year old Churchill a commission as an ensign in the King's Own Regiment, later the Grenadier Guards. In the early 1670s, the young Churchill distinguished himself in battle against the Dutch and impressed the Duke of York further.

But his brother, the king, refused York's request to promote Churchill further. There were stories circulating that the young Churchill was having an affair with Barbara Palmer, the Duchess of Cleveland and Charles II's mistress. Churchill was regarded as the father of her youngest daughter, born in 1672. It is also widely believed that she gave Churchill a gift of £5,000 from money she received from the king.

Despite this, on 13 June 1672, Churchill obtained a military promotion, skipping the rank of lieutenant, from ensign to captain in the Lord High Admiral's regiment. About this time he spent £4,500 purchasing two annuities from Lord Halifax to pay £600 per year for life, thereby creating the foundation for his later fortune.

In the period from 1672 to 1674, Churchill served with distinction on attachment to the French army under the personal command of Louis XIV against the Dutch. He displayed great heroism in the Siege of Maastricht. Following the surrender of its fortress, Louis XIV publicly praised the English soldiers and, among them, personally congratulated Churchill. His French adventure gave Churchill an invaluable insight into French military thinking and tactics, which was to serve him well in future.

Returning to England, Churchill continued to enjoy the patronage of the Duke of York and in January 1675, was promoted to lieutenant-colonel in his regiment. Shortly after returning to court he met fifteen-year-old Sarah Jenyns, who, in October 1673, had been appointed a member of the household of the new Duchess of York, as an attendant to her stepdaughter, Princess Anne, the future queen.

Early in 1676, the Duchess of Cleveland left the court and moved to Paris with her children. Shortly afterwards Churchill became attracted to Sarah Jenyns. Meanwhile, Churchill's debt-ridden parents were busily attempting to arrange a financially advantageous marriage for their eldest son to Katherine, the nineteen-year-old daughter and heir of the playwright Sir Charles Sedley. Nevertheless, Churchill proposed to Sarah in mid November 1676. Sir Winston initially opposed the marriage but in 1677, Sarah's brother died and she received a substantial proportion of her family's estates in Hertfordshire, worth up to £1500 a year. Under these circumstances Sir Winston and Lady Churchill approved of the match between their son and Sarah.

On 18 February 1678, Churchill was promoted colonel of one of the newly raised infantry regiments, and in order to show him further favour the Duke of York altered the date of his commission by one day, to 17 February, giving him seniority over those commissioned the same day. In 1678, Churchill rose further in the army to the rank of brigadier of foot and given authority to enlist recruits.

During 1678, Churchill sold his place as groom in the Duke of York's household, a transaction bringing him a pension of £200 in addition to his current salary as Master of the Robes, his two annuities, and his military pay. As a former maid of honour, Sarah received an annual pension of £300. In addition her share of the Jenyns' estates at Sandridge, at St Albans, Hertfordshire, and at Agney, Kent, provided her with independent assets.

The remaining years of Charles II's reign saw Churchill remain close to the Duke of York, who was exiled first to Brussels and later Scotland by the king as he was so unpopular in Britain. Early in 1682, Churchill accompanied the Duke of York on a visit to Charles II at Newmarket, where he was allowed to return permanently to England. The ship which set sail in May carrying James and his household from Edinburgh ran aground on shoals off the Norfolk coast and sank with a heavy loss of life. Churchill was among the few survivors.

Sarah, his wife, was growing ever closer to Princess Anne, the Duke of York's daughter. With her wedding in 1683, Anne was allowed her own household, separate from that of her parents, but based on the couple's limited income. The chief position in the Princess's household was that of groom of the stole, which provided £400 a year. Churchill encouraged his wife to secure the appointment as a means to promote their own advantage. Eventually, Sarah was given the post, formally inaugurating a connection that lasted for the next 27 years and became the pivot upon which both their political and personal fortunes rose and fell.

For the next two years the Churchills were deeply involved in court life. Later that year Churchill acquired sufficient resources to purchase the remaining share of the Jenyns' estate at Sandridge and Holywell for £11,000 and to begin repairing and extending Holywell House at St Albans as a convenient country seat to raise their family.

The accession of the Duke of York as James II accelerated Churchill's rise. He was appointed ambassador-extraordinary to France to notify Louis XIV of James's accession. Shortly after returning to London, Churchill was appointed a gentleman of the king's bed chamber on 22 April 1685. Then, on 14 May, he was additionally created Baron Churchill of Sandridge, Hertfordshire, taking his title from his wife's inheritance; this was one of only ten English peerages created during James's reign.

Soon after the accession, Churchill proved his loyalty to the new king by playing a leading role in the defeat of the Duke of Monmouth's rebellion at the Battle of Sedgemoor in 1685. James heaped more honour on Churchill but as the king began to replace Protestant office holders with Catholics, Churchill's loyalty to the Crown wavered. It broke finally in 1688, when William of Orange and his wife Mary, James's eldest daughter, deposed him. Churchill agonised but finally abandoned the king who fled to exile.

William gave Churchill the important task of reassembling and reconstituting the army in the face of the impending war with France. Under William and Mary, Churchill found far less personal favour than he had under James II. But he did help William secure Ireland with an imaginative campaign that opened a second front against the exiled James II. However, William could never trust Churchill completely as he corresponded with James and was known to meet his agents. Giving no warning, on the morning of 20 January 1692, Secretary of State Nottingham passed to Marlborough the monarchs' message dismissing him from office and creating for him a serious financial loss of £7,000 to £11,000 in annual income. No official explanation was made, but those close to the king made it known that Marlborough's recent correspondence with James II had been discovered.

Fortunately, relations between Princess Anne and Sarah Churchill proved enduring despite pressure from William and Mary to dismiss her. An invasion scare in May 1692 led to Churchill's brief imprisonment in the Tower of London on charges of high treason. He was finally released on £6,000 bail, but Mary retained her suspicions and personally struck his name from the list of privy councillors, along with the names of those who had stood his bail.

The death of Queen Mary in 1694 led to the elevation of Princess Anne as William's immediate heir. William also restored Churchill to favour in 1698, appointing him as a privy councillor and cabinet minister. As tension mounted with France over the question of the succession to the Spanish throne, William wisely made Churchill his ambassador plenipotentiary on 28 June 1701 to be England's chief negotiator for a new treaty of alliance between the Dutch and Austrian to resist French expansion. He was also commander-in-chief of the 10,000 English troops sent to support the Dutch. Attached to these appointments was a salary of £2,000 a year, plus £1,500 for equipage, an allowance for entertaining, and a supply of appropriate gilt and white plates.

The death of William and accession of Queen Anne in 1702 marked the start of a glorious period for Churchill. He was appointed commander-in-chief of the Allied armies facing the French in 1702 on a £10,000 salary. With his wife Sarah as a close confidante of the new queen and his good friend Godolphin leading the government, Churchill went to work expelling the French from Dutch positions along the river Amass.

By the end of 1702, he had succeeded and was rewarded with the Dukedom of Marlborough by Queen Anne. In 1704, Marlborough fought a brilliant campaign against the combined French and Bavarian forces at Blenheim. It was a stunning victory: the French army suffered a major defeat for the first time in forty years. Two years later he defeated the French again at Ramillies, in 1708 at Oudenarde and in 1709, with a very expensive victory at Malplaquet.

Honours and rewards showered down on Marlborough from a grateful queen. In 1705, the queen granted him the former royal manor of Woodstock, with its historical associations as the birthplace of the Black Prince and of the romantic liaisons of Henry II with his mistress, Rosamond Clifford. The grant included the hundred of Wotton, comprising together a total of some 22,000 acres in Oxfordshire, then estimated to produce revenue of about £6,000 a year. In addition, on 5 February, parliament approved the queen's proposal that a grant of £5,000 made in 1702 should be made permanent for the Duke's lifetime; it also granted the funds to construct a house at Woodstock that would be not only the Duke's family seat, but a national memorial commemorating, and named after, the Battle of Blenheim. In addition, Marlborough received £600 of the Blenheim bounty payment to officers serving in the battle.

In 1706, Marlborough was offered the post as Spain's governor-general in the southern Netherlands, with an estimated income of £60,000 a year and much patronage, and the queen and government in London approved. However, the Dutch made it clear that the appointment was entirely unacceptable. Marlborough eventually declined the post.

By 1710, though, relations between the Marlboroughs and Queen Anne became strained. In late 1711, the satirist Jonathan Swift published his 'Conduct of the Allies', arguing that the whole war had been a Whig plot led by Marlborough and his foreign friends to enrich themselves at the expense of England's Treasury. More than 11,000 copies of Swift's work circulated, which devastated Marlborough's credibility and led to charges of corruption. In December the commissioners for the investigation of public accounts called the allied army's bread contractor, Sir Solomon de Medina, from Holland to testify that he and his predecessor, Antonio Alvarez Machado, had paid 2.5% of the contract to Marlborough between 1702 and 1710, for a total of £64,410, 3s 6d. Moreover, Marlborough had clearly profited by the war, amassing a fortune that Swift estimated at more than half a million pounds.

Given the heated atmosphere of party politics during the parliamentary recess and the charges of improper conduct that were brewing, the queen dismissed Marlborough from all his offices on 30 December 1711. He travelled widely in Europe. When the new king, George I, took the throne in 1714, he said to Marlborough: 'My lord Duke, I hope your troubles are now over.' The first warrant the king signed, on 4 September 1714, restored Marlborough as captain-general of the land forces. Then, on 26 September, he was restored as colonel of the 1st foot guards, on 1 October as master-general of the ordnance, and subsequently as governor of Chelsea Hospital and a privy councillor. He helped supervise the suppression of the 1715 Jacobite Rebellion and remained active in the king's inner circle.

He supervised the continued construction of Blenheim Palace but finally died, exhausted, in 1722. His fortune was reckoned to have been at least £1m. In today's money that would be £13.6bn.

Ralph, The 3rd Lord Cromwell

(c 1394-1456)
Land
Wealth: £40,000
Net National Income: £3.4m
% of NNI: 1.17%

£12.98 billion

The Cromwell family, of whom Oliver, the Lord Protector from 1645 to 1657, is the most famous, had already been around for quite a while in English history, and were rich by way of inheritance.

Before inheriting his title, Ralph, born around 1394, had been knighted for valour by Henry V at Agincourt in 1415. By 1431, he was the Lord Chamberlain, the head man at the Palace. In 1433, he was made treasurer of England, a post he held for 10 years, and out of which he profited mightily.

An inheritance of £1,020 from his wife was worth £2,263 at his death. His movables alone were worth £21,456, not to mention the land they stood on. But his executors had to give back lands he had wrongfully acquired and historians accept that he profited privately from the treasurership, despite being one of the few men to try and straighten out the public finances and reporting them accurately to parliament.

At his death, Ralph was worth approximately £40,000, nearly £13bn in today's money.

Henry Percy, The 9th Earl Of Northumberland

(1564-1632)
Land
Wealth: £350,000
Net National Income: £30m
% of NNI: 1.16%

£12.875 billion

Known as the 'Wizard Earl' because of his interest in alchemy – picked up on his grand tour of the Continent in 1582 – Northumberland spent 16 years in the Tower of London despite his wealth.

His imprisonment followed a link between him and one of the chief conspirators in the Guy Fawkes plot to blow up parliament in 1605. Northumberland had dined with his kinsman Thomas Percy on the night of 4th November. Although a public Protestant, Northumberland had Catholic friends. Although he was initially only arrested as a precaution, with few in power believing him guilty, he was fined £30,000 in 1606, and sentenced to life in the Tower. He served his sentence in some comfort, with a library in his cell, a small court of scientists and children in daily attendance and many other comforts. His daughter married the Earl of Carlisle against his wishes in 1617, but it was the Earl who by and large got his father-in-law out of prison.

Neither the fine nor other tribulations did much to dent the largest fortune of the age and Northumberland died worth £350,000, representing about 1.16% of net national income at the time, which would have made him worth £12.8bn in modern money.

Sir William De La Pole

(d 1366)
Merchant
Wealth: £30,000
Net National Income: £2.6m
% of NNI: 1.15%

£12.76 billion

Neither his parentage, nor his birthplace, nor its date are known, but by 1338, William de la Pole had set up a £111,000 loan for Edward III. This was an unprecedented sum in that age and would be the equivalent of around £11bn nowadays. He raised most of it in the Yorkshire city of Hull.

In partnership with his son, who was mayor between 1332 and 1325, and an MP five times, it was they who got the city its royal charter in 1331. They also supplied munitions and weapons to the Crown for the wars in Scotland. He later arranged huge loans to the Crown, secured against the customs revenues, a precedent that many financiers were subsequently to follow.

A masterful financier and a manager 600 years ahead of his time, de la Pole kept meticulous accounts, controlled his unit costs and kept his own commitment in the big deals well hedged. But he was utterly ruthless and without scruples and walked away from many of his own schemes when they collapsed. He was twice imprisoned and prosecuted for fraud in 1340 and 1353, but came out unscathed.

By 1331, he had land all around Hull, in the city and in County Durham. He had £5,000 on deposit with bankers. He married his daughters into the aristocracy and his son became a peer. They were the only merchant family in the fourteenth century to achieve this piece of social elevation.

When he died he was worth at least £30,000 about 1.15% of net national income at the time. In today's money that would be around £12.7bn.

Violent deaths among the rich list

Rich list member	Wealth
The Earl of Arundel and Surrey (1346-1397)	£55.498bn
Archbishop Thomas Becket (c1120-1170)	£24.641bn
Sir Nicholas Brembre (d 1388)	£3.884bn
The Duke of Buckingham (c1457-1483)	£18.425bn
Sir Simon Burley (d 1388)	£3.884bn
William Catesby (c1440-1483)	£2.996bn
Geoffrey De Mandeville (d 1141)	£5.549bn
Hugh Despencer the Younger (d 1326)	£17.759bn
The Duke of Exeter (1352-1400)	£18.42bn
Piers Gaveston (1284-1312)	£5.549bn
The Duke of Gloucester (1335-1397)	£22.19bn
The Earl of Hereford & Essex (1276-1322)	£6.659bn
Sir Robert Holland (c1270-1329)	£4.106bn
John Howard 1st Duke of Norfolk (1430-1485)	£9.212bn
Thomas Howard, 4th Duke of Norfolk (c1536-1572)	£9.212bn
Viscount Lovell (1454-c1487)	£5.993bn
Richard Lyons (d 1381)	£3.884bn
William Montagu, Earl of Salisbury (1301-1344)	£5.549bn
Roger Mortimer, Earl of March (1286-1330)	£10.605bn
Henry Percy, The 1st Earl of Northumberland (1341-1408)	£11.09bn
Sir Richard Radcliffe (d 1485)	£3.551bn
Earl Rivers (2nd) (1442-1483)	£12.32bn
Earl Rivers (1st) (1410-1469)	£12.653bn
The Earl of Stafford (1593-1641)	£7.88bn
The Duke of Suffolk (1396-1450)	£16.747bn
John Tiptoft, Earl of Worcester (c1427-1470)	£7.88bn
William of Warenne (d 1088)	£73.923bn
The Earl of Warwick (1428-1471)	£15.761bn
The Earl of Wiltshire (c1420-1461)	£6.326bn

William Marshall

(1147-1219)
Land
Wealth: £15,000
Net National Income: £1.3m
% of NNI: 1.15%

£12.75 billion

A pretty face, a strong right arm and an absolute instinct for loyalty were what propelled this fairground roisterer to the regency of England in the course of one of the longest lives at the top in the medieval world.

Born the son of a prosperous minor baron, Marshall never learned to read or write and started out life as the manager of a team of tournament fighters. Clearly a charmer, he won the patronage of Eleanor of Aquataine, her young son Henry I and later that of Henry II. This is characteristic of how he gradually amassed a huge fortune.

He realised early on that royalty was where wealth was and only they could dish it out in large quantities. Which they did. In return for his loyalty, each of his royal patrons gave him land but it was the hand of Isobel, the heiress to Earl Richard of Striguil, that brought the most wealth with it. Huge acreage on the Welsh borders, in Wales itself and in Ireland. Marshall became a baron by their marriage and his lands were confirmed to him in 1189 by Richard the Lion Heart, who had been unhorsed by Marshall in a tournament only the previous year.

When King John, a hapless monarch, died in 1216, he left a son of ten who was crowned that year. Marshall was his regent. John was an unpopular monarch and the child was threatened on all sides. Marshall is said to have remarked that:

If everyone abandons the boy but me, do you know what I shall do? I will carry him on my back, and if I can hold him up, I will hop from island to island, from country to country, even if I have to beg for my bread.

When Marshall died in 1219, he was the richest man in the kingdom. His lands were worth about £15,000 when net national income was £1.3m. In today's money that would be around £12.7bn.

The 3rd Duke Of Bridgewater

(1736-1803)
Land
Wealth: £2.5m
Net National Income: £235m
% of NNI: 1.06%

£12.725 billion

Despised by his mother, Bridgewater received scant education until he was sent to Eton at 12. Here he was birched and bullied, but the experience did not seem to damage him. The death of his elder brother made him a duke, but after breaking off an engagement to the widowed Duchess of Hamilton, he did not marry, and spent most of his life on his estate in Worsley, near Manchester.

Bridgewater became interested in developing the existing coal mining on the estate, which he felt could be delivered at a lower cost if there were better transport links with Manchester. He decided to build a canal, and with the equally uneducated Brindley, created the first aqueduct in Britain since Roman times.

He spent £220,000 on the canal from Worsley to Manchester and its successor canal between Manchester and Liverpool. The second canal very nearly bankrupted him, and Bridgewater cut his spending in his own home to just £400 a year. He refused to mortgage his land for the new canal but raised a loan on the first canal for £25,000 to complete the Manchester to Liverpool scheme. He was vindicated when the price of his coal sold in Manchester was halved. The canals eventually yielded £80,000 a year and he extended his estates in all directions by using the money to buy up any land with coal seams.

Bridgewater also spent nearly £170,000 on underground tunnels and other works extending over 40 miles. He is generally considered the father of the inland waterways of Britain.

When he died, he left a fortune of £2.5m, maybe much more, to his cousin and to his nephew, the First Duke of Sutherland. It would be worth £12.7bn in today's money.

Robert Of Meulan, Lord Of Beaumont and Earl Of Leicester

(1046-1118)
Land
Wealth: £4,000
Net National Income: £350,000
% of NNI: 1.14%

£12.653 billion

The son of a prominent Norman magnate, Robert of Meulan distinguished himself at the Battle of Hastings in 1066. His reward was land in England worth a significant but not spectacular £254. His wealth improved in the early 1080s, when he succeeded to his uncle's lands in the county of Meulan, France. A decade later, he obtained his father's Norman estates.

He later became a key adviser to William Rufus, and after the king's sudden death in 1100, Meulen transferred his loyalty to Henry I. By 1107, in reward for his role in helping Henry acquire Normandy, he was given the earldom of Leicester. His estates in England were by now extensive, especially in the Midlands.

Meulan was, to put it mildly, tenacious about his own enormous property and refused to hand back disputed lands, even on his deathbed. This is consistent with how he dealt with a raid by the French king on his property in Meulan. He attacked Paris, causing so much damage that the Ile de la Cite´ required extensive rebuilding.

He died of natural causes in 1118, worth £4,000, or about £12.6bn in today's money.

Earl Rivers (1st)

(c 1410-1469)
Land
Wealth: £40,000
Net National Income: £3.5m
% of NNI: 1.14%

£12.653 billion

Sic transit gloria mundi (thus fade the glories of the earth) is the only possible epitaph for 1st Earl Rivers. Like so many others of the great and the good in the first five hundred years after the Conquest, he rose to eminence, wealth and power but wound up with the executioners axe whistling down on his collar while it still enclosed his neck.

His name before the earldom arrived was Richard Wydeville (or Woodville), scion of a Northamptonshire family with a very small estate. He fought in France and was knighted and in 1436, married the widow of Bedford, the former Regent of England and Henry VI's aunt by marriage.

Wydeville's career took off with a bang. He became a Lord, Seneschal of Aquitaine and a member of the king's council. Naturally, his wife came with a great estate as dowry but this reverted to her family on her death, something Rivers was determined to compensate for. Then luck struck again. Wydeville's widowed daughter Elizabeth married the king, Edward IV. Wydeville became Earl Rivers and got two jobs which together were worth £1,586 a year, that of treasurer and constable of England.

Every kind of largess was poured onto the Rivers retinue by the king and aristocrats were found to marry all his daughters. But in the undergrowth, Warwick the Kingmaker was plotting and in the process arranged for Rivers' execution and for his widow, Jacquetta, to be charged with sorcery. All five of Rivers' sons died childless, three of them violently.

At the time of his execution, Rivers was worth about £40,000, 1.14% of net national income of £3.5m at the time. This would have made him worth about £12.6bn in today's money.

Earl Rivers (2nd)

(c 1442-1483)
Land
Wealth: £40,000
Net National Income: £3.6m
% of NNI: 1.11%

£12.32 billion

All the medieval biographies speak well of this man on the basis that the royal favours, dubious titles, technicalities, speculation on forfeitures and force that he employed all had their place in normal political life.

Like his father, Rivers was a good soldier and became the Governor of the Prince of Wales, who later became Edward V. He was privately pious and set out on several crusades, ignoring more pressing duties in England. His brother-in-law, Edward IV, did not appoint him to the high posts his father had held. He fell foul of the Duke of Gloucester, busy plotting both the overthrow and murder of his nephew Edward V and the murder of his other nephew the Duke of York, which he duly accomplished, making himself king as Richard III. The king duly sent for the executioner to attend to Rivers, and he did.

When Rivers' head parted from his shoulders he was worth about £40,000 when net national income was around £3.6m, making his 1.1% share of it worth £12.3bn in today's money.

The Earl Of Lancaster

(1245-1296)
Land
Wealth: £50,000
Net National Income: £4.6m
% of NNI: 1.1%

£12.209 billion

Edmund, Earl of Lancaster, known as 'Crouchback', was the second son of Henry III and his queen, Eleanor of Provence.

Edmund came into enormous wealth after the Battle of Evesham in 1264. He urged his father to adopt sweeping confiscation of land belonging to defeated barons in the English Civil War. He received a large share of the spoils and was created the Earl of Leicester, and gained two castles in Wales. He later expropriated all the wealth of the Earl of Derby. In 1267, he was elevated to the earldom of Lancaster. His marriage in April 1270, to the daughter of the Earl of Albemarle brought him great additional wealth.

He spent his last years serving the king, first in the Welsh war of 1277 and later in fighting the French. He died in France while commanding an English army. While dying, he ordered that his body was not to be buried until his debts were paid. He was obeyed and his body was carried over to England in 1297, and honourably buried by the king in Westminster Abbey.

His £50,000 wealth would have been around £12.2bn in today's money.

Sir William Pulteney

(1729-1805)
Property
Wealth: £2.6m
Net National Income: £240m
% of NNI: 1.08%

£12.133 billion

The third son of a baronet and MP, William Johnstone was admitted to the Scottish bar in 1751 aged 22. A contemporary of the great economist Adam Smith, he was an impoverished though highly intelligent young lawyer. Johnstone left Edinburgh for London in 1759, when took a job paying £400 a year in customs and excise. He had the sense to marry well when in 1760 he married Frances, the daughter of Daniel Pulteney MP. The couple returned to Edinburgh but inheritance helped the couple to great wealth.

The unexpected death in quick succession of his wife's cousin, Viscount Pulteney, in 1763, and his father, the Earl of Bath, in 1764, put her in line for the huge Bath fortune. It went initially to Bath's 79-year-old bachelor brother, General Harry Pulteney, but on his death in 1767, it passed to Frances. The Johnstones, who had returned to live in London, immediately adopted the Pulteney name and moved to General Pulteney's home, Bath House in Piccadilly.

William Pulteney developed an interest in politics and he became MP for the Scottish constituency of Cromarty in 1768, following an earlier unsuccessful attempt at Shrewsbury. Seven years later he was elected as MP for Shrewsbury and represented the borough until his death.

Pulteney remained independent and there is no evidence that he actively sought office. His principal interests were in financial and economic matters, which encompassed American and East Indian affairs, agriculture, fisheries, and transport throughout Great Britain. In all of these he had, or developed, a personal financial interest.

Pulteney's American interests appear to have stemmed from the appointment of his brother, George Johnstone, as governor of West Florida in 1763, and existing Johnstone family interests in the West Indies. On the outbreak of the American War of Independence in 1776, he and his brother, by then also an MP, became involved in attempts at reconciliation. George Johnstone joined the Earl of Carlisle's peace mission to America while Pulteney undertook a secret mission, under the alias of Mr Williams, to Paris to attempt negotiations with Benjamin Franklin, the American ambassador to France. Neither initiative bore fruit but subsequently Pulteney made his views known in pamphlets criticising government policy, pointing out the cost of the American war, and supporting a more generous treatment of the rebellious colonists.

Pulteney did not neglect his wife's extensive estates in London and Bath. The Bath estate offered the greatest potential for building development and to exploit this he promoted an act of parliament in 1769 allowing the bridging of the Avon between the old city and the parish of Bathwick on the east bank. Robert Adam, an Edinburgh contemporary and friend, was commissioned to design the estate but in the event only the Pulteney Bridge was built according to his plans.

Frances Pulteney died in 1782, and Pulteney was then responsible for managing the estates on behalf of his daughter, Henrietta Laura, as her mother's heir. Pulteney had always been interested in agricultural improvements and originally experimented at Solwaybank, his own small estate near Lockerbie in Dumfriesshire. He subsequently applied the same principles to his wife's estates in Staffordshire, Shropshire, Montgomeryshire, Northamptonshire, and Somerset.

At Solwaybank there were also fisheries which he developed and improved and his experience here was later applied nationally in Scotland through his role in the British Fisheries Society, of which he was director from 1790 to 1805.

From 1791, as part of the rapprochement with the USA, Pulteney invested heavily in American stock and then began his greatest speculation of all by buying 1m acres in upper New York state, of which a new town of Bath became the centre. Largely through the work of his agent, Colonel Charles Williamson, the scheme was so successful that by 1802, the whole area was opened up and the initial investment of £250,000 was later valued at £2m.

Always a frugal man, Pulteney lived quietly between Bath House and Shrewsbury, where with Telford's assistance he adapted the ruinous castle as a house. In 1794, on the death of his elder brother James Johnstone, Pulteney became fifth baronet and inherited the Westerhall estate together with plantations and slaves in the West Indies.

On 3 January 1804, Pulteney married his second wife, Margaret, daughter of Sir William Stirling, but he died in May 1805 at Bath House.

His British fortune was worth around £600,000 but with his American interest added, he was worth at least £2.6m. In today's money, that would be over £12.1bn.

Sir William Cokayne

(d 1626)
Merchant
Wealth: £300,000
Net National Income: £28m
% of NNI: 1.07%

£11.876 billion

Sir William Cokayne was a much admired Lord Mayor of London and close friend and private counsellor on business matters to James I, who made him a knight.

Much of his later fortune came from the plantation of Ulster in 1612, where he was the 1st Governor of the settlers and where he founded the modern city of Londonderry. In 1872, his livery company, the Skinners, still held its original 34,000 acre stake in the county of Derry. He built on the fortune left to him by his father, a skinners merchant, in 1599, and became successively sheriff of London and an alderman of several City wards.

Having enhanced his fortune in the classic manner by taking the stolen lands of others, he built splendid houses and financed several expeditions to establish new imperial colonies. He gave each of his seven daughters a dowry of £10,000 and saw them all married to aristocrats, but still left his son a rent roll of £12,000. He had land in Leicestershire, Northampton and in London.

At the time of his death he was reckoned the largest commoner landowner in the country. His total estate was reckoned to be worth £300,000, about 1.07% of net national income of £28m at the time. In modern money he would be worth £11.8bn.

Hugh Audley

(1577-1662)
Finance
Wealth: £400,000
Net National Income: £38m
% of NNI: 1.05%

£11.679 billion

Leading seventeenth century moneylender, Hugh Audley came from a family of London mercers. The tenth of eleven children, he was born around 1576, and baptized in 1577. His mother had aristocratic roots as a kinswoman to Baron Coleraine, but Audley was to make his own way in the world.

In 1603, at around the age of 26, he was admitted to the Inner Temple and in the following year obtained the reversion of a clerkship of the court of wards and liveries, in which his maternal uncle was a prothonotary or principal clerk of the court. He is alleged to have paid £3,000 for his position, which he exploited systematically for his personal gain. A close colleague, whose career in the court was exactly contemporaneous with Audley's, and who dedicated himself scrupulously to his duty, died in poverty. Audley became 'infinitely rich', rich enough to afford the loss of more than £100,000, which he is said to have suffered by the suppression of the court in 1646.

Years after this took place, monies due to the court, and its records, were still in his keeping. Audley's practice as a moneylender was extensive: at his death he was owed at least £30,000. He also invested in land, notably the manor of Ebury, in Westminster. He bought this cheaply in 1625-6 from Lionel Cranfield, Earl of Middlesex (1575-1645), who was in debt and desperate for money. The negotiations were prolonged, and during them Audley was described as 'barbarous', a man whose 'looks show his disposition', and one who bore himself 'loftily, respectless and peremptory'.

When Audley took advantage of the financial distress of another landowner to buy land at Buckenham in Norfolk, he appears to have withheld payments which he had promised, and to have harassed one of his creditors with vexatious suits. His reputation as a hard moneylender was such that in 1662, a book was written about his ways by an anonymous author called 'The Way to be Rich, According to the Practice of the Great Audley'. The 'intricacies' of his dealings, and the trouble and sorrow they brought to the men and women from whom he profited, are well attested.

He died on 15 November 1662, at the house of the rector of St Clement Danes, in Milford Lane, London, and was buried on 21 November at the Temple Church. After Audley's death, the estate passed by inheritance to his great-grandniece Mary Davies, wife of Sir Thomas Grosvenor, whose descendants it was to enrich: Mayfair's Audley Street, which runs through it, is named after Hugh Audley.

At his death Audley's wealth was around £400,000 or over £11.6bn in today's money.

Samuel Shepheard

(c 1648-1719)
Merchant
Wealth: £800,000
Net National Income: £77m
% of NNI: 1.04%

£11.528 billion

Thought to have been the son of a London saddler, Samuel Shepheard became a leading London merchant in the late seventeenth and early eighteenth century. His success as a merchant owed much to his initial involvement in first the wine and then the East India trade. During the mid 1690s, he emerged as a prominent critic of the monopoly held by the old East India Company, and early in 1696, with Gilbert Heathcote, he represented the interests of Leeward Islands and East India traders in petitioning the House of Lords to introduce competition.

Shepheard's wealth grew and in 1697 he became a government creditor. A year later he played an active role in establishing the new East India Company (to which he is said to have contributed £35,000) before being appointed a director.

In January 1701, he was elected MP for Newport, his money also securing Andover for his eldest son, Francis, and Malmesbury for his second son. However, Shepheard's conduct during both elections was soon subject to parliamentary scrutiny and resulted in his being sent to the Tower, though he was not impeached. He was rehabilitated in political and business circles during the following year and, while his standing in the East India Company was undoubtedly affected, he himself stood for and won the seat for the City of London in 1705. He sat for three years in the

Commons and kept his trading connections.

In 1708, he was elected one of the first directors of the United East India Company. Shepheard's last major financial activity centred on the formation of the South Sea Company, in which he invested heavily in 1711: he was appointed its deputy governor in 1713 and sub-governor in 1719.

He died that year before the South Sea Bubble burst, leaving an enormous estate worth £800,000 to his wife and sons. That would be worth over £11.5bn in today's money.

The 9th Duke Of Bedford

(1819-1891)
Land
Wealth: £11.067m
Net National Income: £1.075bn
% of NNI: 1.02%

£11.321 billion

The former Cistercian abbey of Woburn in Bedfordshire was granted by Henry VIII to his courtier, John, Lord Russell, later the 1st Earl of Bedford. By the nineteenth century, the Russells were among the most powerful and wealthiest families in Britain and had been raised to a dukedom. Younger sons tended to be active in politics, leaving the dukes to carry on the burden of running the vast estates.

The 9th Duke, who was born in 1819, inherited the title from his first cousin in 1872. For the 25 years up to his inheritance, he had been Liberal MP for Bedfordshire after a short spell in the Guards. His estates ran to 86,335 acres outside London producing an income of £141,793 a year. Adding the London property in Bloomsbury and Covent Garden gave an income in 1882 of around £368,923 and wealth of over £11m.

The 9th Duke lived until 1891, when he shot himself in a fit of insanity brought on by pneumonia. His £11.067m fortune represented around 1.02% of a total net national income of £1.075bn. Today that would be the equivalent of £11.3bn.

Sir John Fastolf

(c 1378-1459)
Land
Wealth: £35,000
Net National Income: £3.4m
% of NNI: 1.02%

£11.321 billion

Described by one of his servants as 'cruel and vengeful' and 'without pity and mercy', Sir John Fastolf was a professional soldier. He made his fortune, starting from humble beginnings, entirely out of the booty, pillage and rape of the Hundred Years' War. From the Battle of Agincourt in 1415, until his retirement in about 1440, Fastolf was on active service in France, remitting his profits back home to buy land, rather than living the high life.

He began with an inheritance of three manors and £46 a year. This improved on marriage to £240. But by the time he had finished remitting his pillage from France he was able to spend £13,855 on land, £9,485 on building and at least £2,500 on silver plate. He even had twenty books, which probably cost as much as the plate. He lost £11,000 of his stolen estates in France when the English were defeated in 1440, and the French recovered them. The key event in his career as soldier was the appointment of his patron, the Duke of Bedford, as Regent of France in 1422. Bedford made Fastolf councillor of France and governor of Anjou and Maine. The chroniclers say of him that:

Although a childless, widowed septuagenarian, he did not stop to consider why he acted as he did or who would benefit from his parsimony, litigation and rigour. He was the complete egotist to the end.

At his death, he was worth at least £35,000, which would be about £11.3bn today.

Ranulf Glanvill

(c 1120-1190)
Land
Wealth: £10,000
Net National Income: £1m
% of NNI: 1.0%

£11.099 billion

Royal patronage was the source of this medieval civil servant's wealth, with more than a little loot and pillage from a number of campaigns thrown in.

Glanvill came from a minor nobility, and so little is known about him personally that his birthday is set as sometime between 1120 and 1130. But his actions as a soldier who defeated the Scots at Alnwick in 1174, and as the king's justiciar, have left their mark, as has his book on law, 'Tractus de legibus et consuetudinibus regni Angliae'.

According to the chronicles he was allowed to keep £1,500 in cash plus horses and plate acquired during the course of his duties as sheriff of Yorkshire. His key patron was Henry II and when Henry died, Glanvill suffered the usual fate of finance ministers in medieval times: he was accused of speculation and theft by the new incumbent Richard I. Richard fined him the colossal sum of £15,000 in 1189.

Thereafter, Glanvill took off on the third Crusade but died in the unbelievable squalor and misery of the siege camp outside Acre in 1190. When he died he was worth about £10,000. In today's money he would be worth £11.09bn.

Bishop Walter Langton

(d 1321)
Church
Wealth: £50,000
Net National Income: £5m
% of NNI: 1%

£11.099 billion

King Edward I found Langton indispensable because, as the chroniclers note:

His devotion to Edward I's interests meant he would go to any lengths, even crime, to achieve his wishes.

He had entered royal service as a youth, eventually becoming the treasurer of the Exchequer and the de facto first minister. Edward defended himself against all comers.

When Edward died and Edward II was crowned the inevitable happened. Langton was tried for a variety of offences including abuse of power, manipulation of justice, extortion, arbitrary arrest and imprisonment on several counts of which he was convicted, and of homicide, devil worship and simony of which he was acquitted.

He was described as the most successful profiteer in the royal administration, probably ever. His abuse of his office was neither unusual nor unique, he simply seems to have made more money out of it, though he complained that the trial cost him £20,000, the equivalent of around £4bn nowadays.

When Langton died he left land, money and mortgages worth an estimated £50,000, about 1% of net national income at the time of £5m. This would be about £11bn in today's money.

Cardinal Thomas Wolsey

(c 1473-1530)
Church
Wealth: £50,000
Net National Income: £5m
% of NNI: 1%

£11.099 billion

King Henry VIII is one of the most famous figures in English history, and his Lord Chancellor Thomas Wolsey only slightly less so. What is less well understood is the extent to which Wolsey, like most chancellors before him and many afterwards, amassed wealth by carefully siphoning off a percentage of royal revenues for himself, something he did with the tacit, if not active consent of the king.

His rise to serious fortune followed his appointment to minor office by Henry VIII in 1509. By 1513, he was sufficiently in place to be the administrative genius behind the equipping and financing of the English invasion of France, which resulted in the victories of Therouanne, Tournai and the Spurs. Wolsey won the favour of the king and almost immediately begun his avid collecting of revenue and asset-rich church appointments. He was Dean of Lincoln Cathedral and Hereford Cathedral, Bishop of Tournai and Bishop of Lincoln before becoming Archbishop of York in 1514. In 1515, he was made a cardinal, which carried rich revenues with the office. He also held the Abbey of St Albans, the richest in England, as well as the bishoprics of Bath and Wells, Durham and Winchester at various times.

In 1515, Henry made him Chancellor. During his period as Chancellor, Wolsey raised taxes significantly and was equally ruthless when political threats to the king appeared, even approving the execution of the Duke of Buckingham. Having lost favour and with it office for failing to obtain a divorce for the king in 1529, Wolsey set off to have himself enthroned as Archbishop of York with a body of 600 horsemen, about the equivalent of an army division today, all on his payroll. But he was arrested on the way and summoned to London to face the usual range of charges and almost certainly to face execution. He avoided this by dying in custody at Leicester.

At his peak, Wolsey was worth at least £50,000, about 1% of net national income. In today's money he would be worth about £11bn.

Henry Percy, The 1st Earl Of Northumberland

(1341-1408)
Land
Wealth: £30,000
Net National Income: £3m
% of NNI: 1%

£11.09 billion

For nine years, this aristocrat and his son, Hotspur, dominated the border with Scotland and can also be said to have dominated English politics. They deposed Richard II in 1399, and had him murdered in February the following year. They installed Henry IV on the throne and became the immediate beneficiaries of all sorts of revenue-bearing honours and were given control of the Scottish border and of parts of the Welsh border. The king made sure they had salaries to go with the jobs. They had a virtual renewal of their licence to make war on and in Scotland, which they had also done under Richard, but Henry refused to finance the wars which could only be done with royal finance.

Hotspur met his end at the Battle of Shrewsbury in 1403, rebelling against the king he had helped install only three years before. His father rebelled twice more, in 1405 and in 1408, when he met his end at the hands of the Sheriff of Yorkshire on Braham Moor.

At the height of their power they were the richest two people in England and their wealth stayed with the family as some of the lands still do with the Smithson successors to the Percys. Their joint estate, much of it accumulated from the booty of war, was worth about £30,000 when they died. This was about 1% of net national income, which would make them worth about £11bn in today's money.

Henry, Earl Of Lancaster

(c 1281-1345)
Land
Wealth: £25,000
Net National Income: £2.5m
% of NNI: 1%

£11.03 billion

Henry's grandfather was Henry III and his father was the famous Edmund Crouchback, Earl of Lancaster. His brother was executed for treason in 1322, charges that Henry resented and disputed to the extent of adopting his brother's title and land after the execution. The post of Steward of England also devolved to Henry on his brother's death. On his father's death in 1296, he inherited the castles and lands of Monmouth, Kidwelly and Carmarthen as well as the extensive lands owned by his father on the Welsh side of the Severn.

He was responsible for the eventual trial and execution of both Despencer the Elder and the Younger in 1326. Having disposed of the dictatorship, Henry deposed and imprisoned the king, Edward II, but was not responsible for his murder. His final success was to see the new king's key adviser, Mortimer, deposed and executed. He became blind in his later years but during his long life he accumulated sufficient lands, estates and the profits of office to make him the richest man in England of his time.

He died worth £25,000, about 1% of net national income of £2.5m in 1345. In today's money he would be worth about £11bn.

The Duke Of Cleveland

(1766-1842)
Land
Wealth: £4.5m
Net National Income: £459m
% of NNI: 0.98%

£10.877 billion

Born with a silver spoon firmly in his mouth, William Vane was educated by private tutor and later at Christ Church, Oxford. At the age of 22, he became MP for Totnes. He succeeded his father as Earl of Darlington in 1792, but was a Whig in politics and supported the political reform which led to the Great Reform Bill of 1832.

Created Marquess of Cleveland in 1827, Vane was elevated to the dukedom of Cleveland in 1833. But sport and hunting preoccupied Cleveland more than politics. He spared no expense on hunting with his hounds on his vast Durham estates, paying considerable sums to his tenants to preserve foxes for hunting. In racing circles, he was known for his magnificent stud, which enabled him to win the 1831 St Leger with his horse Chorister.

Cleveland died in his London home in 1842. Though he left over £1m in his will, his total assets were around £4.5m, or about £10.8bn in today's money.

Sir John Ellerman

(1862-1933)
Finance and Shipping
Wealth: £36.685m
Net National Income: £3.728bn
% of NNI: 0.98%

£10.877 billion

The son of a corn merchant from Hull who had emigrated from Hamburg in 1850, Ellerman went on to become Britain's greatest financier and ship owner at the turn of the twentieth century.

His father died in 1871, when the young Ellerman was just nine, but after a spell living in France, he moved back to England with his mother. Leaving school in Birmingham at 16, Ellerman was articled to a Birmingham accountancy firm, where he passed his exams with top marks. He was able to move to a leading London accountancy firm and was offered a partnership within two years. But at the age of 24, he started his own firm and soon made his mark in the City, establishing investment trusts and mixing with up and coming young financiers.

At the age of 29, Ellerman made his move into shipping, organising a syndicate to take over the eminent shipping firm, Leyland & Co, whose owner had died suddenly. The financial press predicted disaster, but Ellerman proved to be a shrewd operator. He sold Leyland to J.P. Morgan, the American financier, for between £1m and £2m, some 50% higher than its most recent valuation. He was able to use part of the funds to buy an old, established Liverpool shipowner. Reviving the company, he set a pattern for the next quarter of a century, buying up old, established but sound firms where the management had lost its way.

Ellerman ships played a crucial role in both the Boer War and during the First World War: he was adviser on shipping to the government, placing his ships at the government's disposal. In 1916, he made his last great shipping takeover – of a Hull firm – for around £4.1m. But Ellerman was also extending his interests elsewhere. By 1918, he owned over 70 breweries, and in the early 1920s, he had stakes in 22 collieries.

After the war, he also became a leading London landowner, buying nearly 140 acres of prime real estate in Chelsea, Marylebone and South Kensington from the old aristocratic families. But there was no sentiment here: he re-sold a chunk of South Kensington quickly at a 30% profit.

During the war, Ellerman was sensitive about his German roots but there was little criticism of him in the press. It helped that he had large shareholdings in three national newspapers and owned three influential magazines. Ellerman was easily the richest man in Britain by the 1920s. Predicting the 1929 Depression, he was able to rearrange his portfolio accordingly.

On his death in 1933, he left £36.6m in his will. The Inland Revenue must have been trilled, as he made no attempt to avoid death duties. His fortune represented just under 1% of the national income of the day. In today's terms it would be £10.8bn.

Roman Abramovich

(dob 24/10/1966)
Oil and industry

Wealth: £10.8 billion

A £150m divorce settlement would normally impoverish most millionaires, but it was mere small change for Roman Abramovich, whose divorce from his second wife Irina, was announced in March 2007. Even after the settlement, he is still in the list's top sixty. The Russian rich list in *Finans* magazine, published in February 2007, before the divorce, put Abramovich's fortune at £10.7bn.

Abramovich, best known in Britain for the money he has devoted to Chelsea football Club, is of course eligible for this list courtesy of his ownership of Chelsea and the fact that he now spends more of his time in Britain at his Belgravia town house or his 440 acre Sussex estate. Yet Abramovich's background was anything but privileged. Born in a bleak industrial town just south of the Arctic Circle, he was orphaned at three, and raised by his uncle. Moving to Moscow at 14, he did his army service and then started his own business, first making cheap plastic products, later graduating to tyres.

Shrewdly, he moved into the burgeoning oil industry and teamed up with Boris Berezovsky, then the most important of the Russian tycoons. The pair bought the Sibneft oil operation in 1995, for around £120m. Berezovsky went into exile and Abramovich was left in charge of Sibneft. In October 2005, Sibneft was sold to Gazprom, the Russian natural gas monopoly. The stake held by Abramovich and his partners was worth around £7.5bn under the terms of the deal. The vast majority of that will have gone to Abramovich. In addition, Gazprom paid a special £280m dividend to the former owners in June 2006.

Yet that is not the extent of Abramovich's interests. He has another £1bn of holdings in other areas of Russian industry such as food and pharmaceuticals. Huge dividends over the years from Sibneft and sales of stakes in his other operations, such as his aluminium holdings, adds another £2bn. This huge liquidity has given Abramovich the money for his £500m plus spending spree since acquiring Chelsea in 2003, clearing its debts and filling its team with world-class players. It also meant that Chelsea could afford to lose £140m in 2004-05 and £80m in 2005-06.

Abramovich has not forgotten his homeland, giving £200m to the Chukotka region in the Arctic Circle, where he is governor. He is also spending up to £1.5bn acquiring a stake in a leading Russian steel company with a view to becoming a rival to Lakshmi Mittal (q.v.) in that industry.

Aside from his homes in Britain and worldwide, Abramovich can also relax on three yachts with another under construction costing £200m. Even after all the spending, donations and the divorce, Abramovich should easily be worth £10.8bn.

Roger Mortimer, Earl Of March

(1286-1330)
Land
Wealth: £50,000
Net National Income: £5.2m
% of NNI: 0.96%

£10.605 billion

The use of politics to acquire property was honed to a fine art in the fourteenth century, and the main exponent of this ignoble art was Roger Mortimer, Earl of March. Mortimer got off to a good but obscure start by holding Domesday lands at Wigmore and by being related to several other figures in this list, including William Marshall.

Through his wife he inherited extensive lands in Ireland, to which he added when he was king's lieutenant and justiciar. He waged war on Edward II's behalf in Scotland, Gascony, Wales and Bristol with the usual increments to his fortune from confiscated and pillaged lands.

He made an alliance with Queen Isabella, whose lover he was, defeated and executed the Despencers and then had Edward and his brother, the Earl of Kent, murdered. He immediately set out on a campaign of murderous revenge and further theft, all outside the sketchy laws of the period. By 1331, that long lived and most powerful of the Plantagenet monarchs Edward III had had enough of him, had him arrested and then brutally executed despite pleas of clemency from Queen Isabella.

His heirs did well of him as this list demonstrates. He died worth about £50,000 when net national income was £5.2m and his wealth represented 0.96% of that figure. In today's money he would be worth about £10.6bn.

Nathan Meyer Rothschild

(1777-1836)
Finance
Wealth: £3.6m
Net National Income: £395m
% of NNI: 0.91%

£10.1 billion

Nathan Meyer Rothschild broke the news of the British victory at Waterloo to an incredulous British government in June 1815, a day ahead of the official despatch from Wellington. It was a triumphant vindication of Rothschild's determination to obtain vital news as quickly as possible and he built up his own courier network accordingly.

The third son of a Frankfurt banker, Rothschild came to England in 1797, to buy cotton goods for the German market. He took British citizenship and made his home in London, acting as a general merchant as well as financier. During the Napoleonic Wars, he played a key role in helping pay British government subsidies to its allies and for forwarding funds to Wellington in Spain.

After the war, he became the leading financier in the City and was responsible for large loans to European governments such as France, Prussia and Austria. He also dealt in foreign exchange markets and was engaged in trade: for example he ensured that the Rothschilds had a monopoly of the market in mercury.

When he died in 1836, just after purchasing the vast Gunnersbury estate in West London, he was worth at least £3.6m according to Niall Fergusson in his recent history of the dynasty. In today's terms that would be £10.1bn.

Eleanor Of Aquitaine

(c 1122-1204)
Land
Wealth: £10,000
Net National Income: £1.1m
% of NNI: 0.9%

£9.989 billion

Eleanor of Aquitaine, the daughter of King William X of Aquataine, was the greatest heiress of the twelfth century. As a Duchess her lands ran from Poitou to the Pyrenees and she had much else besides.

At the age of fifteen she married King Louis VII of France but he divorced her because she had only produced two daughters by the time she was thirty. A spirited woman, she was rumoured to have had affairs with Geoffrey of Anjou and with her uncle Raymond, Prince of Antioch. But she surprised everyone by marrying Henry of Anjou in 1152. He was fifteen and she was thirty. Her vast estates were joined with those of the Anjous, which made them the richest couple in the world at the time, the more so when he became Henry II of England and acquired the king's lands, the original Crown estate.

She bore him three daughters and five sons but lost her position when she plotted with her elder sons to depose their father. She was put under house arrest and was little seen until Henry's death.

Our estimate of her wealth is probably minimalist. She is reputed to have left £10,000 on her death in 1204, which was about 0.9% of net national income at the time. In today's money she would be worth about £9.9bn.

Geoffrey Fitzpeter

(d 1213)
Land
Wealth: £10,000
Net National Income: £1.1m
% of NNI: 0.9%

£9.989 billion

Geoffrey Fitzpeter was a knight from Wiltshire, without great aristocratic connections. Yet he rose to be Justiciar of England, a cross between Lord Chief Justice and Prime Minister, and held the post from 1199 to his death in 1213.

No one knows how he came to royal notice but by 1181, he was witnessing royal charters and had become sheriff of Northampton and Chief Forester. He sat as a judge at Westminster and in the royal forests, collecting rents and hearing cases.

By marriage he had acquired part of the estates of the earldom of Essex and by 1189, he had lands worth twelve knights' fees. When John became king in 1199, Fitzpeter was supervising the Exchequer, a rich source of 'commission' and was the main tax collector, another rich source of commissions. During the king's many absences, Geoffrey acted as his regent. Oddly, when he lost Normandy, King John showered gifts on Fitzpeter, including the earldom of Essex. The Tower of London was his office, not his prison as it was for so many on this list.

When he died in 1213, he was worth £10,000, 0.9% of net national income of £1.1m. This would make him worth £9.9bn in today's money.

Archbishop Hubert Walter

(1140-1205)
Church
Wealth: £10,000
Net National Income: £1.1m
% of NNI: 0.9%

£9.989 billion

Archbishop Hubert Walter was, successively and sometimes simultaneously, Lord Chancellor, Justiciar, Archbishop of Canterbury and Bishop of Salisbury. He was also a lay brother in one of the most austere orders of the Catholic church, the Cistercians. On a visit to one monastery, while he was Chancellor and the most powerful man in the country, he was so impressed by the piety of one of the monks, Adam of Dryburgh, that he ordered the monk to beat him with a rod, to atone for his sins.

Like all chancellors, even in the distressed country of King John, he amassed a huge amount of wealth. There was an investigation after his death into the number of wardships he had bought and sold. It was also clear that he was using public funds for private investment. But woe betide those who had tried to investigate him before his death. William FitzOsbern, a prominent citizen of London had complained to the king about speculation at the Exchequer. The day before the investigation was to begin, FitzOsbern was hanged on Hubert's orders on a charge of resisting arrest and manslaughter. A French Abbot who arrived the following day on the same investigative mission had dinner with Hubert and was immediately taken ill and died.

When Hubert died he was worth about £10,000, around 0.9% of net national income of £1.1m. In today's money he would be worth about £9.9bn.

The Duke Of Westminster

(1825-1899)
Land and Property
Wealth: £14m
Net National Income: £1.591bn
% of NNI: 0.87%

£9.656 billion

Hugh Lupus Grosvenor became the 3rd Marquess of Grosvenor on the death of his father in 1869. The family fortune – based on the Mayfair property holdings and estates in several counties round Britain – was by then worth around £200,000 a year in annual income.

Grosvenor proved to be a far-sighted landlord and rebuilt his London property. He also built up a fine stud and spent 14,000 guineas buying a horse called Doncaster, which won the 1874 Derby. His art collection was also regarded as one of the finest of its day.

A Liberal in politics, he supported Gladstone, though with reservations about extending the franchise, and he was vehemently opposed to Irish home rule. Loyalty to Gladstone and his huge wealth led to the dukedom of Westminster being conferred on Grosvenor in 1874.

He died after a bronchial attack in 1899, to be succeeded by his grandson. He left around £14m, or around £9.6bn in today's terms.

William Beauchamp, 1st Baron Bergavenny

(1343-1411)
Land
Wealth: £25,000
Net National Income: £3m
% of NNI: 0.83%

£9.329 billion

As a younger son, William Beauchamp was destined for the church and attended Oxford University from 1358 until 1361. But after the deaths of two elder brothers in quick succession, he was made a knight at 24 and began a career as a fighting knight round Europe: he immediately joined the Black Prince on a campaign in Spain and a year later, in 1368, went on a crusade to Prussia. Two years later, he fought in Gascony, in 1373 he participated in John of Gaunt's expedition to France, and in 1381-2 in Edmund, Earl of Cambridge's expedition to Portugal. Edward III gave him a life annuity of 100 marks for his good service.

In 1369, Beauchamp was elevated far above the level of a younger son by the grant under his father's will of land to the value of 400 marks, mostly in the Midlands. In 1372, his prospects were further enhanced: John Hastings, the last Earl of Pembroke of the Hastings family, then childless and at odds with his cousin and heir, Reynold, Lord Grey of Ruthin, willed almost all his lands in England and Wales to Beauchamp, his cousin. The exception was Pembroke, which was left to the king. Beauchamp in return was to bear Hastings' arms and try to obtain the recreation of the earldom.

Hastings died in 1375, but he left an under age son who survived until 1389. However, in 1378, Beauchamp was given custody of Pembroke itself during the heir's minority. He also had dealings in Somerset arising out of his sister's marriage to John, Lord Beauchamp of Hatch. Astute family marriages and other property dealings helped enhance Beauchamp's wealth.

Through all the years of Richard II's reign, Beauchamp managed to steer a way through the intrigue and near rebellion by the powerful barons against the king. He was one of Richard's earliest chamber knights, appointed in 1377, probably because he had been councillor to the Black Prince (he was executor to the Prince's widow in 1385), and was chamberlain of Richard's household from 1378 to 1380.

During the early 1380s, he received various grants, including a life grant of 200 marks a year in 1380-81, and the alien priory of Pembroke in 1383. Campaigning on the Continent and his role as captain of Calais from 1383-1389 kept Beauchamp out of the intrigue against the king. At Calais, he performed with some distinction both on land and at sea and was several times on diplomatic missions. His ability to keep out of trouble meant that he was still able to pick up rewards from the king and he became Baron Bergavenny, and from 1392, received a personal summons to parliament. He was now a nobleman of considerable means. Richard II, though, was forced to abdicate in 1399 and died a year later, having been deposed by Henry Bolingbroke, who became Henry IV. Beauchamp managed to survive and indeed prosper under the new regime. He and his wife obtained a number of grants from Henry IV.

In a violent age, where many a powerful aristocrat lost his head on the block, Beauchamp managed to die a natural death in 1411 at the ripe old age of 68. His fortune at his death was around £25,000 or £9.3bn in today's money.

Thomas Mowbray, 1st Duke Of Norfolk

(1366-1399)
Land
Wealth: £25,000
Net National Income: £3m
% of NNI: 0.83%

£9.296 billion

Thomas Mowbray, the 1st Duke of Norfolk, had a brief but intense life at the centre of British politics. Caught up in the incessant intrigue between powerful aristocrats and the monarch, Richard II, Mowbray barely escaped with his life before dying of the plague in exile on a pilgrimage to the Holy Land aged just 33.

Mowbray's rise to power came at an extraordinarily early age and was due to his close relationship with the king. The second son of Lord Mowbray, he inherited his title – Earl of Nottingham – at the age of 16 after his elder brother died. By then he was a king's knight and had been granted the right to hunt in the royal forests a year earlier. The king also purchased for him, for about £1,000, the marriage of Elizabeth, daughter of John, Lord Lestrange of Blakemere, and in 1383, made him a Knight of the Garter.

During the next few years he remained high in the royal favour: he had his own apartments in the royal palaces at Eltham and Kings Langley. On 30 June 1385, when about to accompany the king on his expedition to Scotland, Mowbray was granted for life the office of Marshal of England when he was just 19. But Mowbray's relationship with Richard II began to cool. Mowbray's first wife had died in 1383, after a few months of marriage, but in 1384, he made a good match by marrying the Earl of Arundel's daughter. While the wedding was attended by the king and queen, the marriage had been agreed without the king's approval. As a result, Richard II ordered Mowbray's lands to be seized.

During 1386, Mowbray became increasingly resentful of the favour that Richard II was now showing to others – especially Robert de Vere, Earl of Oxford – and by the end of the year had grown closer to the group of lords (led by his father-in-law, Arundel and the king's uncle, Thomas of Woodstock, Duke of Gloucester) who had opposed the king and the court during the Wonderful Parliament of October 1386. In early 1387, Mowbray accompanied Arundel to sea, where on 24 March, off Margate, they successfully attacked a Franco-Flemish wine fleet, capturing 8,000 tuns of wine that was then sold in England for 4d. a gallon.

However, their victory earned them nothing but envy from the royalists. Richard II's behaviour during the summer and autumn of 1387, merely served to hasten Mowbray's alienation from the court. The lords who had opposed the king in 1386, heard a year later that he was preparing to turn on them. They assembled their forces at Hornsey and claimed the activities of five of the king's principal favourites, including de Vere, were treasonable. By the end of 1387, they had been joined in their claim of treason by Mowbray and by Henry Bolingbroke, Earl of Derby, the son of John of Gaunt.

King Richard played for time and dispatched de Vere to Chester to raise an army. The combined forces of the five lords met and defeated de Vere's Cheshiremen at Radcot Bridge near Witney on 20 December (although Mowbray apparently arrived too late to take part in the engagement), then returned to London, arrested some fifty of the king's supporters, confronted Richard, and probably deposed him for two or three days.

Their control of the government was now assured, and when parliament met on 3 February 1388, they secured the conviction and execution of eight of the king's supporters (although not de Vere, who had fled abroad after Radcot Bridge). This Merciless Parliament lasted four months, and resulted in the humiliation of the king and the rout of the courtiers.

But Mowbray and Bolingbroke were never as committed to the destruction of the court faction as Gloucester, Arundel, and Warwick. Mowbray rapidly becoming reconciled to the king. Early in 1389, he was granted livery of his lands and formally pardoned his marriage, and at a council meeting on 8 March 1389, it was agreed that he would be granted the wardenship of the east march towards Scotland, to which the custody of Berwick and Roxburgh castles were added in May. He was promised £12,000 a year for this, and agreed to find 400 men-at-arms and 800 archers to serve with him for the months of June and July 1389. Mowbray was appointed as captain of Calais two years later, a post he held until his disgrace in 1398. He was also made chief justice of Chester, Flint, and north Wales for life in 1394.

During these years, Mowbray also enhanced his reputation as a soldier and diplomat. He helped subdue Leinster for the king and was rewarded with the Irish lordship of Carlow. Returning to England he was appointed to negotiate a marriage between Richard II and the French princess Isabella (Richard's first wife, Anne of Bohemia, having died the previous year). Further negotiations with French dukes and the Catholic Church were later entrusted to Mowbray by Richard II.

The mid 1390s saw Mowbray at the height of his influence at court, and he used his position to his best advantage, building up both his landed power and his influence. Between 1389 and 1398, he made grants of land, cash or office, amounting in all to some 40% of his income, to more than seventy persons, thereby establishing a retinue of supporters that could rival that of most earls. Most of these recipients came from the areas in which he already held, or stood to inherit, lands.

The estates which he had inherited from his brother were concentrated in four main areas: first, in the Isle of Axholme in north Lincolnshire, where his manors were grouped around the traditional *caput honoris* at Epworth Castle; second, a string of manors in northern and central Yorkshire, stretching from Hovingham through Thirsk and Kirkby Malzeard to Nidderdale Chase; third, a group of Midland manors based in Melton Mowbray in Leicestershire; and fourth, the honour of Bramber in Sussex, including Horsham, St Leonard's Chase, and Shoreham by Sea, as well as Bramber Castle itself.

These properties were probably worth about £1,400 a year. However, he could look forward to the acreage of his grandmother Margaret Brotherton, Countess of Norfolk, who held lands in Norfolk and Suffolk worth approximately £2,850 a year, which Mowbray stood to inherit at her death.

He also had a dispute with the Earl of Warwick over land in Wales. In 1397, he persuaded Richard II to restore this land to him, and not merely to restore the land itself, but also to order Warwick to hand over seventeen of his Midland manors in trust to Mowbray for a period of eleven years, so that Mowbray could recover the £5,333 that he reckoned he had lost from the land dispute.

Despite this, Richard II never fully trusted Mowbray. When the king suddenly arrested his three main critics – Gloucester, Arundel, and Warwick – in the summer of 1397, Mowbray played a crucial role, imprisoning and later executing Arundel. He also had Gloucester murdered in Calais, smothered to death by a pillow. Mowbray was not happy about his role in these deaths but he had no choice other than to cooperate. He was duly rewarded and in September 1397, was elevated to the dukedom of Norfolk. Mowbray also received his share of the more tangible spoils, in the form of

Arundel's honour and Lewes Castle in Sussex (which bordered his own honour of Bramber), and the seventeen manors in the Midlands forfeited by Warwick.

Such pleasure as he derived from his gains was to be short-lived, however. Mowbray's nerve was at breaking point and he made a serious mistake confiding in Bolingbroke that he suspected the king wanted to have the pair killed. The conversation was reported to the king and Mowbray, now the Duke of Norfolk, was immediately stripped of his office of Earl Marshal and ordered to appear before the king. His goods were seized and he was imprisoned. Bolingbroke sought to introduce a new series of charges against Norfolk. In the end though, after the king rejected a trial by combat between the pair, he had them exiled. Norfolk's exile was much harsher – and for life. He was also deprived of the additional lands forfeited by the earls of Arundel and Warwick, which he had been granted in 1397, and the remainder of his inheritance was seized into the king's hands, with the exception of £1,000 a year with which to support himself in exile.

He went on pilgrimage to the Holy Land via Venice. During his absence, his grandmother Margaret Brotherton, who had been created Duchess of Norfolk in 1397, died on 24 March 1399. Before leaving England, Mowbray had secured letters from the king declaring that if any succession or inheritance should fall to him while in exile, he would be permitted to petition for them, but Richard now revoked these letters and seized Margaret's inheritance for himself. Mowbray was also stripped of the dukedom of Norfolk. Being on pilgrimage, he was not aware of this, and died on his way back at Venice in late 1399 from the plague.

At his zenith, Mowbray's fortune and inheritance should have given him a £25,000 fortune or about £9.2bn in today's money.

The 40 richest Americans of all time

No.	Name	Wealth
1	John D. Rockefeller (1839-1937) *Oil*	£125bn
2	Andrew Carnegie (1835-1919) *Steel*	£66.2bn
3	Cornelius Vanderbilt (1794-1877) *Shipping, railroads*	£63.4bn
4	Bill Gates (1955) *Software*	£53.1bn
5	Robson Walton & Family (1945) *Retailing*	£52.9bn
6	John Jacob Astor (1763-1848) *Fur trade, property*	£51.3bn
7	Stephen Girard (1750-1831) *Shipping, finance*	£36.6bn
8	AT Stewart (1803-1876) *Retailing, property*	£30.7bn
9	Frederick Weyerhaeuser (1834-1914) *Lumber*	£28.5bn
10	Jay Gould (1836-1892) *Investments, railroads*	£27.7bn
11	Marshall Field (1836-1892) *Department stores*	£26.8bn
12	Paul Allen (1953) *Software*	£25bn
13	Henry Ford (1863-1947) *Automobiles*	£23.8bn
14=	Andrew Mellon (1855-1937) *Banking*	£21.3bn
14=	Richard Mellon (1858-1933) *Banking*	£21.3bn
16	James G. Fair (1831-1894) *Mining*	£19.6bn
17	Warren Buffett (1930) *Investments*	£19.4bn
18=	William Weightman (1813-1904) *Chemicals*	£19.3bn
18=	Moses Taylor (1806-1882) *Banking*	£19.3bn
20	Russell Sage (1816-1906) *Finance*	£19.2bn
21	John Blair (1802-1899) *Railroads*	£19.1bn
22	Cyrus Curtis (1850-1933) *Publishing*	£17.2bn
23=	John Pierpont Morgan (1837-1913) *Finance*	£16.5bn
23=	Edward Harriman (1848-1909) *Railroads*	£16.5bn
23=	Henry Rogers (1840-1909) *Oil*	£16.5bn
26	Oliver Payne (1839-1917) *Oil*	£16.2bn
27	Henry Frick (1849-1919) *Steel*	£14.8bn
28	Collis Huntingdon (1821-1900) *Railroads*	£14.6bn
29	Steven Ballmer (1956) *Software*	£14.4bn
30	Peter Widener (1834-1915) *Trams*	£13.8bn
31	Nicholas Longworth (1782-1863) *Property*	£13.4bn
32	Philip Armour (1832-1901) *Meatpacking*	£13.3bn
33=	James Flood (1826-1889) *Mining*	£13.2bn
33=	Mark Hopkins (1813-1878) *Railroads*	£13.2bn
35	Michael Dell (1965) *Computers*	£12.5bn
36	Barbara Cox Anthony (d 2007) & Anne Cox Chambers (1919) *Media*	£12.1bn
37	Edward Clark (1811-1882) *Sewing machines*	£12.0bn
38	Leland Stanford (1824-1893) *Railroads*	£11.9bn
39=	Hetty Green (1834-1916) *Investments*	£11.4bn
39=	James Hill (1838-1916) *Railroads*	£11.4bn

All figures are based on what the wealth of those listed would be worth in 1999.

Source: American Heritage October 1998. Figures for 1998 have been updated by 5.5% to reflect the growth in the US economy in 1999. The wealth of today's American billionaires in the list is taken from the Forbes 400 in October 1999.

Viscount Campden

(1551-1629)
Merchant
Wealth: £250,000
Net National Income: £30m
% of NNI: 1.72%

£9.212 billion

Baptist Hicks, later Viscount Campden, was a merchant, the son of a rich silk supplier in London. Having become a major supplier to the Palace and the courtiers in the late 1500s, he was knighted by James I soon after his coronation in 1603. Hicks was the first knight to keep on his shop after receiving the honour. Despite his position, he found the king's many Scottish courtiers a trial. 'The Scots' he wrote 'are fayre speakers and slow performers' and he would give them no more credit.

By 1609, he was a contractor for Crown lands, and by 1620, he was the MP for Tavistock, Devon. Each of his two daughters had £100,000 as a dowry and he spent £30,000 on his manor house at Campden. He built a sessions house at his own expense for the Middlesex magistrates and was reputed to have given away £10,000 in charity during his lifetime.

He died worth about £250,000, the equivalent of 1.72% of net national income, which at that time was £30m. This would be worth £9.2bn in modern money.

John Howard, The 1st Duke Of Norfolk

(c 1430-1485)
Land
Wealth: £150,000
Net National Income: £18m
% of NNI: 0.83%

£9.212 billion

The 1st Duke of Norfolk, John Howard was the son of a knight of the shires but was, through his mother, the nephew of the Mowbray Duke of Norfolk. (Family names within titles often changed, even when the title marches on.)

He was a supporter of the Yorkist cause in the Wars of the Roses and found favour with the king, who gave him confiscated lands and other rich offices. He was elected an MP in 1455. He raided France with other aristocrats and took lands and hostages for ransom. Over the years he acted as ambassador to France and negotiated several treaties to end the various conflicts between the English and the French. He was given his uncle's dukedom as part of his innumerable financial rewards for his services. He died leading Richard III's vanguard at the Battle of Bosworth in 1485. The king also died there.

The Duke left lands and other wealth worth about £150,000, 0.83% of net national income of £18m. In today's money that would be worth about £9.2bn.

Thomas Howard, The 4th Duke Of Norfolk

(1536-1572)
Land
Wealth: £150,000
Net National Income: £18m
% of NNI: 0.83%

£9.212 billion

The 4th Duke of Norfolk was a popular figure in his own time, and it was his public popularity which saved him from his fate for years. When he was 11, his father was executed for treason and he was placed under the protection of the Privy Council. His father's estate was a significant one and he added considerably to it by marrying the heiress to the Earl of Arundel, and, when she died, by marrying the heiress to the Audley fortune at Walden. When Elizabeth I ascended the throne she immediately brought Howard into the top ranks of the government, making him a Privy Councillor and Earl Marshall.

On being widowed for the third time, he married another great heiress, the widow of Lord Dacre of Gilsland. Howard decided to keep the land in the family by marrying the stepchildren to his own children. In part he succeeded but he was widowed again. His next bride-to-be however, was potentially heiress to the throne. This was Mary, Queen of Scots, who Elizabeth I believed was trying to supplant her. Eventually, Elizabeth had Norfolk tried for treason and executed on Tower Hill in 1572. His death and that of Mary ended any serious opposition to Elizabeth, who reigned until dying a natural death in 1603.

At his death, Norfolk was worth about £150,000. This would be worth £9.2bn in today's money.

Henry Percy, The 4th Earl Of Northumberland

(c 1449-1489)
Land
Wealth: £30,000
Net National Income: £3.6m
% of NNI: 0.83%

£9.212 billion

The huge estates of the present Duke of Northumberland owe much to this energetic soldier and politician, who started out with precious little except his mother's lands.

His grandfather had been killed in action in 1455, and his father was killed in 1461, just six years later. Both had died in wars with the Neville family as each strove for dominance in the region. The struggle was disastrous for the Percy family. Their territories had been confiscated, but the manner in which the heirs of former traitors had their ancestral lands restored, helped them; marrying a putative heir was a good bet and Lord Herbert, one of the great northern magnates, married his daughter to Henry Percy. He survived the rebellions of 1470 and 1471 without losing his head.

However, the old Percy lands were with the Neville heiress Ann and she was married to the king's brother, the Duke of Gloucester. At first Percy clashed with Gloucester but eventually decided that discretion was the better part of valour and became Gloucester's retainer. It was a good bargain. Gloucester left him in control of Northumberland and the East Riding. When Gloucester took the crown after the death of Richard III at Bosworth, Percy assisted the usurpation by executing Earl Rivers and by amassing an army and sending it south to intimidate London.

When he died he had created a new Percy domain and was

worth about £30,000, about 0.83% of net national income when it stood at £3.6m. This would be worth £9.2bn in modern money.

Elizabeth, Lady Of Clare

(c 1294-1360)
Land
Wealth: £20,000
Net National Income: £2.5m
% of NNI: 0.8%

£8.879 billion

Elizabeth of Clare was of high royal blood. Her father was Gilbert de Clare, Earl of Gloucester and her mother, Joan of Acre, the daughter of Edward I.

She married first John Burgh, the heir to the earldom of Ulster and its lands. He died in 1313 but in 1314, she inherited the lands of the Clare family when her brother was killed at Bannockburn. This made her a great heiress and she was abducted by Theobald Verdon in 1316, probably with her consent. Verdon died the same year. Her third marriage to Roger Damory ended with his death in 1321. All three husbands left her huge estates, bringing her a total income of £2,000 a year.

The Despensers, dictators of England (1322-1326) naturally defrauded her of part of her inheritance, but she recovered it. She took a vow of chastity and did not marry again. Her household accounts survived, and are the best medieval set in existence. She had no less than 250 'squires' trotting around the estate in her formal uniform or livery. Elizabeth became a huge benefactress of charities and founded Clare College in Cambridge.

Her estate, worth £20,000 passed to her granddaughter Elizabeth, wife of Edward III's son Lionel, Duke of Clarence. That inheritance was about 0.8% of net national income when it stood at £2.5m. In today's money she would be worth £8.8bn.

The 5th Duke Of Portland

(1800-1879)
Land
Wealth: £8.504m
Net National Income: £1.075bn
% of NNI: 0.79%

£8.768 billion

William Cavendish was the second but surviving son of the 4th Duke of Portland. After service in the Guards and a brief spell as a Tory MP, he inherited the title as the 5th Duke in 1854. His lands were vast: some 183,199 acres in nine counties of England and Scotland. His annual income was around £233,000. A recluse in his later life, he was known for building vast underground passages at his Welbeck Abbey seat. A pity, perhaps, that he was not alive today to build the Jubilee Line.

When he died in 1879, he left in personal items and cash some £1.5m to add to the £7m value of his land holdings. In all, that represented around 0.79% of the then net national income of £1.075bn. Today's equivalent would be over £8.7bn.

The Earl Of Westmoreland

(1354-1425)
Land
Wealth: £25,000
Net National Income: £3.2m
% of NNI: 0.78%

£8.648 billion

Ralph Neville, Earl of Westmoreland, was a close ally of John of Gaunt, the Duke of Lancaster and the fourth son of Edward III. He inherited large estates in the North with four castles. Neville eventually married Gaunt's bastard daughter, Joan Beaufort, in 1397, a move which transformed his career. He was made Earl of Westmoreland in 1399.

In the years following the crowning of John of Gaunt's eldest son as King Henry IV, Westmoreland prospered. His brother was treasurer of England between 1404 and 1407, one of the greatest sources of private profit in the kingdom. Neville showed his loyalty to Henry IV in 1405 and 1408, when he helped put down rebellions by the Percy family of Northumberland. Westmoreland's loyalty was crucial to the survival of the monarch and he was rewarded accordingly with grants of land.

When he died in 1425, he left a fortune of £25,000, about 0.78% of net national income of £3.2m. In today's money he would be worth £8.6bn.

The 1st Viscount Portman

(1799-1888)
Land
Wealth: £8.18m
Net National Income: £1.075bn
% of NNI: 0.76%

£8.435 billion

Edward Portman was born in Dorset in 1799. After the usual Eton and Christ Church Oxford education, he became MP for Dorset at the age of 24, and later for Marylebone, sitting as a Liberal.

The Portman family had large land holdings in the West Country – nearly 34,000 acres in all at 1882 – but it was their London estate round Oxford Street and Marylebone (still largely in family hands) which made them exceedingly rich.

Portman, who was created a baron in 1837, and later raised to be the first Viscount Portman in 1873, left £244,092 in his own personal assets on his death fifteen years later. But the land was worth around £7.9m in 1882 prices, giving an overall fortune of £8.18m, representing 0.76% of the then £1.075bn net national income. Today's equivalent would be over £8.4bn.

Ralph Menthermer, Earl Of Gloucester

(d 1325)
Land
Wealth: £30,000
Net National Income: £4m
% of NNI: 0.75%

£8.324 billion

Ralph Menthermer held the title of Earl of Gloucester during part of his lifetime only because his first wife, Joan of Acre, the widow of Gilbert de Clare, Earl of Gloucester, was a countess. She was also the daughter of Edward I and he locked up the importunate young squire he had just knighted for what he considered to be an inopportune marriage early in 1297. The medieval Gloucestershire love poem 'The song of Caerlaverock' is about the clandestine marriage of the two lovers.

By autumn 1297, the king was appeased and Ralph, styling himself Earl of Gloucester, attended parliament and joined the king in his invasion of Scotland. He prospered there, acquiring the earldom of Atholl, the lands that went with it, and all the lands of Annandale. By 1307, Joan had died, and his stepson was the earl. Menthermer sold his Scottish title for £10,000. He continued to acquire land by grants from the king and was released without ransom after being captured by Robert the Bruce at Bannockburn in 1314, where he had once more joined the fight against the Scots. He lived quietly until his death in 1325.

At the time of his death, scholars reckoned he was, or had been worth, about £30,000, making him one of the richest of the medieval barons. This represented around 0.75% of net national income of £4m. He would have been worth £8.3bn in modern money.

Sir Gregory Page

(1668-1720)
Merchant
Wealth: £600,000
Net National Income: £80m
% of NNI: 0.75%

£8.324 billion

Sir Gregory Page staged a most convenient death for a millionaire, from the point of view of his heir anyhow. A huge shareholder in the stock of the South Sea Company, his executors promptly sold his holding on his death in 1720. It was worth £600,000, and the stock was at its peak. His £600,000 represented 0.75% of an £80m net national income at the time. The equivalent figure today would be about £6.48bn. Had he waited a few more months to expire, his heir, also Sir Gregory Page, might have had nothing. Instead he received a huge addition to the shares he held in his father's and his grandfather's original company, the East India Company.

With the combined fortunes, Page junior bought much of Kent. At one stage it was said that it was possible to walk for a day in north-west Kent without leaving Page land. At Wricklemarsh in Blackheath, now South London, he built a house that was described as:

one of the finest houses in England, resembling a royal palace rather than the home of a gentleman.

He had a wonderful collection of old masters, auctioned by Christie's in 1787.

When Page junior died he was worth £1m, about 0.57% of a fast-growing net national income of £175m. In today's money he would be worth £8.3bn.

Adam Stratton

(d 1294)
Moneylender
Wealth: £30,000
Net National Income: £4m
% of NNI: 0.75%

£8.324 billion

Adam Stratton, also called Adam Argoyles, was the chief moneylender of the late thirteenth century and a master forger to boot.

Stratton started life as a humble clerk or pries from Stratton St Margaret in Wiltshire, but obtained 23 parishes in Canterbury and then entered the service of Isabella de Forz, sister of Baldwin, Earl of Devon in 1263. Through her he was made deputy chamberlain and later chamberlain of the Royal Exchequer on behalf of both Henry III and Edward I. With it, Stratton had custody of the Exchequer records, giving him the opportunity, to forge records and receipts, misappropriate royal funds and pervert the course of justice by using royal justice for private ends.

He came to grief in three stages. First he was caught cutting the seal of a charter of lands in 1278. Convicted of this he continued as Chamberlain. A raid on his premises in 1289, revealed £12,666 in coin, more than half the revenues of the Crown, in his possession. He was charged with a range of offences including homicide and sorcery. Convicted, he paid a fine and still carried on at the Exchequer, until he was convicted of forgery in 1292. That was the end of his career and he lived out his final years living off his many parishes in Kent.

At his peak he was worth £30,000, about 0.75% of net national income of £4m at the time. In today's money that would be the equivalent of £8.3bn.

The 5th Duke Of Buccleuch and Queensbury

(1806-1884)
Land
Wealth: £7.866m
Net National Income: £1.075bn
% of NNI: 0.73%

£8.102 billion

The huge land holdings of the Buccleuch family represent the amalgam of three dukedoms in one family: Buccleuch, Queensberry and Montagu.

By 1882, when John Baterman surveyed the aristocratic landholdings in 'Great Landowners of Great Britain', the Buccleuch estates ran to 460,108 acres, with more besides in the suburbs of London. The 5th Duke, born in 1806 and educated, naturally, at Eton, inherited the title at the age of twelve. He was a far-sighted landowner, investing considerable sums in improving his estates. Between 1835 an 1842, he invested £500,000 in a pier and breakwater at Granton, four miles from Edinburgh. He served briefly in Peel's Tory administration in the 1840s as Lord Privy Seal.

When he died in 1884, his estate was worth around £7.8m, representing about 0.73% of the then £1.075bn net national income. Today's equivalent would be over £8bn.

Lord Hungerford

(c 1378-1449)
Land
Wealth: £25,000
Net National Income: £3.4m
% of NNI: 0.73%

£8.102 billion

Lord Hungerford's father, a former Speaker in parliament, had built up a series of huge landholdings in Wiltshire, Somerset and Berkshire. His son succeeded to these estates and castles in 1398. He was smart enough to back the Lancastrian cause, though he did not really prosper politically until Henry V's reign. He became Speaker of the Commons in 1414, fought at Agincourt a year later, became Henry V's executor and guardian of the infant Henry VI. He was also Lord Treasurer from 1426 to 1432.

Hungerford fought a number of campaigns and was given grants of land in both France and England. He made a great deal of money out of ransoming his captives although he also had to do the same for two of his own sons. He bought about thirty manors, raising his income to £1,800. Unusually, he was educated, civilised and died in his own bed, having given vast sums to religious charities. Hungerford was executor to many landowners, making him probably the most trusted aristocrat who ever lived.

He died worth an estimated £25,000, about 0.73% of the then net national income of £3.4m. In today's money he would be worth about £8.1bn.

Jurnet Of Norwich

(c 1130-1197)
Finance
Wealth: £8,000
Net National Income: £1.1m
% of NNI: 0.72%

£7.981 billion

Jurnet, also known as Eliab HaNadib (the generous), of Norwich was the senior figure in the most prosperous Jewish community in England in its day.

Born in 1130, he lost money in a failed loan to the Crown in 1177. He then had to flee to the Continent and was only allowed back on payment of a £2,000 fine. His son, Isaac, had to pay a fine of £1,000 to inherit his father's estate in 1197. In 1210, Isaac fell victim to the confiscations of King John and was imprisoned in Bristol and later in the Tower of London. In a less than refined form of blackmail, the king excused Isaac execution in return for a fine of £10,000. He got out of the Tower in 1217 and went back to Norwich with royal letters of protection for himself and the Jewish community.

Both his father and Isaac were significant tax collectors for the Crown. The Jewish community at Norwich were educated in the great rabbinical tradition and the two most generous patrons of the Jewish educators were Jurnet and his son, who may have been rabbis themselves. They acquired land and buildings in Norwich, land in the county and helped to boost trade with the Continent. However, by 1273, the line had died out.

At their peak the family were worth at least £8,000, and given the King John fine, probably a lot more. This sum was about 0.72% of net national income in the thirteenth century and would be worth £7.98bn in today's money.

William Cavendish, The Duke Of Newcastle

(1592-1676)
Land
Wealth: £300,000
Net National Income: £42m
% of NNI: 0.71%

£7.880 billion

William Cavendish, the heir to great wealth, was created Earl of Newcastle in 1628. Noted for his lavish hospitality, he spent £20,000 entertaining Charles I in the 1630s. He raised army after army to fight for the royalist cause in the Civil War from 1642-1644. At Marston Moor in 1644, his army was shattered and he went into exile on the Continent. He endured considerable poverty in this period though he did establish a riding school in Antwerp, which achieved fame throughout Europe.

His wife calculated that they lost £900,000 during the war, taking into account unrecovered lands, forced sales, woodlands and other sources of wealth plundered or destroyed, plus sixteen years of unpaid rents. When the monarchy was restored, he recovered most of his lands and in 1665 was raised to the dukedom of Newcastle.

When he died, Cavendish was reckoned to be worth £300,000, about £7.8bn in today's terms.

Michael De La Pole, The Earl Of Suffolk

(c 1330-1389)
Land
Wealth: £20,000
Net National Income: £2.8m
% of NNI: 0.71%

£7.880 billion

Michael de la Pole was the son of the great Hull merchant, William de la Pole, who had been educated as an aristocrat by his father. Like all the key men of his time, he spent a good deal of his time at war, raping and pillaging, mostly in France and Scotland and getting himself captured three times in the process.

He was smart enough to keep in with parliament and was made chancellor in 1383. He was made a lord in 1366 and then an earl in 1385, with the king providing the financial endowment to enable him to uphold the rank. One year later the Wonderful Parliament charged him with various offences, mostly to do with mismanagement of the royal finances, which were in a terrible state. De la Pole had shown public concern about the matter, but this had not led to a solution, or to his refraining from taking vast sums as his fees – fat cats were about in the fourteenth century too. Normally de la Pole's offences would have been ignored, but he had Richard II under his influence and had let corruption and mismanagement get out of hand. The Merciless Parliament of 1388 condemned him to death and forfeited his estates. He escaped the axe by fleeing abroad where he died the next year.

At his peak, De la Pole was worth £20,000, about 0.71% of net national income of £2.8m. In today's money that would be £7.88bn.

Archbishop George Neville

(c 1432-1476)
Church
Wealth: £25,000
Net National Income: £3.5m
% of NNI: 0.71%

£7.880 billion

George Neville was a prelate typical of his time. The son of Richard, Earl of Salisbury, his brother was Warwick the Kingmaker. He benefited enormously from both connections. His father had him made the under age Bishop of Exeter, and his brothers had him made Chancellor of England as his father had been. He became Archbishop of York in 1465. Each of these offices brought enormous revenues and he lived in style at a huge mansion in Rickmansworth. He reputedly possessed movables worth £20,000 in 1472.

Neville supported the return of Henry VI to the throne but his failure to hold London in 1471, led to the defeat and death of his brothers. He continued plotting and eventually Edward IV had him imprisoned in Calais. He was released only to die a sick man in 1476.

At his peak he was worth £25,000 or more, about 0.71% of net national income of £3.5m. In today's money he would be worth £7.8bn.

Sir John Philipot

(d 1384)
Merchant
Wealth: £20,000
Net National Income: £2.8m
% of NNI: 0.71%

£7.880 billion

Sir John Philipot, a native of Kent, made a good marriage bringing with it a manor near Chatham. He became a liveryman of the Grocers company and it was that key position, combined with the patronage of the king, which made him the richest merchant of his age. Edward III sold him the receivership of forfeited goods and merchandise at Calais and later licensed him to export wheat to France.

In the crisis of the Good Parliament in 1377, and its sequel, Philipot and others asserted the rights of the City against aristocratic intervention and wound up lending £10,000 to the new king, Richard II, for the war in France, on the security of three crowns and other royal jewellery. Philipot was one of the treasurers of the campaign funds. Deprived of his Aldermanship in 1383, he died the following year.

At his death he was worth £20,000, about 0.71% of net national income of £2.8m. In today's money that would be worth £7.8bn.

The Earl Of Stafford

(1593-1641)
Land
Wealth: £250,000
Net National Income: £35m
% of NNI: 0.71%

£7.880 billion

Stafford, the son of a Yorkshire landowner, became an MP in 1614. His early years were spent in increasing the yield on his estates. At that time he opposed Charles I but changed sides in 1628. He was made President of the Council of the North, and ruled in an authoritarian fashion. But his real wealth came when he went to Ireland as Lord Deputy in 1633, motivated, as he himself observed by 'the personal profit to be gained from the place'. And profit he gained. While reorganising the administration of the country, he made sure he took his cut of the customs revenues and ensured that the plantation of Protestants and removal of the Irish landowners continued, collecting his share of the fees paid by the planters.

He made more money out of Ireland than almost anyone before him. In 1639, his income from Irish sources was £13,000 a year. But he also made enemies. Even the king, Charles I, was frightened by the ruthlessness of his methods. When the Scots rebelled in 1638-9, Charles summoned Stafford, who persuaded the king to summon the Short Parliament, which refused to grant the king the provisions for an army. Stafford commanded what troops could be mustered and lost the war in the North.

When the Long Parliament met in 1640, years of accumulated resentment by his enemies led to the attempted impeachment of Stafford on charges of high treason. That failed but a bill of attainder, proposed by the many enemies he had made in Ireland and elsewhere succeeded. A crowd of up to 200,000 watched him beheaded on Tower Hill in May 1641.

As his head dropped in the basket his estate was worth £250,000, about 0.71% of net national income at the time. In today's money he would be worth £7.8bn.

John Tiptoft, The Earl Of Worcester

(c 1427-1470)
Land
Wealth: £25,000
Net National Income: £3.5m
% of NNI: 0.71%

£7.880 billion

John Tiptoft was known as the 'Butcher of England' for the rigour with which he pursued traitors in his role as constable of England under Edward IV. Minor offenders and ringleaders were executed by impaling as well as hanging, drawing and quartering.

Tiptoft, the son of the first Baron Tiptoft, inherited his estates, but it was the family's royal connections that allowed him to advance to the earldom of Worcester in 1449. Displaying outstanding ability, Worcester rose effortlessly in royal service to become treasurer of England from 1452-54. Later, under Edward IV, he sold his English offices and went to Ireland as deputy, where he executed his predecessor, the Earl of Desmond.

When the Earl of Warwick launched his coup against Edward IV, Worcester was recalled by the king but was captured by Warwick, and executed to much public rejoicing. He had a religious side which led him to request that he be beheaded with three blows in honour of the Trinity.

His various offices gave him the opportunity to acquire land and wealth. At his death, he would have been worth around £25,000, or over £7.8bn in today's terms.

Roger, Bishop Of Salisbury

(c 1065-1139)
Church
Wealth: £5,000
Net National Income: £700,000
% of NNI: 0.71%

£7.878 billion

This man, a priest of humble origins from south-west Normandy created the English Exchequer, one of the most important single administrative acts of any period in history. He also controlled the treasury at Winchester, the English royal city of the time.

Roger came into his own under Henry I, crowned king in 1100. He became Chancellor in 1101 and also the king's chief minister, in charge of the administration of the country. From 1123 to 1126 he ran England while the king was in France, waging war. He installed his nephews as Privy Councillors and as Bishops of Lincoln and Ely. Though a priest, he had an articulate mistress in Matilda of Ramsbury. Roger installed their sons as Chancellor and Royal Treasurer. A peremptory man, he issued edicts that began: 'On behalf of the king and myself I order...' He amassed a huge fortune in lands and wealth, much, though not all of it, by way of gifts from King Henry and later from King Stephen.

He was undone, almost certainly so that the bankrupt king could have his estates, by Waleran of Meulan, another Croesus of his time. Tried at Winchester in 1139, Roger suffered the Scottish verdict of not proven. He spent the last months of his life undoing his wrongs, having retained his see but having lost most of his wealth.

At its peak, his wealth was worth £5,000, about 0.7% of net national income. In today's money that would be worth £7.8bn.

Sir Gilbert Heathcote

(c 1651-1733)
Merchant
Wealth: £700,000
Net National Income: £100m
% of NNI: 0.7%

£7.769 billion

Sir Gilbert Heathcote was a powerful merchant at a time when the British Empire was still growing and expanding. Born in Derbyshire of a squirearchical family, he came to London in the 1680s and soon had an extensive wine trade with Spain and was acting as military treasurer, for the usual fees, in the payment of the troops in the West Indies. His place in the annals of free trade is assured.

In 1698, one of his ships was seized by the East India Company on the grounds that the EIC was entitled to a monopoly of trade with Jamaica. Heathcote went to the bar of the House of Commons and won the right to trade where he pleased. He then successfully petitioned to have the old East India Company wound up, and promptly became the key shareholder and director of the new East India Company, subscribing £10,000 of its capital.

He was one of the founders of the Bank of England in 1694, and his gain there was around £60,000. Noted for his parsimony, Heathcote served in parliament under four monarchs and also became Lord Mayor of London in 1710. Like many merchants, Heathcote aspired to be a country gentleman and bought a Welsh estate from an old family.

He died in 1733, worth £700,000 and reputedly the richest commoner of his day. That would be worth £7.7bn in today's money.

The Marquess Of Halifax

(1633-1695)
Land
Wealth: £350,000
Net National Income: £50m
% of NNI: 0.7%

£7.767 billion

Born of a staunch royalist in the Civil War, George Savile, later the Marquess of Halifax, had to suffer the indignity of seeing £4,000 of his inheritance paid to Lord Wharton under the orders of a vindictive parliament.

During Cromwell's Protectorate, Savile was involved in royalist conspiracy in 1655-6 in Nottinghamshire and Yorkshire. His estates were passed to his uncles to preserve them from confiscation. When Charles II was restored to the throne, his estates were restored and he became one of the largest landowners in Britain, with estate income of £10,000 a year. His first marriage to a daughter of the Earl of Sunderland came with a £10,000 dowry.

Under Charles II, he played an important role in politics and was created Viscount Halifax in 1668, and raised to a marquess in 1682. While Halifax fell out of favour with James II, he welcomed the accession of William of Orange to the throne and was rewarded with the post of Lord Privy Seal.

Halifax was worth around £250,000 on his death from the effect of vomiting in 1695. In today's money that would be around £7.7bn.

Sir Paul Pindar

(c 1565-1650)
Merchant
Wealth: £250,000
Net National Income: £37m
% of NNI: 0.67%

£7.436 billion

A Northamptonshire man, Sir Paul Pindar was one of the greatest merchants of the age, who created much of his fortune in Europe and the Levant between 1583 and the early 1600s. Initially, this was in Italy where he was factor for a London merchant – Henry Parvish – but where he also acted on his own account and made himself wealthy.

In Turkey he became something of a diamond specialist, bringing back to England the 'Great Diamond' worth £35,000, which he lent to James I for state occasions. His son, Charles I, eventually bought the diamond for £18,000 but appears to have paid for it indirectly by way of grants to manage the customs and licences to produce alum.

In 1626, the king gave him the right to arrest all French ships and goods in England, for a fee. Pindar went on to become an important source of funds for the beleaguered Crown. By 1639, his loans to Charles totalled £100,000 with an 8% interest rate attached. Throughout the Civil War, Pindar supplied the king with funds, but did not suffer any consequences from a victorious parliament. He died aged 85, an unusual age to have achieved, in 1650. The front of his London house is preserved in the Victoria & Albert museum.

His fortune was put at £250,000 by contemporaries. In today's terms, this would be worth over £7.4bn.

Edward Backwell

(d 1683)
Goldsmith
Wealth: £300,000
Net National Income: £45m
% of NNI: 0.66%

£7.325 billion

Edward Backwell is generally considered to be the founding father of the English banking system. The town of Backwell in Somerset is named after the family from which he came, and his ancestors were traced back to the Battle of Poitiers in 1356.

Between 1635 and 1640, he came to London and married the daughter of a London merchant. His date of birth is not known but by 1650, the state papers mention him lending £500 in pieces of eight to the government. Backwell's money making was evident in 1653, when he had a bill for £1,380 for victualling ships.

A year later, parliament bought back Old Bushy Park, near Hampton Court, and other lands he had acquired, probably during the Cromwellian sell off of the Crown estate, for £6,202. The turbulence of the Civil War had made the goldsmiths, already money changers, much safer keepers of deposits than the government, which either seized all the deposits periodically, or devalued the currency.

Despite his financing of Cromwell's government, Backwell prospered after the restoration in 1660. He became the manager of King Charles II's money and handled the sale of Dunkirk to the French for £180,000 in 1662, receiving £1,500 in commission. His goldsmiths shop, under the sign of the Unicorn, was sited next to Lombard Street, which became the premier banking street for the next three centuries.

Backwell declined a knighthood but owned lands around the country. Of the total Exchequer borrowings of £1,828,526 in 1672, £295,995 was borrowed from Backwell and he became an MP in 1679.

His contemporaries reckoned his estate was worth about £300,000 on his death, about 0.66% of net national income of £45m at the time. In today's terms this would be worth £7.3bn.

Breakdown of the rich list by sector

Source of wealth	Number
Brewing/food/retailing	6
Church/politics/judiciary/military	16
Finance/goldsmiths/speculation	26
Industry/textiles/coal/steel/transport	27
Land/property	122
Merchant	53

William Cade

(d 1166)
Finance
Wealth: £6,000
Net National Income: £900,000
% of NNI: 0.66%

£7.325 billion

Of Flemish origin, William Cade was a moneylender in twelfth century Britain. Some of his records survive and they show he lent money on a huge scale in the 1150s and 1160s for many purposes, including to the king. But financing trade was a key element of his business. He raised his own funds, mainly from his own extensive trading, mostly with the low countries.

At his death, he was owed around £5,000. He died worth about £6,000 in 1166. This was about 0.66% of net national income of £900,000 and would be worth £7.3bn in today's money.

The Earl Of Derby

(1508-1572)
Land
Wealth: £120,000
Net National Income: £18m
% of NNI: 0.66%

£7.325 billion

The Earl of Derby was a minor at his father's death and became a ward of the great Cardinal Wolsey. At the age of 21, he took his seat in the Lords and seemed to be on the fast track to success: Knight of the Bath at 25 and cup bearer at the coronation of Anne Boleyn. But in the late 1540s, he started to make his objections known to religious change, so much so that he was commanded to give up his title to the Isle of Man, but refused.

The accession of Queen Mary was welcomed by Derby, who was created lord high steward for her coronation. During her reign, he frequently took part in proceedings against heretics. But his star waned under Elizabeth. His obvious sympathies made him an object of suspicion even though he was made lord lieutenant of Cheshire and Lancashire in 1569, and gave the government timely warning of the insurrection of that year. His sons were, however, implicated in an attempt to release Mary, Queen of Scots.

Derby died in 1572, and his funeral was one of the most magnificent on record. His estates in the North West and other assets were worth around £120,000, about £7.3bn in today's terms.

Sir Richard Gresham

(c 1485-1549)
Merchant
Wealth: £40,000
Net National Income: £6m
% of NNI: 0.66%

£7.325 billion

Descended from a long-established Norfolk family, Richard Gresham went into trade in London, apprenticed to an eminent London mercer. He was admitted to the Mercers' Company in 1507. He started trading on his own account and by 1512 was advancing money to the king. Thus started a long and profitable relationship for Gresham, particularly while his patron Cardinal Wolsey was at the height of his power. After Wolsey's death in 1530, Gresham continued offering the monarchy a discreet service, often abroad in the Low Countries.

He became a sheriff in the City, where he was zealous in burning heretics at the stake. Gresham sought, without avail, to have what would have been London's first stock exchange built in the late 1530s for the convenience of merchants who had to meet in the open air. Elected Lord Mayor of London in 1537, he was knighted shortly after. His close links with Thomas Cromwell who dissolved the monasteries obviously proved useful for Gresham, who obtained large grants of monastic land, in most cases by purchase.

When he died in 1549, he had three country seats in Norfolk, Suffolk and Yorkshire, as well as premises in London. His Yorkshire lands, for example, cost him over £11,737. In all, he was worth around £40,000, or about £7.3bn in today's terms.

The Earl Of Pembroke

(c 1501-1570)
Land
Wealth: £40,000
Net National Income: £6m
% of NNI: 0.66%

£7.325 billion

As a young man, William Herbert, later the Earl of Pembroke, murdered a mercer in Bristol on account of a 'want of some respect in compliment'. He fled to France and served in the French army with such gallantry that the French king wrote to Henry VIII about him. This enabled him to return to England where he married Anne Parr, younger sister of Catherine Parr, who became Henry's sixth queen. Herbert's place was assured.

In 1542 and 1544, he received rich estates belonging to the dissolved abbey of Wilton, where he destroyed the monastic buildings and built the magnificent Wilton House. More land followed in Wales and he became owner of Cardiff Castle. He was also granted the keepership of Baynard's Castle on the banks of the Thames.

When Wilton was invaded by rioters, he dealt with them severely and he raised a force of 2,000 Welshmen from his estates there to help fend off a Cornish attack on Exeter. The heavy expenses of this campaigning was met out of the profit he made from minting a large quantity of silver bullion. This deal netted him £6,709, 19s, profit.

From then on, he followed a path of political intrigue with the supreme ability to come out on the right side. In a dispute between the Earl of Warwick and Protector Somerset over who should rule, Pembroke was courted by both sides, but came out in favour of Warwick. He was richly rewarded and became the Earl of Pembroke. He also acquired Somerset's Wiltshire estates and mansion.

He later supported Lady Jane Grey's succession to the throne, but crucially deserted her for Mary. He served Mary though he was regarded with suspicion. When she died, he switched his loyalty to Elizabeth I, where he was again regarded with some suspicion, especially after he supported a scheme for Mary, Queen of Scots to marry the Duke of Norfolk. He was arrested in 1569, but managed to talk his way out to serve Elizabeth one last time against an open revolt in the North by powerful barons.

He died in 1570, with a £40,000 fortune, or about £7.3bn in today's money.

Sir Robert Viner

(1631-1688)
Goldsmith
Wealth: £300,000
Net National Income: £45m
% of NNI: 0.66%

£7.325 billion

When the liveried Goldsmiths' Company of London meet, they use a small bell and ivory gavel donated by Viner in 1667, to call liverymen to order. Viner, who came from an old Warwickshire family, was apprenticed to his uncle, Sir Thomas Viner, and became his partner in his goldsmith business. Viner joined the Goldsmiths' Company and his rise in the City led to a close and enduring friendship with Charles II. Viner was knighted in 1665 and obtained a baronetcy a year later. Viner was Sheriff during the great fire of London, when his house was burnt down.

During his spell, a prisoner sentenced to death for treason – for counterfeiting the king's signature – escaped, but Viner's royal connections ensured he suffered no penalty for the escape. He was later elected Lord Mayor in 1674.

In the early years of the restoration, Viner was able to live well by taking money on deposit from City companies and lending it to the government and monarchy at much higher rates of interest. But when the Exchequer defaulted on debt repayment in 1672, Viner had £416,724 out on loan to it. He did receive annual interest of £25,000 but his capital was effectively locked up by the government. Viner's creditors pressed him, and he went bankrupt, even though he was able to offer them a fifth of the money in hard cash and an annual payment of over £25,000.

He remained on close terms with the king and died in Windsor Castle in 1688, broken-hearted over the recent death of his only son at 22.

At his peak, Viner was personally worth £300,000, about 0.66% of net national income of £45m at the time. This would be worth £7.3bn in today's money.

Sir John Cutler

(c 1608-1693)
Merchant
Wealth: £300,000
Net National Income: £46m
% of NNI: 0.65%

£7.214 billion

There is no better indication of how seventeenth century administration worked to enrich the rich than Pepy's brief account of Cutler becoming treasurer for the building of St Paul's Cathedral:

It seems he did give £1,500 on condition that he might be treasurer for the work, which they say, will be worth three times as much money. Talk of his being chosen to the office will make people backward to give.

Cutler, like many a self-made man today, fancied being a squire, and bought a manor in Yorkshire in 1657, where he lived in miserly seclusion. But a well-known highwayman, John Nevison, was after him and after a narrow escape, a terrified Cutler went to live in the local village with his servant. Yet as soon as the restoration was in prospect in 1660, he raised a subscription for the king and was the first man knighted at the actual restoration.

A member of the Grocers' Company, Cutler was also an MP for Bodmin. Legend has it that he was a miser, but if so he was a generous one, giving to the poor, the Royal Society, his livery company and to education on a grand scale.

He died in 1693, worth about £300,000, 0.65% of net national income of £46m at the time. This would be worth £7.2bn in today's money.

James Morrison

(1790-1857)
Textiles
Wealth: £4m
Net National Income: £611m
% of NNI: 0.65%

£7.214 billion

Born in 1790 of Hampshire yeoman stock, James Morrison started work in a London warehouse in a humble capacity. But his business skill and marriage to the owner's daughter secured him a partnership in the business. The firm's name was changed to Morrison, Dillon & Co, and it later became the Fore Street Limited Liability Company. It was perhaps the first big discount retailer in Britain, reflecting Morrison's dictum: 'Small profits and quick returns.' He became enormously rich and spent a large part of his fortune on land in six counties round England and Scotland, including the island of Islay.

By 1823, he was worth £150,000 and was always looking for new and profitable investments. Aside from his business, Morrison was a keen politician and became an MP in 1830, supporting the Reform Bill of 1832. His great contribution to British public life involved his work on the various railway acts when he worked on Commons select committees. Many of his proposals were adopted in subsequent legislation. He retired from the Commons in 1847, and devoted himself in his final ten years to building a large library and a magnificent art collection at his Basildon Park estate in Berkshire.

Morrison died in 1857, leaving property in England valued at between £3m and £4m, together with large investments in America. In all, he was worth at least £4m, representing about £7.2bn in today's terms.

Lord Vestey

(1859-1940)
Food production
Wealth: £30m
Net National Income: £4.7bn
% of NNI: 0.64%

£7.145 billion

The Vestey name will always be synonymous with meat and controversy over taxation. The family's huge wealth was largely built up by two brothers in the late nineteenth and early twentieth century. William and Edmund Vestey were both born in Liverpool. Their father, Samuel Vestey, a Yorkshireman by birth, ran a business, buying and selling mainly provisions imported from North America. Both William and Edmund, after an education at the Liverpool Institute, gained experience in the family business.

At the age of seventeen, William was sent to America to buy and ship home goods for his father. Despite his youth, he established a canning factory in Chicago, and purchased the cheaper cuts of meat to make corned beef, which he shipped to Liverpool. This venture was successful, and the management of the cannery was given to Edmund, who had joined the firm in 1883.

Keen to expand the business, William went to Argentina in 1890. Seeing the huge potential for producing meat and other food there, he invested in refrigeration technology to preserve food on the long seaborne voyage across the Atlantic. He began by shipping frozen partridges, and later mutton and beef, from Argentina to Britain. Edmund later joined him and in 1890, the pair established the first cold store in Liverpool, which as the Union Cold Storage Company, was to become one of the world's largest cold storage operations.

The brothers soon diversified into other products, using their extensive network of cold stores to accommodate all types of perishable foodstuffs, and developed their supplies on a worldwide basis. In 1906, they began to ship eggs, chickens, and other produce from China. The China trade led them into another avenue of business, when they purchased two tramp steamers in 1909, and converted them into refrigerated ships. This was the beginning of the Blue Star Line, which they registered in 1911. In the next five years they acquired five more ships, as well as a butchery business, a chain of retail shops in Britain, and small freezing works in Australia and New Zealand. A totally integrated business was established as a result, controlling every stage of the food chain from producer to consumer. During the Great War, the Vesteys' cattle ranches and farms in Argentina were vital for the war effort. It also became their base after the 1914 Finance Act imposed swinging taxes, making the Vestey brothers, in effect, tax exiles.

They returned to Britain in 1919, when William appeared before the royal commission on income tax to argue the need for a return to the pre-1915 tax levels. Unable to convince the government of the validity of their case, in 1921, the Vesteys and their advisers devised a complex and highly successful scheme which not only satisfied their desire to live in Britain and avoid paying any personal tax but also showed them to be as innovative and pioneering in the field of tax avoidances in the food business.

The greater part of the Vesteys' overseas empire was leased to their British company, Union Cold Storage Ltd, for a yearly rent of £960,000, which was used to set up a trust fund in Paris. From the trust the money flowed into the Western United Investment Company in Britain, a Vestey holding company in which the family held the management shares and controlling interest, and thence, tax free, into the pockets of the Vestey brothers.

Once domiciled again in England, Edmund was created a baronet in 1921, and the following year William purchased a peerage from the Lloyd George government, apparently for £25,000. This peerage led to a letter of protest from George V, who felt it wrong that a man who declined to pay national taxes should be so rewarded.

The business prospered after the war and by 1925, Blue Star was the largest refrigerated fleet in the world. In Britain they owned cold stores in several cities as well as 2,365 retail butcher shops. Their operations in Britain were managed from the Union Cold Storage Company Ltd, which had an issued capital of £12m in 1933. The depression did not hamper growth and in 1934, the Vesteys took over the Anglis meat operation in Australia for £1.5m.

When William died in 1940, the business was valued at around £90m. His younger brother Edmund died as chairman in 1953. The family still control the business, though it is now run by professional managers. William's stake at his death was worth perhaps £30m. In today's money that would be around £7.1bn.

Lord Overstone

(1796-1883)
Banking
Wealth: £5.331m
Net National Income: £1.099bn
% of NNI: 0.48%

£7.120 billion

Samuel Loyd, later Lord Overstone, was born the son of a banker in 1790. His father had trained as a preacher and teacher, but joined John Jones & Co, a small Manchester bank, and later married the daughter of the founder. He transformed the bank's fortunes and his own wealth. His son was educated at Eton and Cambridge, becoming a partner in the bank at 20 and an MP three years later. The bank had a London office which was eventually to split from the Manchester operation. Loyd and his father ran the London bank, which was regarded as a well-managed if very conservative operation.

After his father's retirement and death, Loyd left the day-to-day operation of the bank to other partners. He became more interested in public affairs and economics. He was involved in numerous government commissions and was consulted on economic policy. Created Baron Overstone in 1850, his caution as a banker meant that he eschewed the routes taken by other bankers to create high street networks, or for Jones Loyd & Co to become a City merchant bank. As a result, it slowly lost its position as a leading bank. By then, Overstone had little to do with the business and had invested most of his wealth in land.

He died in 1883, leaving over £5.3m in his will, representing about 0.48% of net national income. In today's terms, that would be £7.1bn.

The 6th Duke Of Westminster

(dob 22/12/1951)
Land and property

Wealth: £7.0 billion

The Duke of Westminster stepped down as chairman of his Grosvenor Group on 1 May 2007, after 30 years at the helm of his family's property group. He is also retiring from the Territorial Army where he reached the rank of Major General.

The Duke leaves his property operations in fine fettle with prices rising sharply in central London. He has also spearheaded expansion overseas. In December 2005, Westminster splashed out £35m buying the Paul-Bert and Serpette flea markets in Paris. Traders were said to be delighted that a 'rosbif' is now their landlord.

In recent times, he has also spent another £35m acquiring land for a £40m apartment complex in Sydney, following on from a huge Hong Kong development. But the group, owned by the family trusts of the Duke of Westminster, is not neglecting its home patch. In 2004, plans for one of Bath's biggest ever developments were unveiled. Work will start by Grosvenor on Bath's Western Riverside by the end of 2007. The vast scheme will take 15-20 years to complete. Westminster is also behind the enormous Paradise St development in Liverpool.

Taking such a long view of course has helped Gerald Grosvenor, 6th Duke of Westminster, to become the richest property developer in Britain. The range of his wealth is staggering, taking in vast estates in Lancashire and Cheshire, great swathes of central London, in Mayfair and Belgravia, and tracts of land in Scotland, Canada and around the world.

Grosvenor Group, his main property company, saw its profits rise 23% to £508m in 2006. Its net assets rose to £2.4bn. Within Grosvenor Group are the overseas holdings, the British development work and 100 acres of Mayfair. Separately, some 200 acres of Belgravia are held in family trusts which should be worth around £4bn, not quite twice the Grosvenor Group net assets. That would put a value of around £6.2bn on the total family assets, but when Westminster announced his retirement, the reports spoke of a company with £11bn of assets.

We are slightly more cautious and value the Grosvenor property assets at £6.5bn. Taking in the £62m in dividends that the family trusts have had from the Grosvenor Group since 1999, a valuable art collection and family properties, we reckon that Westminster and his family are now worth around £7bn.

Thomas Chaucer

(c 1367-1434)
Land
Wealth: £20,000
Net National Income: £3.2m
% of NNI: 0.62%

£6.881 billion

His grandfather was a wine house keeper in London. His father was Geoffrey Chaucer, the great medieval poet and author of *The Canterbury Tales*. Thomas Chaucer moved on however, becoming an MP and Speaker of the House of Commons on five occasions. He had the favour and support of Henry IV, then of Henry V and of Cardinal Beaufort, the most powerful official in England after the king. All three just happened to be cousins of Chaucer. His mother was the sister of John of Gaunt's mistress, later his third wife as Duchess of Lancaster. This made Gaunt his uncle at a time when an uncle looked after a nephew, especially if they were loyal.

Chaucer married an heiress and her dowry brought estates through southern England, particularly in Oxfordshire. But Chaucer was also enormously talented as a diplomat and negotiator, defusing row after row between the kings and the Commons. He grew rich on the various lands in the south-west and Hampshire, benefits in kind, and rent-producing offices granted him by the kings and the Cardinal. His daughter became a duchess and immensely wealthy.

When he died in 1434, peacefully in his bed as it happened, he left an estate of about £20,000, around 0.62% of net national income of £3.2m at the time. In today's money this would be worth £6.8bn.

William Beckford

(1709-1770)
Merchant
Wealth: £1m
Net National Income: £165m
% of NNI: 0.6%

£6.659 billion

William Beckford, the son of a prominent Jamaica sugar planter, studied as a medical student in Leyden and Paris before inheriting the vast family fortune when his elder brother died. But politics was his main interest. Elected MP for Shaftsbury in 1747, and later for the City of London, he had a fortune large enough for him to control the MPs from London, Bristol, Salisbury, Petersfield and Hindon. He was an avid supporter of the Tories and of Pitt the Elder as they expanded the empire by taking territory from France. A member of The Ironmongers' Company, Beckford was Lord Mayor of London three times, in 1762, 1769 and 1770.

Though a fairly abstemious man himself, Beckford was known for his lavish banquets. Four of them were regarded by gourmets as the best since the days of Henry VIII.

He died in 1770, leaving £1m to his son, then aged nine, about 0.6% of net national income of £165m. In today's money that would be worth £6.6bn.

Sir Josiah Child

(1630-1699)
Merchant
Wealth: £300,000
Net National Income: £50m
% of NNI: 0.6%

£6.659 billion

The East India Company, a band of English merchants who ran much of India in the sixteenth and seventeenth centuries, mostly by force of arms, was at the heart of Child's fortune. From about 1674, he was a director and thereafter governor or deputy governor of the company until 1689. He got into the company by becoming a shareholder in 1671, having made a fortune from Navy contracts for supplies to the fleet in Portsmouth. He was also a brewer and mayor of Portsmouth.

In the 1680s, the East India Company was in trouble, with parliament and their shareholders. Child secured royal patronage and lots of lucrative franchises and tax collecting duties by paying James II £10,000 a year from 1681. By 1689, his dictatorial conduct had led to the creation of the New East India Company. He had a huge country estate and his daughter married the heir to the Duke of Beaufort.

He died worth £300,000, about 0.6% of net national income of £50m. This would be worth £6.6bn in modern money.

Peter Des Rivaux

(c 1190-1262)
Land
Wealth: £20,000
Net National Income: £3.3m
% of NNI: 0.6%

£6.659 billion

His father, Peter Des Roches, was Bishop of Winchester, the royal city of the period and a powerful Norman baron. Des Rivaux took direct advantage of his inheritance by shadowing his father's career as de facto chief minister of the Crown and financial controller of England. He became Clerk of the Wardrobe but was evicted from office in 1223, only to return in 1232 as his father's deputy. His moment of glory was brief. His father fell in 1234 and Des Rivaux fell with him. Despite this, he continued to serve the king in many capacities and amassed a fortune in church assets. He is important because, though his time at the top was brief, he set in motion administrative changes that sustained English government for centuries.

He died aged 72 in 1262, and was worth about £20,000, around 0.6% of net national income of £3.3m at the time. In today's money he would be worth about £6.6bn. His father, who died in 1238, had left an equally stupendous fortune of around £15,000.

The Earl Of Hereford & Essex

(1276-1322)
Land
Wealth: £30,000
Net National Income: £5m
% of NNI: 0.6%

£6.659 billion

Humphrey Bohun was proof that a good marriage was the route to fortune in the thirteenth century. His father, the Earl of Hereford and Essex had caused trouble for Edward I on the Welsh Marches, yet Bohun made his mark at court and in 1301, married the king's widowed daughter, Elizabeth, Countess of Holland.

Once in the royal circle, Bohun's fortunes improved. His father's £4,000 debt was cancelled and in 1306, Bohun was granted valuable land and castles forfeited by Robert Bruce in Scotland and Essex. He served Edward II in fighting the Scots and the Welsh, and the king rewarded him with favours and helped in bringing diplomatic pressure to bear in Holland for payment of the dowry owing to him. But in the end he took up arms in rebellion against the king and paid for this with his life when he was killed in 1322, at the Battle of Boroughbridge.

His £30,000 wealth at the time of his death would be worth around £6.6bn in today's money.

Thomas Sutton

(1532-1611)
Merchant
Wealth: £160,000
Net National Income: £27m
% of NNI: 0.59%

£6.548 billion

Thomas Sutton, the son of a Lincolnshire court official, went to Eton and later became a student at Lincoln's Inn in London. After an early career as secretary to a succession of aristocrats, he settled on a military career. He served in the North and helped suppress a rebellion there in 1569. He served as an artillery officer at the siege of Edinburgh in 1573, his last military engagement. But it was while serving in Durham that he noted the abundance of coal in the area.

He leased coal-rich land from the Church and the Crown, and by 1580, the coal had made him one of the richest men in England. Sutton then settled in London, married a wealthy widow and proceeded to build up his estates. He had five homes and in 1607, spent £10,800 buying a Cambridgeshire manor. But he was also generous to charities and spent £13,000 establishing a hospital and school at Charterhouse just before he died in 1611. There was much talk after his death of 'rich Sutton's bequest of £200,000'.

This may be a slight exaggeration. While he was the richest commoner in England, his personal possessions were valued at over £60,410 and his land produced £5,000 of annual income. In all he was worth about £160,000, representing 0.59% of net national income. In today's terms that is £6.5bn.

Sir Maurice Abbot

(1565-1642)
Merchant
Wealth: £200,000
Net National Income: £35m
% of NNI: 0.57%

£6.326 billion

Sir Maurice Abbot was a businessman with lucrative interests spanning the globe including the East India Company, the Levant Company, a company to exploit the discovery of the Northwest passage and another colonising Virginia in America. He started out at a considerable advantage, his family having sufficient clout to have one of his brothers made Archbishop of Canterbury and another made Bishop of Salisbury.

He was born in Guildford and was apprenticed early in the drapery business, becoming a liveryman of the Drapers' Company. By the early part of the 1600s, he was in virtual control of the English merchant fleet and in 1621, was elected MP for Kingston upon Hull. He was very active in public affairs and was the de facto governor of London when the king left to fight the Scots in 1639. This was the year that Abbot was made Lord Mayor of London. A royalist, he lent money to the king and obtained lucrative contracts to collect customs and take a cut. For this privilege he paid £12,000 plus a loan to the king of £20,000. Abbot's biographer wrote that he was 'one of the earliest examples we have of the creation of enormous wealth by the application of great personal abilities to commerce'.

Abbot died in 1642, worth at least £200,000, about 0.57% of net national income of £35m at the time. In today's money that would be £6.3bn.

The Earl Of Wiltshire

(c 1420-1461)
Land
Wealth: £20,000
Net National Income: £3.5m
% of NNI: 0.57%

£6.326 billion

In a short life of 41 years, James Butler, Earl of Wiltshire, the most unattractive of Henry VI's favourites, amassed a fortune that outshone his contemporaries but which, like his earldom, did not survive him.

He started out as heir to the Earl of Ormond, a huge landowner in Ireland. He even became Lieutenant of Ireland. But he hardly ever visited his estates there, preferring the court in England and the acquisition of further land in the West Country. Apart from his own lands, he was appointed steward of his lands in Dorset and Somerset by the Duke of York. He married a sister of the Duke of Beaufort, a great Welsh and West Country landowner.

Wiltshire was granted many fee-paying favours by the king, but his war record was dreadful, and eventually fatal. In 1451, he fled the Earl of Devon's private army, which burnt his manor to the ground. In 1455, he escaped from the Battle of St Albans in disguise. In 1460, he fled abroad to escape the Yorkists. He did the same after defeat at both the Battle of Mortimer's Cross and at Towton in 1461. At Cockermouth in Cumbria his luck ran out. He was captured and executed at Newcastle in 1461.

At his peak he was worth £20,000 when net national income was just £3.5m. This would make him worth £6.3bn in today's money.

Sir Samuel Fludyer

(c 1705-1768)
Industrialist
Wealth: £900,000
Net National Income: £160m
% of NNI: 0.56%

£6.215 billion

Sir Samuel Fludyer, a merchant and MP, was caught out in a minor smuggling racket in 1768, and was chastised by the Lord Chancellor. The biographers say that this hit him so hard that shortly after he died of embarrassment.

He was a director of the Bank of England, which was a private company and made his fortune through dealing in North and West Country cloth. A religious dissenter when it mattered, he demonstrated the power of the City by amassing a fortune, becoming an MP and eventually Lord Mayor of London, despite his religion.

His vast lending to the government was accompanied by the lucrative victualling contracts he obtained. In 1762, for example, he subscribed £19,000 to one loan. Many of his contracts were for the supply of troops in America but he did not live to see the colony depart to independence.

At his death, he was worth £900,000 according to *The Gentleman's Magazine* of 1768. That would have been about 0.56% of net national income of £160m at the time. In today's terms he would be worth £6.2bn.

Gopi & Sri Hinduja

(dob 29/02/1940 and 08/11/1935)
Industry, property and finance

Wealth: £6.2 billion

Flexing their financial muscles on the global stage has put the Hinduja brothers in the limelight of late. Early in 2007, they bid, unsuccessfully, to buy a stake in Hutchison Essar, India's second-largest mobile phone company, which would value the business at over £9bn. This was followed with the news that the Hindujas were weighing up the acquisition of a stake in Telecom Italia, the former Italian monopoly, after being approached by a party seeking to offload a holding.

That the brothers are now so prominent on the international stage is no accident. In June 2005, the brothers celebrated victory in the New Delhi High Court, having been acquitted of accepting kickbacks in the long-standing Bofors affair. They were alleged to have accepted bribes from the Swedish arms firm Bofors to clinch a $1.3bn deal to sell 410 howitzers to the Indian army in 1986.

With the decks cleared, many doors that were previously closed to them are now opening. Aside from telecoms they have now gone into two new areas: insurance and real estate development. On the latter, they are now developing hundreds of acres of land in Hyderabad, Bangalore, Chennai and Mumbai. Their Hinduja Group is to revive its proposal to set up a 1,040-megawatt capacity, coal-based power project in India in partnership with Gulf Oil. The Hindujas have applied to increase their stake in a local bank, their vehicle operation has posted record profits and is moving into the luxury bus market and looking at export opportunities and a joint venture with China.

Investment also continues apace in other Indian-based operations while their Middle East oil business is moving into pharmaceuticals. Sri and Gopi Hinduja are the two London-based of four brothers (the others are in Europe and India), though they have been forced to spend much of their time recently in India defending themselves against the Bofors charges.

The brothers inherited a business empire from their late father based in the Middle East, and links with the late Shah of Iran. The listed companies in the group include Ashok Leyland, Gulf Oil, Hinduja TMT and IndusInd Bank. In total, the revenues for the group are around £7bn annually. It is also reckoned to be debt free.

In the midst of the battle for Hutchison Essar, it was reported in *The Times* that the Hinduja family had assets of around £8bn. Certainly there is no question mark over their ability to mount a takeover for Hutchison Essar. Indeed, up until the summer of 2006, they held a 5% stake in Hutchison Essar, which they sold for £225m as at that stage Hutchison was not a seller of its stake.

Perhaps the most significant rise in their wealth has been in their widespread holdings in the property sector – both in India and across the world – where values have increased by up to 250%. Their industrial holdings in Ashok Leyland, Gulf Oil, HTMT and Ennore Foundries have also increased in value by some 60%.

The Hinduja family also showed its financial clout in the summer of 2006, when it acquired one of London's most expensive and sought-after properties, previously owned by the queen. The brothers paid £58m for a 100 year lease on the 60-room property at Carlton House Terrace on the Mall, and plan to spend another £40m to £50m converting it for use by their joint families. We are slightly more cautious in our valuation and settle for a current valuation of £6.2bn for the Hinduja family.

Sir Thomas Cook

(c 1410-1478)
Merchant
Wealth: £20,000
Net National Income: £3.6m
% of NNI: 0.55%

£6.104 billion

One measure of Cook's wealth was his capacity to pay a fine of £5,333 in 1468, having had a charge of treason reduced to one of concealing a treason. Yet no one knows where or when he was born or who his family were.

He first came to note in London in 1425 as a drapery apprentice, but around the time of his trial he was running a stock worth £1,600 and collecting ancient tapestries and expensive plate to decorate his City mansion. His fortunes were intimately mixed up with the affairs of various royals, including Edward IV's sister Margaret, whose wedding to the Duke of Burgundy he financed. He lent money to Queen Margaret and to Edward IV, who professed outrage at finding Cook amongst the Lancastrian plotters against him. Contemporaries reckoned Edward went after Cook as much for the money as for any legal reason, and the king was joined by his in-laws and the queen who tried to get 10% of the fine for themselves. Cook was both an MP and Mayor of London and died surrounded by wealth.

At his peak he was worth £20,000 or more, 0.55% of net national income which stood at £3.6m at the time. In today's money he would be worth £6.1bn.

The 1st Earl Of Kent

(c 1420-1489)
Land
Wealth: £20,000
Net National Income: £3.6m
% of NNI: 0.55%

£6.104 billion

Edmund Grey, a well-connected aristocrat, managed the unusual feat of combining politics, military activity and lucrative fee-earning activities in the fifteenth century. He was the commissioner for hearing (oyer) and trying (terminer) criminal cases in London and the adjoining counties and entitled to a percentage of the fines levied, naturally. He helped to raise loans in various counties, for the king and for warfare. Later he became Lord High Treasurer of England, mainly as a reward for switching the vanguard of the royal army at the Battle of Northampton to the side of Warwick, and the Yorkist succession.

His rise to fame started with his parentage. His father was Sir John Grey KG and his uncle was the Duke of Exeter. He was plundering Aquitaine before he was twenty and went on to plunder parts of England on behalf, first of the Lancastrians, and later of the Yorkists. He married a daughter of the Earl of Northumberland. His first title was that of Lord Grey of Ruthin, but he was created Earl of Kent in 1465, by a grateful Edward IV, with all the usual rents and fees.

When Kent died he was worth £20,000, mostly in land. This was 0.55% of net national income of £3.6m. It would be worth £6.1bn in modern money.

Lord Walter Mauny

(d 1372)
Land
Wealth: £15,000
Net National Income: £2.7m
% of NNI: 0.55%

£6.104 billion

Lord Walter Mauny came to England in 1327, with Queen Philipa of Hainault the bride-to-be of Edward III. Although a mere esquire, he was well connected in Normandy, and eventually inherited lands there from both his parents.

Between 1332 and 1360, he was almost continuously at war, either on land as one of Edward III senior commanders or at sea as an Admiral. In 1337, he attacked the island of Cadzand in the Scheldt estuary and took most of the population prisoner, later ransoming them for £8,000. He fought in Scotland, Brittany, Gascony, the Low Countries and at Calais.

Famous for acts of personal chivalry and bravery, Mauny married one of the great heiresses of her age, Margaret Marshall, later the Duchess of Norfolk. For his actions, he received huge tracts of land from the king. He was personally pious and founded at least one monastery for the Carthusian monks.

When he died he was worth £15,000, 0.55% of net national income of £2.7m at the time. This would be worth £6.1bn in today's money.

Sir John Moleyns

(d 1361)
Land and crime
Wealth: £15,000
Net National Income: £2.7m
% of NNI: 0.55%

£6.104 billion

The son of an MP, John Moleyns made his fortune in the early fourteenth century by debt collecting, bounty hunting and as a general hard man for Edward III. Unlike most of the aristocratic thugs, such as Folville and Coterell, who terrorised the English Midlands at the time, he was literate and saw where the main chance was, which was with the royals. He entered royal service in 1325, and did well until he was found out, which was difficult because royal servants had the protection of the king.

To obtain the manor of Stoke Poges, he murdered his wife's uncle, coerced her grandfather into handing over the manor and suborned the judges sent to investigate. The law caught up with him in 1340, but he was later pardoned and taken back into royal service where he became a one-man crime wave, committing offences of kidnap, chicanery, theft of land, abuse of office and forest offences. He was also steward of the queen's household at the time.

In 1357, Moleyns was imprisoned for abuse of office and horse stealing and died in prison in 1361. His heirs inherited most of his empire, which ran to lands worth £800 a year and personal possession such as coin, jewels, armour and wine, which took royal agents several days to list. At his peak, he was worth £15,000, about 0.55% of net national income of £2.7m. In today's money that would be £6.1bn.

Viscount Lovell

(1454-c1487)
Land
Wealth: £25,000
Net National Income: £4.6m
% of NNI: 0.54%

£5.993 billion

The beautiful medieval manor at Minster Lovell in Oxfordshire was having a new chimney installed in 1708, when the builders discovered a vault. Upon opening it, they found a skeleton sitting at a table with a book open, pen and paper beside it. The tableau dissolved into dust in minutes. This is how the richest man of his generation died, of starvation in his own house, having fled there over two hundred years earlier to escape a vengeful Henry VII who Lovell had tried to depose in 1487.

Lovell was born to wealth and was a high aristocrat. In 1483, he was Chief Butler of England and a close friend and adviser to Richard III. While he lasted Lovell prospered. He fought at Bosworth in 1485, but escaped when Richard was killed. The remainder of Lovell's life was spent in revolt against Henry VII. His last battle was at Stoke in 1487, where it was thought that Lovell was killed, until he was spotted swimming the Trent on horseback. He made it back to Minster Lovell, and to the vault.

His capacity to raise revolts and wage war was related to his vast wealth and lands, which peaked at £25,000 at a time when net national income stood at £4.6m. This would be worth £5.9bn in modern money. Most of his assets were attained in 1485, and handed over to Henry VII's mother.

Cecily Neville, The Duchess Of York

(1415-1495)
Land
Wealth: £20,000
Net National Income: £3.7m
% of NNI: 0.54%

£5.993 billion

Cecily Neville was the last of the twenty-three children of Ralph Neville, Earl of Westmoreland (d 1425) and the mother of two kings, Edward IV and Richard III. Married to the Duke of York she lived to see her husband, three of her sons, including Richard III, and four grandsons, die violently.

In her early days she was so extravagant, and so wealthy, that her husband had a manager appointed to look after her expenditure. To receive a new queen she had a dress made that had 325 pearls stitched to it, and a half pound of gold thread woven on it. She spent as much on clothes (£608 in 1443-44) as many earls had to live on. In her later years, she became renowned as one of the most pious women in the country, spending most of her days in religious readings or devotions. She was rich through inheritance, from her father's family, and later from the estates of her husband and sons.

She died worth £20,000, 0.54% of net national income of £3.7m. In today's money that would be £5.9bn.

Sir Julius Wernher

(1850-1912)
Diamonds and gold mining
Wealth: £11.5m
Net National Income: £2.181bn
% of NNI: 0.527%

£5.902 billion

The son of a leading railway engineer from Hesse in Germany (who was a friend of Brunel and Robert Stephenson), Julius Wernher was educated in Frankfurt. While he had a life-long interest in engineering, he opted for a career in business, serving an apprenticeship in a bank. On the outbreak of the Franco-Prussian War in 1870, Wernher served as a cadet in the dragoons of the 4th Cavalry division and in the Army of Occupation, without being in the least bit touched by the wave of military and imperial sentiment then sweeping over Germany.

After the war he went to London, where he first worked as a bookkeeper in a firm of German druggists and then in a bank. He had the luck to secure an introduction to Jules Porgès, a leading diamond merchant in Paris and London. Diamonds were just being discovered in South Africa and the young Wernher was sent there to open an office with his boss. Wernher made himself master of the delicate business of diamond buying. When his boss returned home in 1873, Wernher was its sole representative in Kimberley, the centre of the diamond trade. Porgès came to trust him absolutely.

By 1875, Wernher, still just 25, was a member of the Kimberley mining board. In that same year, Alfred Beit joined him in Kimberley, and a lifelong business partnership was born. They both became partners in Jules Porgès and in 1884,

Wernher returned to London and traded in diamond shares, while Beit remained in Kimberley to look after their interests.

Wernher moved back and forth between London and Kimberley in the early to mid 1880s while he helped establish the London Diamond Syndicate in 1886, which stabilised the price of diamonds. Skilful manoeuvring by Wernher and Beit, aided by Cecil Rhodes, meant that they were ultimately able to merge the various diamond operations in Kimberley into a new company De Beers Consolidated Mines in 1888.

After Porgès retired at the end of 1889, the firm was reconstituted, in January 1890, as Wernher, Beit & Co. of London. Wernher, the hard-headed practical businessman, and Beit, the financial genius, formed a most successful partnership which was only terminated by Beit's untimely death in 1906.

The discovery of the Witwatersrand goldfields in 1886 brought the firm into a new arena. Deep-level mining properties were established by Beit and Wernher and in 1893, they formed the company Rand Mines to develop their sites. By the end of the century, the group's mines accounted for nearly 50% of the value of the Witwatersrand's total gold production.

Still based in London, Wernher's career reached its pinnacle in 1905 when he was created a baronet. He was managing over seventy South African companies from his London office, and formed a huge new company – Central Mining and Investment Corporation – to buy gold shares and steady the volatile markets.

With his health failing, Wernher merged his various interests in 1911. A year later, at the time of his death, the gold mines under the control of his group produced 3.5m ounces of fine gold and earned over half of the profits of the whole of the Witwatersrand. He did not have it all his way though. His reputation for prudence did not prevent Wernher being swindled out of £64,000 in 1906 by a Frenchman called Henri Lemoine, who claimed he could make synthetic diamonds. Wernher left an estate of around £11.5m and bequeathed huge amounts of his wealth to charities and education both in Britain and South Africa. In today's money his fortune would have been around £5.9bn.

Rich list members born in the 11th century

Rich list member	Lifespan
Bayeux, Odo of	c1030-1097
Mortain, Robert of	c1031-1090
Meulan, Robert of, Lord of Beaumont and Earl of Leicester	1046-1118
Belleme, Robert of, Earl of Shrewsbury	c1052-1130
Flambard, Bishop Ranulf	1060-1128
Bishop of Salisbury, Roger	c1065-1139
Warenne, William of	d 1088
Rufus, Alan	d 1093

Peter Des Roches

(d 1238)
Land
Wealth: £15,000
Net National Income: £2.8m
% of NNI: 0.53%

£5.882 billion

Little remembered in modern histories, Peter des Roches was one of the towering figures in the English administration of the thirteenth century. A military commander of considerable talent, an ecclesiastical administrator of genius, he was totally and resolutely dedicated to the concept of absolute royal power.

A foreigner, such was his contempt for the English barons that they rebelled against des Roches's patron King John, and forced Magna Carta on him at Runnymead in 1212. Out of favour during the minority of Richard III, he came back to favour after Richard was crowned and historians say that it was des Roches's running of the Exchequer that made Richard's reign possible. He defended the king against the Pope, at one time being the only bishop left in the country, though he later went to fight for the Pope in Italy. In 1237, his son was appointed to head the royal finances and at the same time acquired huge fee earning privileges in twenty-one English shires.

At his peak Peter Des Roches was worth £15,000, about 0.53% of net national income of £2.8m. That would be worth £5.8bn in today's money.

Sir Charles Duncombe

(d 1711)
Banker
Wealth: £350,000
Net National Income: £65m
% of NNI: 0.53%

£5.882 billion

Sir Charles Duncombe came from minor country gentry, but was apprenticed to Edward Backwell (q.v.) sometime in the early to mid sixteen hundreds as a goldsmith. But by 1672, Duncombe was independent and trading from the Grasshopper in Lombard Street.

Banker to the Earl of Shaftesbury, he received a timely warning of Charles II's plan to close the Exchequer, and was able to withdraw his cash and clients' deposits in time. When he retired from banking in 1695, he sold his shares in the Bank of England for £80,000. Earlier he had bought the largest estate in England ever bought by a commoner, Helmsley in Yorkshire, for £90,000.

Duncombe was an MP and held a variety of revenue-generating posts in government. He was, like the other great city magnates, elected Lord Mayor in 1708.

When he died in 1711, he was worth about £350,000 according to contemporary record. This was 0.53% of net national income of £65m at the time. In today's money he would be worth £5.8bn.

Lord William Latimer

(1330-1381)
Land
Wealth: £15,000
Net National Income: £2.8m
% of NNI: 0.53%

£5.882 billion

As chamberlain to Edward III between 1371 and 1376, when the king had lost his grip on affairs, Latimer controlled both written and personal access to the king. It was a rewarding role for Latimer, who came from Yorkshire, but he did not inherit his father's income as his mother outlived him. With just £333 annuity from his father, he was dependent on royal service for his wealth.

In his early years he fought in France, from the Battle of Crècy in 1346, where he served as a sixteen year old through to the 1360s. His rewards for service were prodigious. He acquired estates in France, made money from ransoming French aristocrats, became warden of the Cinque Ports and northern forests, and acquired valuable wardships. All these activities allowed Latimer to build up the capital to lend money to the Crown at a profitable rate of interest. He also sold licences for wool exports free of custom duties and purchased royal debt at a discount. Latimer profited from these schemes at a time of great financial stringency and he naturally made enemies. At the Good Parliament of 1376, he was impeached, fined and lost his office. But he recovered the king's favour, though no longer held the office of chamberlain.

Latimer died in 1381. At his height, his fortune was around £15,000, representing 0.53% of net national income at the time. In today's terms that would be over £5.8bn.

Sir Robert Clayton

(1629-1707)
Merchant
Wealth: £300,000
Net National Income: £60m
% of NNI: 0.5%

£5.549 billion

Robert Clayton is a genuine case of the self-made man. He was born in 1629, one of several children of a poor farmer from Northants, but rose to be an MP, Lord Mayor of London, a Director of the Bank of England, Vice President of the Irish Society and a knight.

Clayton's break came when he was apprenticed to his uncle, a London scrivener. His uncle died leaving him a large sum of money and later Clayton's partner and former fellow-apprentice, John Morris, died in 1682, leaving him a large estate. Clayton was a major real estate developer and devised new forms of mortgages and trusts to protect borrowers, mostly the aristocracy. A liveryman of the Scriveners and Drapers' companies, he was extremely active politically, defending the interests of the City and its Corporation against Charles II, and risking his life in doing so. When William came to the throne in 1688, Clayton was one of the common council sent to welcome him. His reward was a place on the board of customs. Proof of his wealth came in 1697, when he had no trouble in lending the king £30,000 to pay off his troops.

He died in 1707, and his huge estate, worth £300,000 at his death, went to his nephew. Clayton and his wife of 46 years had no children of their own. His estate represented 0.5% of net national income of £60m and would be worth £5.5bn in today's money.

Geoffrey De Mandeville

(d 1144)
Land
Wealth: £4,000
Net National Income: £800,000
% of NNI: 0.5%

£5.549 billion

Geoffrey de Mandeville's father was sheriff of Essex and castellan of the Tower of London. He left his son a swathe of land stretching across the home counties north of London, as well as the castles of Saffron Walden and Pleshey.

De Mandeville supported King Stephen against Stephen's cousin, Empress Matilda, and was awarded the keepership of the Tower of London, made sheriff of the city and of Middlesex, Essex and Herefordshire as a hereditary right. De Mandeville returned to the king's side. Stephen soon had second thoughts about his loyalty and arrested de Mandeville in 1141. He was forced to hand over all his castles to the king.

In response, de Mandeville initiated a rebellion in 1143, in which both sides wrecked such havoc that the chroniclers noted that 'Men said openly that Christ and all his saints slept'. He was killed at the siege of Burwell when, having taken his helmet off to mop his brow, an arrow came straight down on him.

At his peak, de Mandeville was worth about £4,000, when net national income was just £800,000 and his share of it was about 0.5%. In today's money he would be worth £5.5bn.

Marquess Of Dorset

(1451-1501)
Land
Wealth: £20,000
Net National Income: £4m
% of NNI: 0.5%

£5.549 billion

Thomas Grey, later the Earl of Dorset, was in the thick of the Wars of the Roses intrigue in the fifteenth century. In 1471, he fought for Edward IV at Tewkesbury and in the same year took part in the murder of Edward, Prince of Wales. Honours were showered on him: firstly a knighthood and later in 1475, he was created Marquess of Dorset. When his half-brother, Edward V, took the throne, Dorset rose further and became constable of the Tower. But the accession of Richard III ended his promotion.

In 1483, a reward was offered for Dorset's capture. He organised rebellion and when that failed became a fugitive, fleeing to Brittany. He backed Henry Tudor's claim to the throne but despairing of its success, was prepared to return to England and throw his lot in with Richard III. Henry, hearing of Dorset's plans, persuaded him to stay in France while he went to claim the throne at Bosworth. Henry recalled him to England and restored Dorset to his lands that had been seized by Richard. But Dorset was again under suspicion of supporting a rebellion against Henry and was sent to the Tower. After Henry had consolidated power, Dorset was released and played a loyal role in supporting the king until his death in 1501.

His two marriages to important heiresses bought him land and estates, and his £20,000 fortune would have been about 0.5% of the £4m national income of the day. In today's terms that is £5.5bn.

Piers Gaveston

(c 1284-1312)
Land
Wealth: £25,000
Net National Income: £4.8m
% of NNI: 0.5%

£5.549 billion

The notorious favourite of Edward II, Piers Gaveston was the younger son of a French knight with lands in Gascony and on the French border. The young Gaveston was taken into the service of Edward I and he became a servant to the king's heir, Prince Edward. The two became lovers and Gaveston fought with the Prince against the Scots, eventually deserting to joust in France. He returned to England but was exiled because of his continuing intimate relationship with the Prince.

On Edward's accession in 1307, Gaveston's fortunes improved sharply. Created Earl of Cornwall, he was granted lands worth around £4,000 a year, married the new king's niece and was appointed keeper of the realm (regent). At the coronation in 1308, he took pride of place, and later cornered royal patronage. His gains from royal service were prodigious. He was regarded as more extravagant even than the king and chroniclers of the day reckoned that he exported royal treasure and drafted blank charters to enrich himself.

But Gaveston's close relationship with the king, his lifestyle and his contempt for the barons created some powerful enemies. He was exiled in 1311, and on his return at the end of the year, he was besieged at Scarborough Castle. He surrendered and was seized by the powerful Earl of Warwick who had Gaveston condemned in a kangaroo court and executed in June 1312. Gaveston was taken to Blacklow Hill (which belonged to the Earl of Lancaster), and killed by two Welshmen, who ran him through with a sword before beheading him as he lay dying on the grass. The country 'rejoined and all its inhabitants glad' at his death.

His wealth was around £25,000, which was 0.5% of the £4.8m net national income of the day. In today's terms that is over £5.5bn.

William Montagu, The Earl Of Salisbury

(1301-1344)
Land
Wealth: £25,000
Net National Income: £5m
% of NNI: 0.5%

£5.549 billion

The Montagu family were established in the West Country at the time of the Conquest in 1066, and had prospered in royal service. Born in 1301, William Montagu formed a close friendship with Edward III during his early military career. This friendship lasted throughout his life and was the source of most of his great wealth.

He started well by leading a coup d'etat against Edward's enemies, Isabella and Mortimer. For that he was given lands worth £1,000 a year. Made Earl of Salisbury in 1337, he was created Earl Marshall the following year and granted more West Country land plus the Lordships of Denbigh, Wark on Tweed, the Channel Isles, Lundy and the Isle of Man. He spent most of his life fighting wars and died from a jousting accident aged just 43.

At his death he was worth £25,000, 0.5% of net national income when it stood at £5m. In today's money that would be worth £5.5bn.

The Duke Of Queensberry

(1724-1810)
Land
Wealth: £1.502m
Net National Income: £300m
% of NNI: 0.5%

£5.549 billion

The subject of a sonnet by Wordsworth beginning 'Degenerate Douglas' and a satirical poem by Burns, William Douglas, later the Duke of Queensberry, was universally known as 'Old Q'. Perhaps the most notorious rake of his generation, it was said that at seventy he was 'oggling and hobbling down St James's Street'.

As a young man, Douglas was a keen follower of the turf and built up a top class stud. He was also remarkably astute in his betting and relieved the Duke of Cumberland and others of large sums of money. On the death of his cousin in 1778, he succeeded to the dukedom of Queensberry. He served as a Lord of the Bedchamber to George III, but supported the Prince of Wales's bid for a regency during George's madness. When the king recovered in 1789, Queensberry's 'ratting' led to his dismissal.

In later years, he was a generous patron of opera, owing to his eye for the prima donnas and dancers. Though he died in 1810 unmarried, he was the victim of a cruel hoax: he and another great landowner gave large dowries to one Maria Fagniani on her marriage to the Earl of Yarmouth, both supposing her to be their daughter. It was widely reckoned in polite society that both were wrong.

Old Q left personal property worth about £1.1m in his will. His land had a capital value of over £400,000, garnering annual income of £13,384. In all, he was worth over £1.5m. In today's terms that would be £5.5bn.

The Lord Rhys

(d 1197)
Land
Wealth: £5,000
Net National Income: £1m
% of NNI: 0.5%

£5.549 billion

Rhys ap Gruffydd was probably the last magnate to really rule Wales, doing so through an extraordinary mesalliance with his old enemy Henry I whereby they invaded Ireland together in 1171. Historians note that this agreement was as much to get rid of the Norman Marcher Lords who were threatening Gruffydd's Welsh domains as to please the Norman king. But it made Gruffydd justiciar, effectively Henry's viceroy.

In this position he amassed huge tracts of land in Wales, extending his family possessions throughout the kingdom. He bound himself to the most powerful Anglo-Norman families of Wales and the Marches through marriage. He managed to hold on to his possession right up to his death in 1197, peacefully in bed, an unusual end for a warrior king at that period. His four brothers were killed at the beginning of his reign when they had to fight the Normans for their lands in Wales.

Gruffydd's estate was worth about £5,000 on his death when net national income stood at £1m. His 0.5% share of net national income would be worth £5.5bn in today's money.

Bishop Hugh Du Puiset

(c 1120-1195)
Church
Wealth: £5,000
Net National Income: £1m
% of NNI: 0.5%

£5.543 billion

He may have been a bishop, but Hugh du Puiset fathered four sons by his mistress, Alice de Percy. He was never a great theologian. Indeed his biographer describes du Puiset as 'reputedly one of the most avaricious public figures in twelfth-century Britain'. His father was a notorious gangster who terrorised wide areas of northern France. His patronage secured du Puiset a place in the church.

By the 1160s, he had ingratiated himself with Henry II. The Bishop enriched himself by the perks of office through what is termed 'purchase and exchange'. When Richard came to the throne in 1189, he was desperate for money and approached the Bishop. Du Puiset promptly turned over about 3,600 marks – money he had raised for a crusade – to the king. In return he made Richard grant him a half share in the justiciarship and the earldom of Northumberland.

Du Puiset died of overindulgence at a Shrove Tuesday feast in 1195. After his debts were paid his estate was worth £5,000, about 0.5% of net national income of £1m. In today's money that would be worth £5.5bn.

Richard Crawshay

(1739-1810)
Industry
Wealth: £1.5m
Net National Income: £300m
% of NNI: 0.5%

£5.517 billion

Richard Crawshay, the great South Wales ironmaster, was born the son of a prosperous yeoman farmer in Yorkshire. The family name was then Crashaw. At 15, the young Crashaw had a violent argument with his father and left home for London with a horse. After about twenty days he arrived, exhausted, penniless and friendless. But he managed to find work as an odd-job boy in a warehouse belonging to the owner of a cast iron business in Upper Thames Street. He proved a willing worker and at 24, having changed his surname to Crawshay, he took over ownership of the business when his employer retired.

In the mid 1770s, while arranging a sale of cannon made at Cyfarthfa Ironworks, Merthyr Tydfil, Crawshay first met the works proprietor, Anthony Bacon. The two became partners and expanded the business for cannon both at home and in the export market. Bacon died in 1786, and Crawshay saw the Merthyr works for the first time. While Bacon had left his inheritance to his son, Crawshay leased properties on the site. He invested heavily in new technology – particularly the new 'puddling' method of ironmaking – which expanded his business enormously.

Within eight years of arriving in Merthyr, Crawshay was sole owner of the whole flourishing ironworks, making his family the wealthiest and most powerful in Wales. The Napoleonic

Wars proved to be particularly profitable for leading cannon makers. The guns of Nelson's flagship, Victory, had been cast at Cyfarthfa. Crawshay did not live to see the end of the war. He died in 1810, and his elaborate funeral procession stretched 24 miles from Merthyr to Llandaff Cathedral in Cardiff.

He left £1.5m in his will, representing about 0.5% of the £300m net national income of the day. In today's terms that would be £5.5bn.

Hans Rausing

(dob 25/03/1926)
Industry

Wealth: £5.4 billion

Hans Rausing, the reclusive Swedish industrialist, is one of Britain's most charitable donors, having given away over £146m in the last few years. He has also given £343,000 to the Conservative Party over the past two years, providing financial support for the office of Oliver Letwin, who is in charge of David Cameron's policy reviews.

Based in Wadhurst, East Sussex, Rausing is a tax exile who helped develop the Tetra Pak (later Tetra Laval) operation founded by his late father in 1944. It revolutionised the packaging of products such as milk and juices. In the early 1980s, he moved to Britain to escape Sweden's punitive tax regime and sold his 50% stake in the company to his late brother Gad, for around £4.4bn in 1995.

Since then he has been investing heavily in new products such as Ecolean, the new environmentally-friendly packaging material made from chalk. Having taken control of the Swedish-based firm in 2000, it is a coup for Rausing that Marks & Spencer is now using Ecolean to wrap a range of its own-label butters. It follows a decision by Carrefour, the French supermarket operation, to use Ecolean in all its stores. But Ecolean will require more of the Rausing millions, having chalked up losses in 2003 and 2004. It recently laid off thirty staff as well. Rausing has also invested in a Swedish crystal company and bizarrely a Ukrainian ketchup maker.

Rausing's charitable trusts have also given enormous sums to charity of at least £20m a year but usually around £40m annually. Last year, among the donations by the Marit and

Hans Rausing Charitable Foundation was a £1.5m grant to a Swedish University medical faculty to research treatments for brain tumours.

It is not just Rausing who is generous to charitable causes. His London-based daughter, Lisbet, supports the conservation charity, Fauna and Flora International, where she is a vice president. She also helps conserve the golden eagle at her 48,000 acre Scottish Highland estate where she is spending upwards of £20m on a new and extraordinary granite house. Her donations to charity and worthy causes will soon reach £15m a year. Her sister Sigrid, the youngest daughter of Hans, also has a Scottish estate from where she is waging a battle against a wind farm proposed on Sir Jack Hayward's (q.v.) neighbouring estate.

The hefty investments and the increasing charitable work will have limited the growth in the Rausing fortune. Cautiously we value the Rausing family at £5.4bn, which is mid-point between the valuations in the 2006 Swedish rich list in *Veckans Affarer* and the figure in *Forbes'* recent list of world billionaires.

Sir William Craven

(c 1545-1618)
Merchant
Wealth: £125,000
Net National Income: £26m
% of NNI: 0.48%

£5.337 billion

Born in around 1545 at Appletreewick, a village near Skipton in Yorkshire's West Riding, the young William Craven was later apprenticed to the London merchant tailor Robert Hulson. He became free of the company in 1569. Craven then seems to have started business with Hulson, who gave him his shop and warehouse at the intersection of Bread Street with Watling Street for a period of three years after his death. He never engaged in overseas trade, and his fortune was made through the domestic wholesaling of cloth. He supplied cloth worth almost £600 for Queen Elizabeth's funeral.

Later in his career his activities extended to moneylending on a major scale, and his debtors included Sir Robert Cecil, the 2nd Earl of Essex, and the 9th Earl of Northumberland. Craven was relatively uninvolved in the affairs of his livery company, serving only in the office of second warden in 1593, but he enjoyed a long and distinguished career in civic politics, which began with his election to the court of common council for Bread Street ward in 1582. He was sheriff in 1601, and a beneficiary of the bonanza of honours at the accession of the new Stuart king, from whom he received a knighthood in 1603. He was Lord Mayor of London in 1610-11, but did not undertake any major policy initiatives.

Over the course of his career he was associated with the conventional charitable projects through which Londoners proved their godly credentials. He subscribed to the new Merchant Taylors' almshouses on Tower Hill in 1595, and founded a grammar school in his native parish of Burnsall in 1605, for the support of which he conveyed properties in the London parishes of St Mary Woolnoth and St Michael, Cornhill, in 1615.

Another object of his benefactions was Christ's Hospital, of which he was a governor from 1593, and a most assiduous president from 1611 to 1618, scarcely missing a meeting. In 1611, he gave the hospital £1,000, a gift which he unsuccessfully attempted to keep anonymous, and the money was used in the purchase of the parsonage and advowson of Ugley in Essex. In 1613, St John's College, Oxford, with which the Merchant Taylors were closely associated, received from him the living of Creeke in Northamptonshire, on condition that it should be reserved for one of the ten senior fellows of the college.

Craven laid the foundation stone of the rebuilt Aldersgate on 31 March 1617, bringing to fruition a project cherished by his friend William Parker. It was typical of their interest in the beautification of the City and its churches, for Craven had been involved in the rebuilding of Holy Trinity the Less in 1606, and left £100 for the repair of the church of St John the Evangelist, where he had been apprenticed. His will also included bequests to the London hospitals and prisons, the poor of a number of London parishes, Burnsall, and Tiverton, Devon.

Craven married in or before 1597, Elizabeth (d 1624), the third daughter of William Whitmore, and the sister of Sir George Whitmore (Lord Mayor, 1631-2). Although Craven himself had not invested in land, his enormous fortune ensured that his widow and their surviving sons were able to carve out sizeable estates after his death. When Lady Craven died in 1624, it was reported that she had left an estate of £8,000 per annum to her eldest son and £5,000 per annum to the younger. Craven's fortune was around £125,000 or over £5.3bn in today's money.

Sir Lawrence Dundas

(c 1710-1781)
Land
Wealth: £900,000
Net National Income: £188m
% of NNI: 0.47%

£5.216 billion

One of the great eighteenth century pillagers of government contracts, Lawrence Dundas started out with few prospects. He was the younger son of an impoverished branch of the Dundas family. Born in Scotland, he worked in his father's drapery shop setting up in business as a merchant contractor. Realising that the key to contracts for the army was to have political clout, Dundas spent vast sums on trying to buy his way into parliament. He failed in 1754, but recouped his losses with contracts to supply troops in Germany during the Seven Years' War. He was able to build up a considerable reputation and a fortune estimated then at between £600,000 and £800,000. Using his financial clout, he lent money to the Earl of Shelburne, who had the ear of the Prime Minister, Lord Bute, and in return Dundas was raised to the baronetcy.

Next he started buying up estates in Yorkshire with a view to obtaining their parliamentary representation. But Dundas was not finished. In 1763, he spent £40,000 on an estate and London home fit for a man of his position. But his greed over the German 'pillage' during the war led to questions by the Treasury and disputes over his accounts. Nothing seems to have come of this, presumably because Dundas was canny enough to build up his political power base and become a useful ally to have, with at least six seats in his pocket in Scotland and Yorkshire.

Of course the old Scottish and English aristocracy treated him with contempt as an 'upstart.' They liked his money but would not give him a peerage. But like so many self-made men, Dundas wanted to be one of them and continued making speeches in the Commons and manoeuvring his group one way and another: all to no real avail. He even lost one of his seats in 1780. In Edinburgh, he was up against a distant family member, Henry Dundas, backed by the Duke of Buccleuch, and lost a particularly dirty campaign. In previous battles with the Dundas-Buccleuch faction for control of Edinburgh council, Dundas was attacked in handbills as 'the stout Earl of the German Plains', ridiculing his origins, pretensions and presumably the manner in which his fortune was acquired.

Crippled by gout, Dundas died in 1781, leaving a fortune of around £900,000 according to *The Gentleman's Magazine* of the time. That would have been around 0.47% of the £188m net national income of the day. In today's terms that represents just over £5.2bn.

John Holles, The Earl Of Clare

(1564-1637)
Land
Wealth: £150,000
Net National Income: £32m
% of NNI: 0.46%

£5.105 billion

The son of a large landowner in Nottingham and a grandson of Lord Sheffield, another land magnate, John Holles married a Stanhope heiress in 1591, with more land in Nottinghamshire.

During the reign of Elizabeth I, he fought against the Armada, in Ireland and against the Turks in Hungary. Of a quarrelsome disposition he nonetheless became Baron Holles of Houghton for a payment of £10,000 and the Earl of Clare in 1624, for a further fee of £5,000. But during the reigns of James I and Charles I, his abrasive nature led to two appearances before the Star Chamber and a fine of £1,000. Clare was active but not successful in court politics.

He died worth £150,000, about 0.46% of net national income of £32m at the time. In today's money that would be worth £5.1bn.

William Dension

(1770-1849)
Finance
Wealth: £2.3m
Net National Income: £508m
% of NNI: 0.45%

£4.994 billion

William Denison's grandfather was a Leeds woollen merchant, but his father went to London to make his fortune. Denison himself was born in the City in 1770, and pursued a banking career, ending up as senior partner of Denison, Heywood & Kennard in Lombard Street. His father had bought Yorkshire estates, including Seamer, near Scarborough from the Duke of Leeds for £100,000.

Denison, who was also a backbench MP for most of his life from 1796 onwards, died in 1849. His will was reckoned at the time to be worth £2.3m. The Yorkshire estates had risen to £500,000 in value and his land in Surrey some £100,000. The rest was in cash and securities. His fortune represented about 0.45% of net national income at the time, or £4.9bn in today's money.

William Lambton

(1764-1797)
Coal mine owner
Wealth: £1m
Net National Income: £220m
% of NNI: 0.45%

£4.994 billion

The Lambton family went back to the twelfth century in north Durham, but they moved from prosperous gentry to the super-rich class and one of the wealthiest commoner families in England in the eighteenth century. Coal was discovered beneath the Hedworth estate (which had come to the Lambtons by marriage in 1696) on the banks of the Wear.

Lambton's father, an army general, became an MP and was succeeded in parliament by his son in 1787. Young Lambton was a radical firebrand, closely aligned with Fox and in favour of parliamentary reform. He spoke eloquently and passionately in the Commons against war with France in 1793, in favour of press freedom and against the suspension of habeas corpus in the early and difficult days of the war with revolutionary France.

In 1794, his father died leaving him an annual income of around £35,000 a year. But Lambton's health was poor. He went to Italy to recover in 1796, but died of consumption at Pisa a year later. He was worth around £1m, or 0.45% of the £220m net national income at the time. In today's terms that would be £4.9bn.

John Mansel

(d 1265)
Politics
Wealth: £15,000
Net National Income: £3.3m
% of NNI: 0.45%

£4.994 billion

The son of a cleric, John Mansel was one of Henry III's key servants, particularly in foreign policy. Educated at court, he was employed in the Exchequer from 1234, and for the next thirty years until his death in 1265, he held a number of key posts. Mansel was well rewarded with income from various appointments running into thousands of marks a year. He also had a reputation as a fighting cleric until a stone crushed his leg in France in 1243.

Regarded as 'almost the Wolsey of his age', Mansel stirred up jealous opposition and was forced into exile in 1263. He died abroad and his £15,000 fortune would have been about 0.45% of net national income, or £4.9bn in today's terms.

Sir Horatio Palavicino

(c 1540-1600)
Financier
Wealth: £100,000
Net National Income: £22m
% of NNI: 0.45%

£4.994 billion

Not many people got the better of Elizabeth I, but Horatio Palavicino was one. A banker and diplomat, who came from a powerful aristocratic banking family in Genoa, Palavicino made his mark in the Low Countries. The family fortune was based on handling the papal monopoly in alum, which was in great demand in the cloth trade. In 1578, he sold the family stock of alum in Antwerp to the Dutch rebels fighting their Spanish masters in return for an import monopoly on alum. When the Dutch could or would not pay cash for the alum, Elizabeth I underwrote a loan to them for £29,000. It was an expedient way of keeping alive Dutch resistance to Spain, her deadly enemy. But it meant that she effectively owed that £29,000 to Palavicino.

A year later, when Sir Thomas Gresham, the English government's chief financial agent died, Palavicino was seen as the only person with the skills and reputation in high finance to succeed him. He became a naturalised Englishman, was knighted and given a full diplomatic post as ambassador to the Protestant princes of north-western Europe. But he lost Elizabeth's favour when in 1592, she found that while she had only repaid £4,425 of the 1578 loan, Palavicino had cleared over £41,000 in interest alone.

From 1594 to his death in 1600, he was busy increasing his wealth and buying up land. He speculated in the corn market, driving up prices in times of famine, he handled art and antiques for clients, ransomed Spanish prisoners from the Armada of 1588, and lent money at punishing rates of interest. He tried but failed to corner the world supply of pepper.

At his death he had assets of £100,000 including 8,000 acres of land in three counties. His wealth represented about 0.45% of the £22m net national income of the day. In today's terms that would be £4.9bn.

Rich list members born in the 12th century

Rich list member	Lifespan
Becket, Archbishop Thomas	1120-1170
Glanvill, Ranulf	c1120-1190
Du Puiset, Bishop High	c1120-1195
Aquitaine, Eleanor of	c1122-1204
Norwich, Jurnet of	c1130-1197
Walter, Archbishop Hubert	1140-1205
De Mandeville, Geoffrey	d 1144
Marshall, William	1147-1219
Espec, Walter	d 1158
Cade, William	d 1166
De Lucy, Richard	d 1179
Lincoln, Aaron of	d 1186
Des Rivaux, Peter	c1190-1262
Rhys, The Lord	d 1197

Sir Philip & Lady Green

(dob 15/03/1952 and 03/08/1949)
Retailing

Wealth: £4.9 billion

In the news recently over his 55th birthday bash costing £6m on the Indian ocean island of Kunfunadhoo, newly knighted Sir Philip Green will be more concerned about the state of his retail empire. Profits fell at both his Arcadia and Bhs chains in 2005-06, and the days of record £1.2bn payments to his wife Tina Green – as owner of the 92% stake in Arcadia – are long gone.

Monaco-based Green who made his name as a discount retailer in the 1980s and early 1990s, rewrote all the rules about how to turn round businesses when he took over Bhs in 2000 for £200m. Within two years it was making £172m profit on £876m sales. In three years it paid out £423m in dividends, of which around £398m went to the Green family. But profits fell sharply in 2005-06 from £109.5m to £42.2m on sales down slightly at £860.5m. Green has pledged to reverse the decline and will invest £100m in freshening up Bhs stores, which face a fresh challenge from a revitalised Marks & Spencer.

Green admitted to taking his eye off the ball following the £850m acquisition of Arcadia in 2002. Arcadia, best known for its brands like Topshop and Dorothy Perkins, has been hugely successful but even it could not shrug off the retail environment. Profits at its parent company, Taveta Investments, fell from £253m to £202m in the year to September 2006, though sales rose 1.8% to £1.8bn.

Collectively, we value Bhs and Arcadia at around £3.1bn on the latest figures. That values the Green family stake at nearly

£2.9bn. We add another £1.6bn for past dividends and £400m for other assets, homes, yachts and the proceeds of earlier property deals and the like that Green has worked on. In all, we reckon a £4.9bn figure is a fair valuation until we see signs of an upturn in the fortunes at Arcadia and Bhs.

The 4th Earl Cadogan

(1812-1873)
Land
Wealth: £4.803m
Net National Income: £1.075bn
% of NNI: 0.44%

£4.883 billion

The Cadogan fortune stems from the exploits of William Cadogan, an Irish soldier who served in Marlborough's army with distinction in the battles against France in the early eighteenth century. By the end of the war, this Dublin lawyer's son was Colonel of the Coldstream Guards and an MP.

In 1716, he was created Baron Cadogan of Reading. His brother, who later inherited the title, made the family fortune by marrying one Mary Sloane in 1717. She was the daughter and heir of Sir Hans Sloane, Lord of the Manor of Chelsea. That inheritance – now the 100 acres round Sloane Square – has become some of the most valuable real estate in the world. By the nineteenth century, the Cadogans' wealth had pushed them into the forefront of the British aristocracy. The 4th Earl, born in 1812, was not willing, however, to lead an idle life. He served in diplomatic posts in the key embassies of St Petersburg and Paris, and had been a Tory MP.

When he died in 1873, Cadogan left a relatively small will of around £80,000 in personal wealth. Yet the annual rental value of the Chelsea land around that time was £180,000 according to Professor Peter Lindert in an article entitled 'Who Owned Victorian England?' in the journal *Agricultural History* (1987). Cadogan's asset wealth would have been not far off 30 times the rental income – perhaps £4.8m, representing 0.44% of the then £1.075bn net national income. Today's equivalent would be £4.8bn.

Robert Cecil, Earl Of Salisbury

(1563-1612)
Land
Wealth: £110,000
Net National Income: £25m
% of NNI: 0.44%

£4.883 billion

Robert Cecil was the second son of Lord Burghley, Elizabeth I's great Minister. His heir was regarded as stupid, so Burghley devoted his affection and training on his younger son, who proved to be a genius at statecraft. At 21, he entered the Commons and at 27 was in effect Secretary of State without the title. But it was his skill rather than his father's patronage that had helped his advance. Noted for his caution, prudence and hard work, he was well regarded by Elizabeth, and when his father died in 1598, Cecil succeeded him as Master of the Wards: He had already been made Secretary of State proper two years earlier.

Cecil eased the succession of James I smoothly, earning the title Marquess of Salisbury as a reward. He became in effect Prime Minister when he was made Lord Treasurer in 1608. By then he had proved to be a vital administrator for James and after he died in 1612 from overwork, royal administration and finances descended into disorder and crisis. Lawrence Stone in his book 'Crisis of the Aristocracy' reckoned Salisbury's annual income to be over £20,000. It was enough to allow him to build the magnificent Hatfield House in Hertfordshire.

His wealth would have been around £110,000, equivalent to 0.44% of the £25m net national income. In today's terms that would be over £4.8bn.

Sir Robert Peel

(1750-1830)
Industry
Wealth: £1.5m
Net National Income: £336m
% of NNI: 0.44%

£4.883 billion

Born in Oswaldtwistle, Lancashire in 1750, Peel joined his father's calico printing business in Blackburn at the age of 23. When his father died in 1795, he left a £140,000 fortune, but Peel built on that substantially. By then he had moved his operation to Tamworth in Staffordshire, where he had acquired the estate of the Marquess of Bath in 1790. This enabled him to install modern machinery without falling foul of the increasingly militant Lancashire handloom weavers. Peel became MP for Tamworth in 1790, where he was an enthusiastic supporter of Pitt, and for the next thirty years sat in the Commons, promoting the interests of industry.

Peel's heir, also Robert, was born in 1788. It was said that on hearing the news of his birth, the elder Peel fell on his knees, and returning thanks to God, vowed that he would give his child to his country. He did and the son became the pride of his life. 'Bob,' the elder Peel is said to have remarked 'if you are not prime minister some day, I'll disinherit you.' Though the elder Peel died in 1830, this dream was posthumously fulfilled – his son became prime minister in 1841.

Peel's fortune on his death was around £1.5m according to the historian Eric Hobsbawm in his book 'Industry and Empire'. That would represent around 0.44% of the £336m net national income of the day, or £4.8bn in today's terms.

Alfred Beit

(1853-1906)
Mining
Wealth: £8.049m
Net National Income: £1.874bn
% of NNI: 0.43%

£4.816 billion

One of the great financiers of the British Empire, Alfred Beit was born to a prosperous Hamburg merchant in 1853. His family were descended from Portuguese Jews but were Lutheran by religion. The young Beit showed little aptitude academically and was educated privately until he entered the office of an Amsterdam diamond merchant at the age of 18.

After learning the trade he joined another Amsterdam firm, D Lippert & Co, and was sent in 1875, aged 22, to the Cape Colony in South Africa as its representative. For three years he worked in Kimberley, the diamond mining centre, before returning to Hamburg three years later in 1878. His Amsterdam training kicked in and he saw that Cape diamonds had an entirely undeserved reputation as an inferior stone. As a result they were being sold in Africa at a price far below their worth in Europe. Beit borrowed £2,000 from his father by way of capital, he returned to Kimberley in the same year, and set up under his own name as a diamond merchant. Foreseeing the growth of Kimberley, he is said to have invested most of his capital in purchasing ground on which he put up a number of corrugated iron offices. For twelve of these the rent ultimately received by him was around £1,800 a month, and later he is believed to have sold the ground for £260,000.

In Kimberley, Beit became associated with two men who were

to have a profound impact on his later life. First in 1882, he teamed up with Julius Wernher, a fellow diamond merchant. By 1890, the pair worked together through the firm, Wernher, Beit & Co. More importantly, Beit made the acquaintance of Cecil Rhodes, and became a close friend. He soon joined Rhodes on the board of the original De Beers Diamond Company (founded in 1880) and played an important part in Rhodes's great scheme for the amalgamation of the chief diamond mines of Kimberley as De Beers Consolidated Mines. It took effect in 1888, after Beit had advanced an unsecured £250,000 loan to Rhodes.

Beit also shrewdly started investing in gold prospecting in the Rand area. When it was declared a public goldfield in 1886, Beit acquired large tracts of land and, hiring the best mining engineers of the day from America, sunk deep level shafts to search for gold, despite initial public scepticism.

Beit, who had become a naturalised British subject, was deeply interested in Rhodes's scheme of northern expansion. On the formation of the chartered British South Africa Company in 1889, for the conquest of the extensive territory afterwards known as Southern and Northern Rhodesia (and later as Zimbabwe and Zambia), Beit became an original director. He first visited the country in 1891. He later joined the boards of the various Rhodesian railway companies. But when extensive prospecting failed to locate goldfields of any significance between the Limpopo and Zambezi rivers, Beit's interest in the Rand redoubled.

But he became impatient with the rule of President Kruger. Rhodes and Beit together placed Starr Jameson with an armed force on the Transvaal border (December 1895) leading to the infamous Jameson Raid. Beit's role in the fiasco cost him £200,000. Censured for his part in the affair by the British South Africa committee of the House of Commons in 1897, he resigned his directorship of the British South Africa Company.

During the Boer War of 1899-1902, Beit spent immense sums on the Imperial Light Horse and on the equipment of the Imperial Yeomanry, and before and after the war he poured money into land settlement, immigration, and kindred schemes for the development of South Africa.

On Rhodes's death in March 1902, Beit succeeded to much of his friend's position. He became the chief figure on the boards of the De Beers Company and of the chartered company, which he rejoined in that year. But Beit's health had long been poor, and in the autumn of 1903, when he visited southern Africa for the purpose of examining the administration of Rhodesia, he suffered a stroke near Salisbury. In the early spring of 1906, he was sent to Wiesbaden on account of heart trouble, but by his own wish he was brought home to England, and died at his country residence, Tewin Water, Welwyn, Hertfordshire, on 16 July 1906.

The unmarried Beit left over £8m in his will, mostly to his brother. But his gifts to charities, hospitals, and education amounted to £2m. In today's money, his fortune would have been over £4.8bn.

The 1st Earl Of Dudley

(1817-1885)
Land
Wealth: £4.721m
Net National Income: £1.075bn
% of NNI: 0.43%

£4.772 billion

The early Dudleys did not have much luck in the scramble for land in the sixteenth century. The 3rd Baron Dudley lost Dudley Castle and relied on charity from friends having suffered at the hands of usurers, which led to him being styled 'Lord Quondam'. Queen Mary restored the castle and the valuables to the family. By the nineteenth century, the Dudley estates ran to around 25,554 acres, not much by contemporary standards. But there were huge coal seams around Birmingham, vital to the Industrial Revolution and the prop for the Dudley fortune.

William Ward, the 11th Lord Dudley was born in 1817, just as the demand for coal was taking off. He succeeded his father to the baronetcy in 1835, and was raised to the earldom of Dudley in 1860.

At his death in 1885, he left £1m in personal assets. Adding in his land and coal assets gives a £4.72m fortune representing around 0.43% of the net national income. Today's equivalent would be over £4.7bn.

George Bowes

(1701-1760)
Coal
Wealth: £600,000
Net National Income: £140m
% of NNI: 0.42%

£4.661 billion

George Bowes was one of the largest coal owners in eighteenth century Durham. He formed a cartel with two other prominent coal mining families called the 'Grand Alliance', which dominated the north country coal trade through the century. He was mayor of Durham in 1739, and sat as MP for the county from 1727 to his death in 1760, speaking on behalf of local coal interests.

He left a £600,000 fortune, equivalent to 0.42% of the £140m net national income. In today's terms, that would be £4.6bn.

The 3rd Marquess Of Bute

(1847-1900)
Land
Wealth: £4.609m
Net National Income: £1.075bn
% of NNI: 0.42%

£4.661 billion

Though he was described as 'the richest man in the world' in the nineteenth century, this was not quite accurate. He may not have been the Bill Gates of his day, but the huge coal seams in Wales and Ayrshire certainly made the Butes enormously wealthy. The 2nd Marquess, described as the 'maker of modern Cardiff' died suddenly in 1847 of a heart attack, leaving his huge inheritance to his six-month old son, who became the 3rd Marquess.

With a passion for history and antiquarianism, he was later to use his coal revenues to transform the Georgian Cardiff Castle, one of his residences, from 1865 onwards into a medieval-style nobleman's home. Among his treasures was an elaborate bed, richly sculpted and inlaid with minerals, which was recently discovered after disappearing in 1949. Bute's total acreage in 1882 was computed at 116,668 by Bateman in 'The Great Landowners of Great Britain'.

He died in 1900, leaving just over £2m in his will. But at the time Bateman did his work, his total land and personal wealth was around £4.6m, representing 0.42% of the then £1.075bn net national income. Today's equivalent would be over £4.6bn.

Sir James Campbell

(1570-1642)
Merchant
Wealth: £150,000
Net National Income: £35m
% of NNI: 0.42%

£4.661 billion

Sir James Campbell followed his father's trade of ironmonger in London. He made his way up the political ladder in the City: sheriff in 1619, alderman in 1620 and Lord Mayor in 1629. Knighted by the king in 1630, Campbell built up a huge fortune of at least £150,000 by his death twelve years later. With no children, he bequeathed nearly £49,000 to various charities. His fortune was equivalent to 0.42% of net national income at the time, or £4.6bn in today's terms.

Sampson Gideon

(1699-1762)
Moneylender
Wealth: £600,000
Net National Income: £145m
% of NNI: 0.42%

£4.661 billion

Sampson Gideon's father, a Portuguese merchant, had settled in London in the seventeenth century. At the age of 20, Gideon founded his fortune by speculation in Change Alley and in coffee houses over lottery tickets, government bonds and various company shares, including the South Sea Company. His capital was around £1,500 when he started. Within two years, he had increased that to £7,900 and when he became a broker in 1729, at the age of 30, his capital stood at £25,000.

In the 1740s and 1750s, he was vital to successive governments in raising and lending money for war in Europe and the colonies. In the 1745 Jacobite Rebellion, he put his fortune on the line to stop financial panic sweeping London as Bonnie Prince Charlie moved south to Derby. In the crucial years of 1758-59, it was Gideon's skill as a financier that produced the money needed for the war effort in the famous 'year of victories'.

At this time, Gideon did little to add to his fortune so busy was he with government business. He did however build a fine house in Kent and collect some remarkable Old Master paintings. The only reward he wanted from the government was a peerage, but the king refused because of lingering prejudice against Jews. His son, who was raised as a Christian, did receive a baronetcy, while his youngest daughter married into the aristocracy.

Gideon's estates were valued at around £580,000 at his death. His personal assets would have taken his fortune to around £600,000, representing 0.42% of net national income. In today's terms that equates to over £4.6bn.

William Denison

(1713-1782)
Textiles
Wealth: £700,000
Net National Income: £195m
% of NNI: 0.407%

£4.515 billion

A proud Yorkshireman, William Denison came from a long line of cloth makers and cloth merchants from Great Woodhouse near Leeds. Little is known of his early years though he was likely to have been educated at Leeds Grammar School and probably served an apprenticeship in the Leeds cloth trade.

He first came to prominence in the 1750s, when he refused to serve the office of Mayor of Leeds on no fewer than four occasions (he had been elected to the corporation in 1750). The corporation brought a case at York Assizes in 1759, settled on condition that Denison agreed to pay its costs and his brother Robert act in his place.

His fortune, largely self-made, appears to have been based on the export of Yorkshire cloth primarily to the Italian market. Clearly it was already substantial by the late 1750s, when he began to buy land on a large scale, a passion which by the 1770s, left him with many thousands of acres scattered across Yorkshire, Durham, Lincolnshire, and Nottinghamshire.

Certainly Denison's interests were never confined to the cloth export trade. By the end of the 1770s, when the Mediterranean trade was at a standstill, he was dealing extensively in annuities for some of the more extravagant members of the aristocracy, buying government stock, and threatening to sell some of his landed property because the returns on it were inferior to those he could make in the funds.

In 1779, Denison served office as high sheriff of Nottinghamshire with great reluctance, claiming he never spent more than a fortnight a year on his Ossington estate.

On all his properties he was an exacting landlord and a keen agricultural improver, revealing a good knowledge of up-to-date farming practices and woodland management. This fitted with his immensely shrewd nature and the pride he took in his wealth. Although he appears to have visited his scattered estates each year, he was firmly based in Kirkgate, Leeds, in a house surrounded by the bustle of an industrial town, with his work and packing shops crowded into the yard behind. Short on public spirit, he was generous to the poor. In the winter of 1775-6, he provided the poor of Kirkgate with thirty loads of corn and four hundred corves of coal.

Denison did not marry and when he died in 1782, local papers in Leeds later reckoned his fortune to be upwards of £700,000. It passed to his sister's son, who changed his name to Denison and immediately sent his nine sons to Eton. Many were later to distinguish themselves as leading members of the Victorian establishment. Denison's £700,000 would be worth £4.5bn in today's money.

Robert Clive, 1st Baron Clive Of Plassey

(1725-1774)
Soldier and statesman
Wealth: £500,000
Net National Income: £123m
% of NNI: 0.401%

£4.491 billion

The eldest of thirteen children, Robert Clive was farmed out by his parents to live with an aunt and uncle. His father, a lawyer and MP, was a long established member of the Shropshire gentry. A boisterous youth, Clive went to a number of schools and learnt bookkeeping at the age of 14. He did not follow his father into the legal profession but in 1742, at the age of just 17, he secured a job as a clerk with the East India Company in Madras.

Leaving London in 1743, he took a full fifteen months to get to India after a spell in Brazil en route. Clive arrived in Madras in June 1744, impoverished by debts incurred during the journey and without any connections or acquaintances in the small British settlement of Fort St George. These circumstances made for a miserable existence, and in February 1745, Clive confessed that 'I have not enjoyed one happy day since I left my native country.' He even attempted to commit suicide, his life being saved by the fact that his pistol twice misfired.

In 1746, he transferred to the accountant's office, where he acquired a wide range of technical skills while dealing with the company's commercial affairs. He also sought to improve himself and broaden his education in other ways. Madras fell to the French in September 1746, but Clive escaped and entered the East India Company's own private army as an ensign.

Over the next two years his reputation in battle grew and he was promoted to lieutenant. By the end of 1749, Clive had returned to civil employment, and his military success earned him the lucrative position of commissary for the supply of provisions to the company's troops. The profitable opportunities opened up by the levying of commission on all goods purchased on the army's behalf were considerable, and in a short period of time Clive was able to lay the foundations of his private fortune.

After illness in 1750, Clive resumed his company military career with the rank of captain in July 1751. His reputation was further enhanced when he seized the fort of Arcot with a force of 800 men and held it for 50 days under siege by the French and their allies. Building on his success at Arcot, Clive then went on in quick succession to take a number of forts, defeat the enemy at Arni, twice recapture Conjeeveram, rout a small French force during a night-time engagement at Kaveripak, and lay waste to the town of Dupleix Fatehabad.

In 1752, he played a crucial role in a campaign which led to the capture of the fort at Trichinopoly. The heavy fighting took its toll on his health and at the end of 1752, he returned to Britain newly married. Just before he returned, Clive had arranged for all of his estate in India to be invested in diamonds. His private wealth stood at £40,000. A careful spender, Clive was generous towards his friends, and paid off family debts, including much of the £8,000 mortgage on his family seat. He made a brief foray in parliament as a Cornish MP but was unseated after the result was disputed in the Commons.

The cost of the campaign hit Clive hard and he welcomed the offer of more work in India with the Company. He arrived in Bombay late in 1755. For the next two years he fought against a local nawab (including relieving the notorious Black Hole of Calcutta) and later the French, ending in 1757 with his victory at Plassey, which paved the way for British hegemony in India.

Clive was generously rewarded, receiving presents worth £234,000 in 1757, and two years later, following the successful defence of Bengal against invasion by the son of the Mughal emperor, he received a grant of land revenue worth around £27,000 a year to the recipient. Known as a jagir, it allowed Clive to invest £30,000 in Golconda diamonds at Madras in 1757, and during the aftermath of Plassey he was also able to negotiate the purchase of 230,000 bills to be drawn on the Dutch East India Company. He also became Governor of Bengal, a post he held until he returned to England yet again in 1760, with a fortune of around £300,000.

He was elected unopposed as MP for Shrewsbury in April 1761. Clive again took great trouble to look after the well-being of his family and close friends. He did this through a series of generous gifts and settlements, providing a new house for his parents on the Styche estate. He started buying land and property including an Irish estate, which was renamed Plassey to mark Clive's greatest triumph. Lord Montfort's 7,500 acre Shropshire estate was bought for £70,000 in 1761, and the nearby 6,000 acre Walcot estate and house were purchased for £92,000 in 1763. A fashionable town house, 45 Berkeley Square in London, was rented from Lord Ancram, and this too was eventually acquired for an outlay of £10,500.

Despite – perhaps because of – his growing reputation and wealth, Clive was to face grilling in parliament over his jagir for years to come. But his time in India was not done. Serious military setbacks forced the East India Company to seek his return, and in return he was able to secure the jagir. Setting sail in June 1764, he reached Bengal nearly a year later to find that a British victory had transformed the military situation.

Wisely resisting the temptation for expansion, Clive

consolidated the company's economic and political position in Bengal. He established a dual system of government which enabled the company firmly to secure de facto control of Bengal and its adjacent territories with access to the wealth.

Clive's success was noted in London and the East India shares rose sharply. Clive was able to profit by this through what would be deemed insider dealing today. In September 1765, he had made use of his inside knowledge of developments in Bengal to advise friends in Britain to buy company stock, and he ordered his own London attorneys to raise large loans, liquefy his assets, and make substantial purchases on his behalf. These instructions were followed with great zeal, and by the beginning of 1767, Clive owned £75,000 of India stock, although the full extent of these stock market transactions was partially concealed from public scrutiny (and later parliamentary examination) by the use of nominee holding accounts. Clive secured a generous profit from enhanced dividend payments and the timely sale at a high price of half of his accumulated stock in the spring of 1767.

Thereafter he continued to conceal his East India holdings so that 'the World may not know what sum or sums of money I have in that stock'. Brazenly he later robustly denied any wrongdoing when his stock market transactions were examined by a House of Commons committee of inquiry.

As far as the company's internal affairs were concerned, Clive's second governorship of Bengal was characterized by a programme of rigorous, wide-ranging reforms. He set the general tone of his administration on 9 May 1765, when, in an action which caused considerable resentment, he insisted that, as previously instructed by the directors, members of the Bengal council sign covenants which prohibited present taking by company servants. It caused resentment and disaffected individuals all returned to Britain nurturing deep grievances, determined to pursue personal vendettas against Clive. His unpopularity increased yet further when, at the behest of the directors, he began to regulate the private trading activity of company employees.

As far as the company's military forces were concerned, Clive set about reorganizing and redeploying the army in an attempt to more effectively meet a new set of defensive priorities. Serious problems were encountered, however, when Clive tackled the issue of financial retrenchment and the rationalization of the army's pay and allowance structure. During the early months of 1766, discontent within the company's officer corps translated itself into a campaign of active resistance and near mutiny which Clive put down with characteristic efficiency and firmness.

In a hostile political climate Clive could not be seen to be profiting from present taking or private trade. Thus, in order to avoid any further charges of double standards, he gave away large sums of money to his friends, and the substantial bequest of 5 lakhs of rupees, made to him in Mir Jafar's will, was used to establish a fund to provide financial relief for disabled or impoverished company soldiers. In 1765, he wrote:

With regard to myself, I have not benefited or added to my fortune one farthing, nor shall I; though I might, by this time have received £500,000.

Even so, during his second governorship Clive was still able to remit home over £160,000, a sum arising from jagir payment arrears and the final settlement of his Indian affairs. His workload took its toll on Clive's health. Only large doses of opium helped him through the pain. He left India for the last time, setting sail from Calcutta on 29 January 1767. Arriving back in July 1767, he was once more honoured with many official marks of gratitude. He estimated that his personal fortune now stood at just over £400,000, but public condemnation of his private wealth, as well as criticism of his actions as governor, began ever more to force him onto the defensive. His cause was not helped by the fact that, as a foretaste of things to come, in early 1767, the East India Company had been subjected to the first parliamentary inquiry into its affairs.

Despite poor health though, Clive set about spending his fortune. He spent £30,000 acquiring another Shropshire estate. A Monmouthshire estate was bought for £43,000 the next year, followed by a smaller £5,400 purchase there. Clive was seeking to establish a foothold there to pave the way for a seat in parliament. But he later abandoned his efforts in Monmouthshire in 1772, selling all his land there for £57,000, a handsome profit of £8,400. By then he had returned to the Commons as MP for Shrewsbury in 1768. As ever, he faced opposition from those who felt aggrieved by his recent Bengal reforms. His right to the jagir was still challenged even though it had been extended by a narrow majority of stockholders in September 1767.

Clive continued his land accumulation, spending £25,000 in 1769, on the purchase of the Claremont estate in Surrey from the widow of the Duke of Newcastle. Two years later the Oakley Park estate was bought from Lord Powis, and he also purchased the Okehampton estate in Devon. Clive's wealth was now such that he sanctioned the demolition of a Vanbrugh-designed Palladian mansion at Claremont and built in its place a house designed by Capability Brown and Henry Holland.

The final years of Clive's life were marked by parliamentary scrutiny of the East India Company and his role. In 1772, the Commons established a select committee of inquiry to look into the East India Company from 1756. Clive, a member of the inquiry, was also subjected to searching cross-examination. Clive received some much needed relief from his personal troubles, being at last installed as Knight of the Bath in June, and he was then appointed Lord Lieutenant of both Shropshire and Montgomery during the autumn of 1772. The report was published and followed by parliamentary debate where the enquiry chairman indicated that he would make a motion declaring that Clive had illegally acquired £234,000 after the Battle of Plassey. A majority of MPs backed Clive though and it was eventually resolved that, although he had indeed received £234,000, he had not abused his powers to do so. Indeed a motion backing Clive was carried unanimously.

Now semi-retired he went to Italy and it was reckoned that Clive spent much of the winter of 1773-4 in Italy in the company of several companions but not his wife. The purpose of the trip was twofold: to escape harsh weather and to procure works of art for the new house at Claremont, which was now approaching completion at a cost of around £30,000. The summer of 1774 was then spent in Shropshire, where guests were entertained and preparations were made for the forthcoming general election. In early November, however, Clive fell ill, as a common cold steadily worsened. He travelled first to Bath for the waters and then moved on to London. By the time he arrived at Berkeley Square on 20 November he had been in considerable pain for some time, and his old ailments had returned with a vengeance. He resorted to large doses of opium, which brought some respite, but on 22 November, having abandoned a game of cards being played with friends, he was found dead on the floor of an adjoining room. Clive, in great discomfort, had taken an excessively large dose of opium which led ultimately to a fatal seizure or epileptic fit.

His asset wealth was at least £500,000 when he died. In modern money that would easily be nearly £4.5bn.

The Earl Of Gloucester

(1291-1347)
Land
Wealth: £10,000
Net National Income: £2.5m
% of NNI: 0.4%

£4.440 billion

The son of a minor West Country baron, Hugh Audley went to the court of Edward II as a newly created knight in 1311. He became a leading figure at court and in 1317, married Margaret de Clare, widow of the former royal favourite, Piers Gaveston (q.v.). She was also co-heiress to the estates of her brother, the 9th Earl of Gloucester who had died at Bannockburn in 1314.

For three years, Audley was one of a small group of courtiers who kept a tight grip on Edward II's royal patronage and favour. He later became involved in rebellion against the Crown and was captured after the Battle of Boroughbridge. For four years he was imprisoned, only escaping execution through his wife's influence. He lost most of his estates but when Edward II was overthrown in 1326, his lands were restored. This did not prevent Audley from joining a revolt against the corrupt government of Queen Isabella, which cost him a £10,000 fine. This was eventually remitted but it showed the sort of wealth he could muster. Audley was astute enough to back the coup which raised Edward III to the throne. He served the new king and was created Earl of Gloucester in 1337, a title which he owed to his wife's inheritance. Audley served the king until his death in 1347 – surprisingly by natural causes. His £10,000 of wealth would be worth around £4.4bn in today's money.

Baron Grey Of Ruthin

(d 1353)
Land
Wealth: £10,000
Net National Income: £2.5m
% of NNI: 0.4%

£4.439 billion

Baron Grey was a younger son of a baron, and on his father's death in 1323, he inherited the castle of Ruthin, plus lands in Wales and southern England. In the 1340s, he served the king in Scotland and France. He later acted as a commissioner of array for Bedfordshire and Buckinghamshire, where most of his estates were situated.

Grey died in 1353, with a £10,000 fortune, representing around 0.4% of net national income, or £4.4bn in today's terms.

Sir Peter Warren

(1703-1752)
Navy
Wealth: £500,000
Net National Income: £125m
% of NNI: 0.4%

£4.439 billion

A Hornblower type, Peter Warren was born into a naval family in 1703. At the age of twelve, he joined the navy, and at eighteen passed the all-important lieutenant's exam. Through the 1720s and 1730s, he rose to command various naval ships in America and the West Indies. In 1744, he commanded a small squadron, which captured twenty valuable prizes, including one with cargo of £250,000. The squadron later moved to attack the French fort of Louisbourg, and the fort and a harbour full of ships fell to Warren in June 1745.

Canny Warren kept the French flag flying and as the port was a port of call for French ships returning from the West Indies, many came into the harbour to be captured by Warren's ships without a fight. He captured prizes with cargoes worth over £940,000 using these tactics. The lion's share of the prize money naturally went to Warren as senior officer. He was promoted to rear admiral after these successes and later retired to London to enjoy his spoils as an MP.

Warren was regarded as one of the richest commoners in the country, worth £500,000 when he died in 1752 of 'inflammatory fever'. This represented around 0.4% of the then £125m net national income. An equivalent figure today would be £4.4bn.

Sir Joseph Herne

(c 1639-1699)
Merchant
Wealth: £200,000
Net National Income: £50m
% of NNI: 0.4%

£4.438 billion

The eighth son of a merchant tailor, Joseph Herne was born in London and baptised in 1639. His early years remain a mystery but in 1671, he joined the East India Company, and a year later married Elizabeth, the daughter of Sir John Frederick of Old Jewry, London. It was a shrewd match. Frederick was himself a major figure in trade with the Peninsula, and Herne succeeded him as head of their joint firm in 1685. The Hernes had seven sons and three daughters. Herne was elected to the committee of the East India Company in 1678, and served continuously through to 1686, and then from 1687 to 1694 and from 1698 until his death.

It was after the revolution of 1688, however, that Herne's career took off. He was elected MP for Dartmouth on 28 November 1689 (and represented the constituency until his death), and was knighted on 15 September 1690. He invested widely in a number of the new industrial and trading concerns of the early 1690s, and, in partnership with the goldsmith-banker Sir Stephen Evance and others, used his international trading connections to handle the government's military remittances, first to Ireland (1690-91) and then, between May 1691 and October 1694, to the Continent. It was his credit that kept the artillery train in Flanders from starving late in 1694.

After being elected governor of the East India Company for

1690-92, Herne defended the company's monopoly and also appears to have been party to some extremely shady deals to break up the opposition group in 1693-4, and to have engaged in bribery to help secure a new charter for the company in 1694; all this brought a parliamentary storm on his head in the spring of 1696. But when in 1698, a new company finally won the trade in return for a loan of £2m, Herne brought the 'old' company into the subscription so that it could continue in the trade.

In 1698, Herne also joined the so-called tobacco contractors who had won from Peter the Great the lucrative right to export tobacco from England to Russia. But Herne did not enjoy the fruits of this trade, He died suddenly of a brain haemorrhage on 26 February 1699, worth 'near £200,000', or £4.4bn in today's money.

The Hon. Henry Cavendish

(1731-1810)
Land
Wealth: £1.175m
Net National Income: £300m
% of NNI: 0.39%

£4.328 billion

A grandson of the second Duke of Devonshire, Henry Cavendish was born in 1731. After leaving Cambridge in 1753, he spent the rest of his life in scientific discovery and experiments at his home in Clapham Common, London. A virtual recluse who barely spoke to anyone, Cavendish would only leave his house for meetings of the Royal Society. He was the first person to convert oxygen and hydrogen into water. He died in 1810, after virtually his only illness.

As he lived very modestly, his fortune had piled up to around £1.175m at his death, equivalent to 0.39% of the £300m net national income of the day. In today's terms that would be £4.3bn.

Sir Isaac Goldsmid

(1778-1859)
Finance
Wealth: £2.5m
Net National Income: £640m
% of NNI: 0.39%

£4.328 billion

The son of a City bullion broker, Isaac Goldsmid entered the firm of Mocatta & Goldsmid, bullion brokers to the Bank of England and the East India Company. He became a member of the stock exchange and amassed a large fortune, largely through financial dealings with Portugal, Brazil and Turkey. He was created a baron by the Portuguese government for settling a complex dispute with Brazil. But in England, aside from his financial affairs, Goldsmid's main effort was directed to Jewish emancipation and he sought to have a Jewish Disabilities Bill passed by parliament. While the reformed Commons of 1833 passed the bill by a large majority, it fell in the Lords. But Goldsmid persevered with the cause and that of prison reform. He had the distinction of being the first Jew to be raised to a baronetcy in 1841.

He died in 1859, leaving around £2m in cash and other assets plus land worth around £36,000 a year in income. In all, he was worth about £2.5m or equivalent to 0.39% of the £640m net national income. In today's terms that would be £4.3bn.

Earl Fitzwilliam

(1815-1902)
Land
Wealth: £4.164m
Net National Income: £1.075bn
% of NNI: 0.38%

£4.217 billion

Earl Fitzwilliam, a huge landowner in Ireland and England, was born in 1815, and sat as a Liberal MP for Malton in Yorkshire and later for Co. Wicklow. In 1857, he succeeded his father to the title and large estates running to over 115,000 acres in nine counties. The great bulk – over 89,000 acres – was in Co. Wicklow, with another 22,000 acres in Yorkshire.

Fitzwilliam died in 1902, leaving £2.95m in his will. Based on his rental income of £138,801 in 1882, and taking account of his personal assets, he was easily worth over £4.1m at the time, representing around 0.38% of the then £1.075bn net national income. Today's equivalent would be over £4.2bn.

Archbishop William Melton

(d 1340)
Church
Wealth: £20,000
Net National Income: £5.2m
% of NNI: 0.38%

£4.217 billion

Unusually, Archbishop Melton proved to be an efficient and honest administrator in fourteenth century England. A Yorkshire-born cleric, Melton was recruited into government by Edward I and Edward II. He had two spells as treasurer of the Exchequer and one as Chancellor. In 1317, he was nominated by the king to be Archbishop of York, and he went there to live until his death in 1340.

He was a prodigious pluralist, holding several ecclesiastical benefices. As Archbishop, he proved to be kind to the poor and relieved his poor tenants of their debts. But he was able to afford it. As Archbishop he made a total of at least 388 loans totalling £23,551, some at hefty interest rates. He died in 1340, leaving substantial bequests to his nephews and nieces. He built up a large Nottinghamshire estate for one nephew, raising the Meltons into a leading county family.

In his death, Melton was worth around £20,000, equivalent to about 0.38% of the £5.2m net national income. In today's money that would be £4.2bn.

The Marquess Of Rockingham

(1730-1782)
Land
Wealth: £750,000
Net National Income: £195m
% of NNI: 0.38%

£4.217 billion

The Marquess of Rockingham was a great landowner in Yorkshire and Ireland who ran his estates wisely to the point where he was able to garner an annual income from them of £24,000 in 1761. An active parliamentarian, who spent his early career promoting the interests of Yorkshire wool growers, Rockingham was also a keen follower of the turf and a member of the newly formed Jockey Club.

He inherited his estates and title in 1750, when his father died. At 35, he became First Lord of the Treasury, i.e. Prime Minister, where he was regarded as a man of honour and integrity. But he was too inexperienced to keep power in what was dubbed 'an administration of boys' by George II. In 1766, his administration fell. But he returned to office in 1782, with a stronger hand to negotiate American Independence, which he had long advocated.

But he had been in office a bare three months when he died of influenza at 52. His estates were worth at least £750,000, equivalent to around 0.38% of the £195m net national income of the day. Today's equivalent would be around £4.2bn.

Sir Hugh Clopton

(d 1496)
Merchant
Wealth: £15,000
Net National Income: £4m
% of NNI: 0.37%

£4.106 billion

Sir Hugh Clopton, a wealthy mercer in fifteenth century London, originally hailed from Clopton near Stratford-upon-Avon. His ancestors had owned Clopton Manor since Henry III's time. His business skills and wealth lead to political power and honours: he became Lord Mayor in 1491, and was knighted in the same year. His large fortune enabled him to buy the family estate from his elder brother, and he had the distinction of building a house in Stratford which was later to be Shakespeare's main home from 1597, until his death in 1616.

Clopton died in 1496, leaving considerable bequests to his native town, including 100 marks to 24 Stratford maidens. He was worth around £15,000 at his death, the equivalent of about 0.37% of the £4m net national income of the day. Today that would be £4.1bn.

Sir Robert Holland

(c 1270-1329)
Land
Wealth: £15,000
Net National Income: £4m
% of NNI: 0.37%

£4.106 billion

From a county family in Lancashire, Robert Holland devoted much of his life to loyal service in the cause of Thomas of Lancaster. He entered Lancaster retinue in 1298, serving with him continuously for the next 22 years in Scotland and domestic politics. He was richly rewarded with a stream of grants from 1300 onwards, including 25 manors worth £550 a year.

Holland married a co-heiress and with Lancaster's support in 1314, secured the highly favourable partition of her estates. With his grants from Lancaster and his wife's land, Holland's land income was around £1,270 a year from land in sixteen counties. But Holland deserted him in 1322, and his refusal to send his troops from the Midlands contributed to Lancaster's destruction. Lancaster's followers did not forget and Holland was murdered in 1329.

His fortune was around £15,000, equivalent to around 0.37% of the £4m net national income of the day. In today's figures that would be £4.1bn.

Philip Rundell

(1746-1827)
Merchant
Wealth: £1.2m
Net National Income: £321m
% of NNI: 0.37%

£4.106 billion

Born of a large Somerset family, Rundell was apprenticed to a Bath jeweller at 14. After serving his apprenticeship, he moved to the City of London. Within three or four years the young Rundell was a partner in the firm. In 1786, Rundell bought his partner out and took on a new partner, John Bridge, and they worked in harmony for forty years. In 1798, Rundell purchased John Duval, Sons & Co, which gave Rundell & Bridge the Crown jewellership. By the time he retired in 1823, Rundell had built the firm into a dominant position in the jewellery business.

He died in 1827, worth around £1.2m, equivalent to 0.37% of the £321m net national income. In today's money, that would be £4.1bn.

Sir David Yule

(1858-1928)
Industry
Wealth: £15m
Net National Income: £4.15bn
% of NNI: 0.361%

£4.005 billion

One of India's wealthiest businessmen at the height of the Raj came from humble Scottish roots. David Yule's grandfather was a linen and wool draper and Yule was educated at Edinburgh's Royal High School. After that he spent three years in Oldham, the Lancashire mill town, learning the cotton trade. This was to prove useful when in 1875, he went out to India to work in Calcutta for his two uncles, Andrew and George Yule who were building what was to become a huge conglomerate based in Calcutta. He initially managed one of their subsidiaries, the Bengal Cotton Mills, but rose to become a partner in the parent firm, Andrew Yule & Co in 1887. His uncles retired back to the UK and Yule acquired the shares of one of them and replaced him as resident partner in India.

David Yule acquired a reputation as a shy and reclusive man, who preferred to live in the mill compound than to move to the fashionable areas of Calcutta favoured by other Europeans. It is said that he never took a holiday, and did not pay a visit to Britain for eighteen years after his arrival in India.

The range of the company's business interests increased dramatically under his direction. He was largely responsible for increasing the firm's involvement in the jute industry. In 1895, he had formed the Bengal Assam Steamship Company. The success of this venture encouraged him, in 1906, to form Port Shipping Ltd, Calcutta's largest lighterage company.

The firm had acquired substantial interest in the Indian coal industry, and in 1908, Yule consolidated its interest in this field when Andrew Yule & Co. became managing agents of Bengal Coal Ltd. Yule was also enthusiastic about the prospects for estate management in India, and in 1902, formed Midnapore Zemindary Company (MZC) to acquire and develop land in Bengal. The MZC estates comprised 2,400 square miles, on which the company promoted agriculture, forestry, fisheries, and other rural industries. He received a knighthood in the Durbar honours list of 1912, and in 1922, he was created a baronet.

By 1917, Andrew Yule & Co. managed more than sixty companies and was one of the leading businesses in Calcutta. Nevertheless, Yule decided to dispose of the firm as he had no son to inherit the business. In 1919, he sold the goodwill and business of the firms for £600,000 to a newly created company Andrew Yule & Co. Ltd, in which the major shareholders were J. P. Morgan & Co. and some of the leading partners in Morgan Grenfell & Co. Yule retired from active participation in the affairs of Andrew Yule & Co. Ltd in 1922, and returned to England to settle at Hanstead House, Bricket Wood, near St Albans, Hertfordshire.

In 1926, with his friend Sir Thomas Catto and the former viceroy of India, Lord Reading, he purchased United Newspapers from David Lloyd George, after giving undertakings that the *Daily Chronicle* and other titles published by the company would continue to support the policies of progressive Liberalism and that Reading would act as chairman. The following year, Yule acquired two Calcutta newspapers, *The Statesman* and *The Englishman*.

On 3 July 1928, Yule died of heart failure. In his obituary in *The Times* he was described as 'one of the wealthiest men, if not the wealthiest man, in the country'. His fortune in India and Britain was reckoned to be around £15m at his death, or just over £4bn in today's money.

Richard Thornton

(1776-1865)
Finance
Wealth: £2.8m
Net National Income: £768m
% of NNI: 0.36%

£3.995 billion

The value of inside information was well demonstrated in 1812, by Richard Thornton, an insurer and merchant based in the City. Learning of the defeat of Napoleon at Moscow before the news was public, he secured a large contract for the delivery of Russian imports to Britain at peak wartime prices, even though with Napoleon on the retreat, the prices would inevitably fall. Thornton made a huge profit and earned the lasting sobriquet, 'the Duke of Danzig'.

The son of a Yorkshire yeoman farmer, Thornton was educated in London and then apprenticed to his uncle, a hop merchant, before branching out on his own in 1798. The Napoleonic blockade and the British government's need for naval stores offered exceptional opportunities for profit. Thornton ran blockade-braking armed merchantmen through the Baltic in 1810, and made a fortune in trade described as 'the most lucrative in the world'. After the war ended, Thornton redirected his trading efforts to the East Indies, and became a financier supporting Spanish loans. By the 1840s, he was the leading merchant, financier, ship owner and marine insurance broker in the City.

He retired from active trading in the 1850s and died in 1865, at 89, leaving £2.8m in his will, one of the largest ever recorded up to that point. It represented 0.36% of the £768m net national income of the day. In today's terms that would be £3.9bn.

Thomas Guy

(1644-1724)
Bookseller and printer
Wealth: £300,000
Net National Income: £85m
% of NNI: 0.353%

£3.916 billion

Thomas Guy, the founder of London's Guy's Hospital, was born in nearby Southwark the son of a lighterman, coalmonger, and carpenter, and his wife from Tamworth in Staffordshire. His father died when Guy was eight and his mother returned to Tamworth, where she married again in 1661; her family were well known in the area, having furnished generations of parish officials. Guy was probably educated at Tamworth Free Grammar School, and in 1660, having returned to London, was apprenticed to John Clarke, bookseller, in Mercers' Hall Porch, Cheapside. Eight years later he was admitted a freeman of the Stationers' Company.

In 1668, Guy bought a newly built shop near the Stocks Market in the City, at the junction of Cornhill and Lombard Street, with a stock worth £200. Guy wanted to offer bibles for sale, but this was the sole privilege of the king's printers, who were also members of the Stationers' Company. Their bibles were of inferior quality, and Guy joined other booksellers in illegally importing Dutch bibles and becoming subjected to endless harassment and seizures. The Stationers' Company had had a monopoly since the reign of Elizabeth I to produce prayer books, primers, psalters, and almanacs, which formed the legal basis for what was known as the English Stock.

However, not all its members shared in this monopoly. Oxford University also had the right to print bibles, but did not have the presses to do so. The Stationers' Company paid the university £200 a year not to produce bibles, but was not printing many itself. In 1679, Bishop Fell and Dr Yates contracted with Guy and Peter Parker to become university printers at Oxford, and they set up a press which met the demand for cheap, mass-produced bibles. Guy and Parker were chosen as less senior members of the Stationers' Company who were willing to break ranks. In 1691, the Company ousted them from this contract, after they had started to bind up psalms with their bibles, once again to meet a need that English Stock was failing to satisfy. This contract had established Guy in the trade and was the foundation of his success. In fourteen years he is said to have amassed £15,000, and he named his shop the Oxford Arms.

Guy later acquired a reputation as a miser, but proved to be very charitable. As early as 1678, he had founded an almshouse with a library in Tamworth for six poor women, which was enlarged in 1693 to accommodate fourteen men and women. Prior to this, he had contributed funds to the grammar school, and in 1686, to Lord Weymouth's workhouse, where the poor were to be educated and employed. In 1701, he paid for a new town hall in Tamworth.

Having campaigned unsuccessfully in 1690 to represent Tamworth in parliament, he was elected in November 1695, in the Whig interest. He remained an MP until July 1708, when he failed to get re-elected. Guy was clearly very upset at being rejected, and threatened to pull down his town hall. He declined an invitation to stand again, and in his will specifically excluded the citizens of Tamworth from access to his almshouse, while including all the neighbouring parishes.

By 1708, Guy was an eminent figure among London booksellers; however, he eschewed all the pomp and expense of guild life. In 1694, he was elected sheriff of London but paid a £400 fine rather than take up office. It was this sort of behaviour which gained him a reputation for being tight-fisted.

By the late 1670s, Guy had money to invest. He dealt in seamen's pay-tickets (at a 30-50% discount), a high-risk commodity at the time. This arrears of sailors' pay formed the beginnings of the national debt. Guy also lent money to the English Stock and made large private loans to landowners. Although Guy has been accused of being a stockjobber, he had already invested in sailors' tickets when in 1710, they were put into the South Sea Company. In 1720, Guy bought over £42,200 of the original expanded South Sea stock when the company took on three-fifths of the national debt. Guy began to sell out his shares at £300 each and had sold them all by the time they reached £600. It was this which made his vast fortune.

In 1704, Guy became a governor of St Thomas's Hospital, by which time he had left the management of his business to his partners Varnum and Osborne. He was greatly influenced by Dr Richard Mead, who prompted him to found a new hospital. In 1721, Guy bought some land from the governors of St Thomas's, intending the new hospital to be part of the same foundation. When the building had reached a second storey, however, he decided on a separate administration. The building cost £18,793 and was roofed just before his death.

Guy died on 27 December 1724, at his home in London at the junction of Cornhill and Lombard Street. He left estate in Staffordshire, Warwickshire, and Derbyshire to more than 100 relatives and acquaintances, mostly in sums of £1,000. He left £1,000 to discharge poor debtors in London, Middlesex, and Surrey, in sums not exceeding £5 each (600 people were helped by this benefaction). To Christ's Hospital he left £400 annually for the board and education of four poor children, and money was left to his Tamworth almshouse. Guy's will left £219,499 to the Guy's Hospital. The rest of his estate, about £80,000, went to distant relatives. His £300,000 fortune would be worth around £3.9bn today.

Sir Edward Brampton

(c 1440-1508)
Land
Wealth: £15,000
Net National Income: £4.2m
% of NNI: 0.35%

£3.884 billion

Sir Edward Brampton was born in Lisbon in around 1440, and came to Britain when he was aged about 28. A Jew by birth, he converted to Christianity and fought for Edward IV during the political upheavals of 1469-71. His skills appear to have been in naval warfare, and in 1472, he was given joint command of a naval force and rewarded for his service to the king with property in London. In 1480, he was given a large Northamptonshire estate by the king and a year later served under the Duke of Norfolk on a naval expedition against the Scots.

From the mid 1470s, Brampton also built up trading and business interests and became master of the Drapers' Company in 1477-78. He lent money to the monarch and was paid through taking a cut of custom revenues, and obtained cloth for the royal wardrobe. His Portuguese links were also useful in developing trade there. He also took the precaution of keeping on the side of the Portuguese king, being re-naturalised a subject in 1479, and obtaining trading privileges. He was in Portugal negotiating for a bride for Richard III when the Battle of Bosworth ended Richard's life and reign in 1485. Brampton never returned to England and his Northamptonshire estates were seized by Henry VII.

He died in 1508, and at his peak would have been worth £15,000, the equivalent of 0.35% of the £4.2m net national income. In today's terms that would be over £3.8bn.

Thomas Brassey

(1805-1870)
Industry
Wealth: £3.2m
Net National Income: £893m
% of NNI: 0.35%

£3.884 billion

Born of a Cheshire farmer in 1805, Thomas Brassey trained as a chartered surveyor. At 21, he was made a partner by his employer and in 1834, met George Stephenson for the first time. Brassey won a contract to build a viaduct on the Grand Junction railway line, then under construction. In 1836, as railway building took off in Britain, Brassey was at the centre of the construction activity.

His extraordinary business skills led to a global business. Apart from British railways, he was active in France, Italy, Canada, the Crimea, Australia, Argentina, India and Moldavia. In 1866, he managed to build a line in Austria on time despite its war with Prussia. But the toll of his huge workload led to illness and Brassey's death in 1870.

He left a £3.2m fortune, about 0.35% of the £893m net national income at the time. In today's terms that would be just over £3.8bn.

Sir Nicholas Brembre

(d 1388)
Merchant
Wealth: £10,000
Net National Income: £2.8m
% of NNI: 0.35%

£3.884 billion

A first generation Londoner, Nicholas Brembre was an ally of Richard II. Marrying a rich heiress, his wife brought with her considerable property and cash with which he was able to start a valuable trading empire. He was a leading wool exporter and dealt in iron, wines and woad, and a merchant, grocer and pepperer. His contacts on the Continent were important in extending his trade. Brembre also lent large sums to the Crown. On one occasion, he advanced £2,970 to Richard II. But his close relations with the king could not prevent Brembre from falling foul of the Lords Appellant in 1388. He was accused of treason, and despite the king's efforts, was executed.

His wealth at his death was around £10,000, or around 0.35% of the £2.8m net national income. In today's terms that would be over £3.8bn.

Sir Simon Burley

(d 1388)
Land
Wealth: £10,000
Net National Income: £2.8m
% of NNI: 0.35%

£3.884 billion

A penniless squire from Herefordshire, Simon Burley served the Black Prince and Edward II, before transferring to the service of Richard II in 1377. He became vice-chamberlain at a time when there was no effective chamberlain and ruthlessly exploited his position to his own advantage. As a result, his annual income mutiplied nearly one hundred-fold from around £13.66 a year as a squire to £1,333.66, the endowment of a duke. His wealth came from lands given by the king and some Burley had bought. But he was not above dubious activities: he secured ownership of land which Edward III had intended for religious foundations. But he did not live long enough to enjoy the fruits of his greed. He fell foul of the Lords Appellant and was executed in 1388.

His wealth at his death was around £10,000, or around 0.35% of the £2.8m net national income. In today's terms that would be over £3.8bn.

Sir Francis Child

(1642-1713)
Banker
Wealth: £250,000
Net National Income: £70m
% of NNI: 0.35%

£3.884 billion

The son of a Wiltshire clothier, Francis Child spent eight years as an apprentice to a London goldsmith. He was admitted to the Goldsmiths' Company in 1664. He married into an old established goldsmith family and eventually inherited the bulk of the family fortune. He became the first banker to give up the trade of goldsmith and was regarded as the father of banking.

In 1689, Child was knighted by William III and became Lord Mayor in 1698. His term of office left him around £4,000 out of pocket. But it was money Child could afford. In the late 1690s, he was lending the government large sums of money, presumably at lucrative interest rates. In 1692, for example, he was part of a syndicate that lent £50,000. Child became an MP in 1698, but did not make much of a mark in the Commons.

He died in 1713, having established the family seat at Osterley Park, now in the London suburbs near Heathrow. His £250,000 fortune was the equivalent of 0.35% of the £70m net national income at the time. Today that would be over £3.8bn.

Sir Stephen Fox

(1627-1716)
Placeman
Wealth: £250,000
Net National Income: £70m
% of NNI: 0.35%

£3.884 billion

A good head for figures and loyalty to Charles II even in his difficult exile made Stephen Fox enormously wealthy. Born in Wiltshire, he received an early drilling in bookkeeping, before joining the staff of the Percy family of Northumberland. He helped Charles II escape to France after the defeat at the Battle of Worcester in 1651, which led to Cromwell's protectorate.

Through Charles's exile, Fox was able to procure frequent supplies of money for the king and carried out several important missions. He was the first to break the news of Cromwell's death to Charles and after the restoration in 1660, Fox's stock rose sharply. He was granted a Hampshire manor. In 1661, he became paymaster-general, and served under Charles, James I, William and Queen Anne in a number of key posts.

His various appointments made him a huge fortune, but not through corruption. In 1680, his friend Evelyn wrote that by then Fox was worth at least £200,000 'honestly got and unenvied, which is next to a miracle'. Fox gave large bequests to charity, building schools and almshouses round the country. He was also credited with inspiring Charles II to found the Chelsea Hospital for disabled soldiers in 1681.

At his death in 1716, he left around £250,000, equivalent to 0.35% of the then £70m net national income. Today that would be over £3.8bn.

Sir William Hewett

(d 1567)
Merchant
Wealth: £50,000
Net National Income: £14m
% of NNI: 0.35%

£3.884 billion

A Yorkshireman who made his fortune in London as a clothier, William Hewett became master of the Clothworkers' Company in 1543. He seems to have emerged unscathed from the attempt by Lady Jane Grey to take the throne. With other prominent citizens he had countersigned the letters patent of Edward IV leaving the throne to Grey in 1553, but as sheriff was charged with executing her and her husband by Queen Mary. He became Lord Mayor in 1559, the first member of the Clothworkers to reach that position.

Knighted by Elizabeth, Hewett was assiduous in building his fortune. He had a country house in Highgate, a manor in Essex and various manors and estates in Yorkshire, Derbyshire and Nottinghamshire. His annual income from his estates was around £6,000 a year. All the fortune went to his one surviving child, his daughter Anne, who was 23 when he died in 1567. As a child she had been dropped in the Thames by a maid, and rescued by her father's apprentice. The apprentice later married Anne. Hewett preferred him as a husband for his daughter even above other suitors, such as the Earl of Shrewsbury, which was quite democratic for the time. The apprentice, Osborne, was later a Lord Mayor himself.

Hewett's fortune was around £50,000 on his death, equivalent to 0.35% of the then £14m net national income. Today that would be over £3.8bn.

Richard Lyons

(d 1381)
Merchant
Wealth: £10,000
Net National Income: £2.8m
% of NNI: 0.35%

£3.884 billion

A bastard, Richard Lyons had an obscure background, though he had apparently completed his apprenticeship as a vintner when he started buying property in London in 1359. By the mid 1360s, he had leases on taverns and around fifty properties in the capital and was also actively buying up manors and land in Essex and Kent. He also lent money to the Crown and was impeached for that in 1376.

There was no evidence of real corruption: his impeachment and forfeiture of his assets was regarded as political as Lyons was too close to unpopular politicians and seemed to have been a scapegoat. His land was held in trust and most of it escaped forfeiture but £2,443 of movables were discovered in his London home and seized. Lyons started up his business again in 1379, and was richer than ever when he was murdered in the Peasants' Revolt of 1381.

He was worth around £10,000 then, equivalent to 0.35% of the £2.8m net national income. That would be over £3.8bn today.

Richard Renger

(d 1239)
Merchant
Wealth: £10,000
Net National Income: £2.8m
% of NNI: 0.35%

£3.884 billion

It is reckoned that Richard Renger was a London vintner, but he inherited much property from his father. The family descended from a Norman servant of the first Norman bishop of London. The family moved to a higher station through marriage.

At his death in 1239, Renger was worth perhaps £10,000, equivalent to 0.35% of the then net national income of £2.8m. Today that would be over £3.8bn.

Peter Thellusson

(1737-1797)
Merchant
Wealth: £800,000
Net National Income: £225m
% of NNI: 0.35%

£3.884 billion

Born in Paris, Peter Thellusson's father was a leading French banker. Thellusson himself came to London in 1762, and was naturalised as an Englishman in the same year. Initially he acted for Dutch and French bankers in London, but later branched out on his own. He was particularly active in the West Indies and acquired large estates there, as well as property in England.

He died in 1797, leaving £100,000 in his will and between £600,000 to £800,000 in trust. In all we reckon he was easily worth £800,000 at his death, around 0.35% of the then £225m net national income. Today that would be over £3.8bn.

John Farquhar

(1751-1826)
Industry
Wealth: £1.1m
Net National Income: £316m
% of NNI: 0.348%

£3.861 billion

Good quality gunpowder was the making of John Farquhar's fortune. Born of humble parents in Aberdeenshire, his exceptional intelligence was evident from an early age. He was awarded a bursary to attend the Marischal College of Aberdeen at fifteen. After four years of study, he was entitled to the award of MA, and he soon moved on to London. From there he secured the post of surgeon's mate on an East India shop heading for China, but he jumped ship and became the surgeon on a vessel making for Calcutta instead.

On arrival in Bengal, he became a writer employed in a merchant's office near Barrackpore and he began to dabble in his own private commercial activity. In his spare time he amused himself with chemical experiments. At the time, the gunpowder manufactured at Pultah for the British was of poor quality. Farquhar was selected by Lord Cornwallis, governor-general of Bengal, to help with research into the quality problems. His work was invaluable and he was made superintendent of the factory, and ultimately became sole contractor to the government.

He made his fortune and in 1814, returned to England with a then £500,000 fortune. His business acumen enabled Farquhar to increase this considerably. He invested in government stock and became a partner in the City firm, Basset, Farquhar & Co as well as taking a stake in the Whitbread brewery.

Farquhar took up residence in Upper Baker Street, Portman Square. He was a bachelor and eccentric figure, whose sole attendant was an old woman, and his house soon became conspicuous for its neglected appearance. He himself was often mistaken for a beggar in the street. Farquhar nevertheless retained a sharp sense of business acumen. Despite living frugally, he was also fond of purchasing estates. In 1822, he bought Fonthill Abbey from William Beckford for £330,000, and lived there occasionally until its tower fell in late 1825.

Farquhar died suddenly of apoplexy at his home in New Road, Regent's Park, on 6 July 1826. At the time of his death, his wealth amounted to well over £1m. In today's money that would be over £3.8bn.

Sir Henry Garraway

(1575-1646)
Merchant
Wealth: £120,000
Net National Income: £35m
% of NNI: 0.34%

£3.774 billion

One of seventeen children of a London customs official, Garraway travelled widely on the Continent in his youth. Later he was to build up extensive trading links with the Low Countries, France, Italy, the East Indies, Greenland, Russia and Turkey. By 1639, he was governor of the great trading companies which traded with the last three of these countries and was immensely rich as a result.

A member of the Drapers' Company, Garraway lived near Drapers Hall in the City. As a sign of his wealth, he offered to rebuild the house he leased from the company, which he did at a cost of over £1,000. Garraway's wealth and rank made him a natural candidate for Lord Mayor of London, a post he took up in 1639. But it was a difficult time to hold such a prominent office with the Civil War looming. Though he was loyal to Charles I, that loyalty must have been tested by the king's demands for money and/or troops from the City. On one occasion, when Charles demanded that the Lord Mayor raise a regiment of 4,000 men for the king's service in the North, the City's common council refused to either raise or equip such a force. Garraway found a neat if expensive compromise when he paid for the regiment out of his own pocket.

Knighted by the king in 1640, Garraway valiantly stood up for the royalist cause against an increasingly hostile environment. Time and again the City's common council or sheriffs refused to help in raising money for the king. Garraway's position as a prominent royalist worsened when the Civil War began. In 1643, he was imprisoned for not contributing to parliament's demands for money. He was stripped of his posts and flung into the dungeons at Dover Castle, though he was released to die in London in 1646.

His sons inherited large estates in Sussex, Kent, Devon, Northumberland, Westmoreland and Yorkshire. Parliament did not interfere with this inheritance though there were apparently some difficulties over Garraway's lands in Cornwall. The local commissioners for sequestrations claimed that the Garraway family were known enemies of parliament, which his sons claimed to be 'scandalous and untrue'. Garraway's interests from trade and his estates – even in the difficult period of the Civil War – would have been worth around £120,000 at prevailing prices or over £3.7bn today.

Giles Loder

(1786-1871)
Merchant
Wealth: £3.2m
Net National Income: £917m
% of NNI: 0.34%

£3.773 billion

Giles Loder, an obscure Russian merchant, was based in Old Broad Street in what is now the heart of the modern City. His son became a baronet, while his grandson was ennobled as Lord Wakehurst. His son owned 10,200 acres providing around £11,527 annual income, while Loder himself bought a Northamptonshire estate for £335,000.

Though he left around £2.9m in his will, with his assets and land, he would have been worth around £3.2m, or about £3.7bn in today's terms.

Archbishop William Courtenay

(1342-1396)
Church
Wealth: £10,000
Net National Income: £3m
% of NNI: 0.33%

£3.662 billion

Born the fourth son of the Earl of Devon, William Courtenay did what all fourth sons of nobility did at the time, and joined the church. At the age of 13, he held his first benefice worth around £66 a year, and was Bishop of Hereford at 27, while still under the canonical age of thirty. His aristocratic background smoothed his passage to promotion, but Courtenay did have the brains to go with the job. At 24, he was a doctor of law and a year later, chancellor of Oxford University. In 1381, before his fortieth birthday, he became Archbishop of Canterbury, and was regarded as one of the ablest primates of the later Middle Ages.

He frequently clashed with leading aristocrats and even the king. In 1385, he condemned King Richard for plotting the death of John of Gaunt, warning him to mend his ways and sack his evil councillors. This enraged the king so much that he overstepped convention and tried to kill Courtenay with his sword. He survived and died peacefully in 1396, having sought through his life to be a churchman rather than an agent of the Crown.

His family assets and the trappings of the Church, though, would have given him some considerable wealth – perhaps £10,000 – which would translate into about £3.6bn in today's terms.

Henry Despencer

(c 1341-1406)
Land
Wealth: £10,000
Net National Income: £3m
% of NNI: 0.33%

£3.662 billion

Another younger son of a noble who went into the Church, Henry Despencer achieved rapid promotion at an early age as a result of his background rather than qualifications. At around the age of 29, he was Bishop of Norwich, and carved out a career as a warrior-churchman. He was also noted as a great landowner and peer of the realm. But he made enemies. In 1377, Despencer quarrelled with the town of King's Lynn and was attacked and wounded by townsmen. The people of Norwich apparently plotted his death in 1382, and he made a name for himself when fully clad in helmet, chain mail and with sword in hand, he attacked a camp of rebel peasants in 1381, and executed the ringleader.

Despencer led an ignominious crusade to Flanders in 1383, which led to his impeachment, subsequent imprisonment and the seizure of his lands. But he was released to accompany Richard II to Scotland and on a naval expedition to Flanders. His support for the king and rebel earls led to further imprisonment and he died in 1406.

At its peak, his wealth would have been around £10,000 or some £3.6bn in today's terms.

John Eldred

(1552-1632)
Merchant
Wealth: £100,000
Net National Income: £30m
% of NNI: 0.33%

£3.662 billion

While still a young lad, John Eldred left his native Norfolk to move to London, where he prospered in business. But his real fortune came as a result of his four-year stint in the Middle East. He left London in 1583, at the age of 31. Travelling to Baghdad and further south to what is now Basra, he seems to have efficiently gathered together up to seventy barges of merchandise, mainly spices. He took them up the Tigris to Baghdad and then with a huge caravan of camels, took the goods to Aleppo in what is now Syria. For four years he made Aleppo the headquarters of his trading operation and made two more trips to Baghdad.

He left Arabia in 1587 for England and arrived in London three months later in the ship Hercules, which he later wrote was 'the richest ship of English merchants' goods that ever was known to come into this realm'. Eldred was set up for life and by taking these risks, was clearly one of Britain's earliest entrepreneurs. He then proceeded to gentrify himself, buying the manor of Great Saxham in 1597, where he built a large manor house, popularly known as 'Nutmeg Hall'. He became a major shareholder in the East India Company when it was formed and served on its board.

The change of regime which came with the death of Elizabeth I did nothing to hurt Eldred's wealth. Under James I, he was a contractor and commissioner for the sale of lands, a farmer of customs and the holder of a patent for tin making. No doubt all these activities further enhanced his fortune.

He died peacefully in 1632, so avoiding the turmoil of the Civil War. His fortune by then would have been around £100,000 – about £3.6bn in today's money.

Rich list members born in the 13th century

Rich list member	Lifespan
Merton, Bishop Walter	c1205-1277
Cornwall, Richard Earl of	1209-1272
Fitzpeter, Geoffrey	d 1213
Menahem, Elijah of	c1232-1284
Des Roches, Peter	d 1238
Renger, Richard	d 1239
Basing, Adam De	1240s
Lancaster, Earl of	1245-1296
Mansel, John	d 1265
Holland, Sir Robert	c1270-1329
Hereford & Essex, Earl of	1276-1322
Lancaster, Henry Earl of	c1281-1345
Gaveston, Piers	c1284-1312
Scrope, Sir Geoffrey	c1285-1340
Mortimer, Roger, Earl of March	1286-1330
Pulteney, Sir John	c1290-1349
Gloucester, The Earl of	1291-1347
De Rokesle, Gregory	d 1291
Clare, Elizabeth Lady of	c1294-1360
Stratton, Adam	d 1294
Lancaster, The Duke of	1299-1361

Walter Espec

(d 1158)
Land
Wealth: £3,000
Net National Income: £900,000
% of NNI: 0.33%

£3.662 billion

A second generation Anglo-Norman landowner, Walter Espec inherited land in Bedfordshire, but later acquired substantial property in Yorkshire centred on the castles of Wark and Helmsley. From his Yorkshire base, Espec proved to be one of Henry I's most loyal followers in what was a potentially subversive region. Not only was he a royal justice for many northern counties but he collected royal taxes in Yorkshire and Durham.

Espec proved his real worth during the Scottish invasion of 1138, three years after Henry's death. His castle at Wark had to withstand a vigorous siege, and he later organised and rallied the northern barons in their victory over the Scots at the Battle of The Standard in the same year.

He died in the mid 1150s with no surviving children, but his wealth went to found a priory, a monastery and two Cistercian houses. In total his wealth was around £3,000, around £3.6bn in today's money.

John Hende

(d 1418)
Merchant
Wealth: £10,000
Net National Income: £3m
% of NNI: 0.33%

£3.662 billion

John Hende was a successful and socially ambitious London merchant in the late fourteenth and early fifteenth centuries. A draper by trade, Hende reckoned that debts owing to him and his stock of merchandise were worth around £4,000 to £5,000. He had around the same again in land, with manors in Kent and a mill, several manors and a quay in Essex. His income from his London property was put at around £54, six years before his death, while the Kent manors raked in £41 annually.

Hende died peacefully in 1418, leaving around £10,000, about £3.6bn in today's money.

The Earl Of Iveagh

(1847-1927)
Brewing
Wealth: £13.48m
Net National Income: £4.145bn
% of NNI: 0.33%

£3.662 billion

Edward Guinness, later the 1st Earl of Iveagh, was the driving force behind the expansion of Guinness from being a small Dublin brewer when he joined the firm in 1868, to the largest single brewery in the world making 1.2m bulk barrels by 1886. Guinness, with the help of a highly competent professional management team, invested over £1m in that period in new facilities, all from the brewery's own retained profits. In 1886, the company was floated on the stock market valued at £6m. In scenes reminiscent of the mid 1980s, the offer was twenty times oversubscribed, and the shares rose to a 60% premium on their first day's trading. The family and their banking advisers retained control from the start. Guinness started with a significant minority stake after the float but gradually bought his way back to a controlling stake.

He gradually handed over control of the company to his professional managers in the 1890s, remaining as chairman until the First World War. Created Earl of Iveagh in 1919, he devoted his final years to charitable work. In 1925, he rescued Kenwood House in London and filled it with a large part of his huge art collection. When he died in 1927, it was granted to the Nation intact.

Iveagh left an estate valued at over £13.4m, or around £3.6bn in today's terms.

The Marquess Of Wharton

(1648-1715)
Land
Wealth: £250,000
Net National Income: £75m
% of NNI: 0.33%

£3.662 billion

The Marquess of Wharton's father supported parliament in the Civil War, but acquired an unfortunate reputation for cowardice at the Battle of Edgehill in 1642. His son showed none of this when he fought a duel with a rival at the age of 25 over the hand of a rich heiress. He lost the duel but the rival 'gave him both his life and his mistress too, since he had the courage to fight for her'. His bride came with £10,000 in cash, a house in Chelsea and an estate in Malmesbury yielding £2,000 a year. Wharton was not happy in marriage and improved his swordmanship so he would never lose a duel again.

He became one of the greatest rakes in the country and a flavour of his lifestyle may be gauged by a 'grievous prank' as one commentator called it, which he pulled off in 1682. While drunk, Wharton and his brother forced the doors of a parish church in Gloucestershire in the middle of the night, rang the bells, tore up the Bible and 'pissed against a communion table'. The rector was willing to turn a blind eye to the sacrilege, but a newly-appointed bishop heard of it and fined the pair £1,000.

In the reign of James I, Wharton – by now an MP – was regarded as one of the opposition. Luckily, he did not take part in the Duke of Monmouth's rebellion in 1685, though Monmouth had been a racing crony. That year Wharton had spent £3,000 securing his re-election to parliament. But his position and wealth sharply improved when he became an early backer of William of Orange. He joined the future king at Exeter with around 20 followers, and in the election of 1689, was re-elected as MP for Buckinghamshire. His interests carried both seats in Malmesbury, his home base, and his brother represented Westmoreland, giving Wharton some political clout. He served on several Commons committees and was rewarded with a post in the Royal Household worth over £1,000 a year.

He died peacefully as a peer with his valuable estate assets bringing in a handsome £8,000 a year income. His total asset wealth of about £250,000 would be around £3.6bn today.

Richard Wyche

(1554-1621)
Merchant
Wealth: £100,000
Net National Income: £30m
% of NNI: 0.33%

£3.662 billion

A descendant of a former Lord Mayor of London in the fifteenth century, Richard Wyche followed family tradition and became involved in lucrative trading with the East Indies as a merchant. He married well, the daughter of Sir Richard Saltonstall, another wealthy London merchant. Wyche's fortune would have been around £100,000 at prevailing prices, or £3.6bn today.

His son, Sir Peter Wyche (d 1643), took his fortune to the court of Charles I. In 1626, he was knighted by the king and two years later made a gentleman of the privy chamber. Appointed English ambassador to Constantinople, Wyche junior secured a reduction of duty on English cloth. His wife astonished the Sultana by making a visit to the Sultan's harem. In 1641, Wyche returned to London, and promptly lent a large sum of money to the king, which hit the family fortune. But Wyche did not live to see the outcome of the Civil War, dying at Oxford in December 1643.

Sir John Banks

(1627-1699)
Merchant
Wealth: £180,000
Net National Income: £50m
% of NNI: 0.33%

£3.661 billion

The son of a prosperous Maidstone businessman, Banks made his mark in public life at the age of 25 in 1652, when he joined a syndicate to victual the navy. It was to be the start of a profitable career in finance and politics, which took Banks into naval contracts for canvas and saltpetre, trade with the Levant, the East Indies and New England in cloth, lead, pepper and diamonds. He built up large estates in Kent from where he made a further turn on the sale of grain, hops, cattle, timber and fruit, not to mention the rents from his tenant farmers.

Banks would have been at home in the modern City. He was quick to recognise the value of liquidity and had the means to advance large sums rapidly to a stretched government – at considerable profit. Shortly after Charles II was restored to the throne, Banks took over the repayment of a royal debt of £2,700 and made a 63% profit in six months, with a baronetcy thrown in as well. Banks had political skills too, serving in two parliaments during Cromwell's Protectorate and eight under the Stuarts, with no difficulty. He steered a moderate line and cultivated influential friends with some success. He was a director and later governor of the powerful East India Company. Banks' eldest daughter married the Lord Chancellor's son. It worked. By 1678, despite the sneering of aristocrats, he was worth £100,000.

At his death in 1679, it had risen to £180,000, equivalent to 0.33% of the £50m net national income at the time. In today's terms that would be £3.6bn.

Thomas Western

(c 1624-1707)
Industry
Wealth: £200,000
Net National Income: £60m
% of NNI: 0.33%

£3.661 billion

One of Britain's first armament tycoons, Thomas Western was a prominent seventeenth and early eighteenth century ironmaster. Born in London in 1624, the son of a grocer, Western's route to a fortune began in 1651, when he married Martha Gott, daughter of Samuel Gott, a London ironmaster. Though he was a member of the Grocers' Company, Western shrewdly saw the money to be made in guns and became an ironmonger himself in the 1650s.

Western leased Brede furnace in Sussex in 1660, from Samuel Gott, MP, his wife's brother. Afterwards he received orders for guns and shot from the Board of Ordnance, breaking into the monopoly held by the Brownes, the king's gun-founders. Regular wars helped his business. By February 1666, Western had delivered fifty-four guns and 200 tons of shot, becoming the largest supplier after the Brownes in the second and third Dutch wars. He shared the gun contracts under the Thirty Ships Act with Mary, widow of John Browne, casting over 550 guns in 1678 and 1679. The orders declined in the 1680s and during James II's reign he was said to be:

as much against the King's Government and interest as any, and as hott and violent as the worst.

As a result he was not allowed to hold civic office. Naturally he became a strong supporter of William III. Western's son Samuel, and Peter Gott, his nephew and son-in-law, became whig MPs.

Western claimed in 1690, to have supplied since 1689, 'several great guns and other provisions of war', and was 'willing further to provide the like at reasonable prices...to a total not exceeding £30,000'. Under a second Thirty Ships Act, Western took the largest share, casting almost 1,400 guns, worth £48,500, between 1692 and 1699. He was the most important gun-founder under William III.

Western also developed a thriving international arms trade. He bought iron from the Netherlands and Sweden, exporting it to Guinea and the East, and he shipped about £2,500 worth of guns, shot, and iron with the East India Company annually in the 1670s. He hired out ballast and guns to merchantmen, and was probably responsible for a series of large iron mortars for the Venetian Republic in 1684. Western cast brass guns for the East India Company and the Board of Ordnance in the 1670s and 1680s in collaboration with William Wightman at the Moorfields foundry.

A shareholder in the Royal African Company and the Bank of England, he also invested in land, owning two estates in East Anglia, in addition to property, woods, and ironworks in the Sussex weald. In London he lived at Dyce Quay, Billingsgate, and twice served on the common council as well as being deputy lieutenant of London.

At his death, Western was one of the most important ironmongers in England. He owned Brede furnace and leased others such as Ashburnham, Robertsbridge, and Waldron as he needed them. He sent iron round the world, both as armament on ships and as cargo.

He died in 1707, at his Essex manor house and was naturally buried under an iron slab from his own furnace, in the local churchyard. Western was said, at his death, 'to be worth £200,000'. That would be around £3.6bn in today's money.

Thomas Coutts

(1735-1822)
Finance
Wealth: £1m
Net National Income: £310m
% of NNI: 0.323%

£3.583 billion

Thomas Coutts learnt all about the need for discretion while growing up in Edinburgh during the 1745 Jacobite Rebellion. The fourth son of a merchant banker, he was ten and a pupil at the local high school when Edinburgh was besieged. His father, John Coutts, was on the town council from 1730, and served as Lord Provost from 1742 to 1744. He took care to keep on good terms with George II's ministers in Scotland, Lord Ilay and Lord Milton, because his family in Montrose had Jacobite leanings and his wife, Jean, daughter of Sir John Stuart and Margaret Kerr, had relatives who were similarly suspect. It was reckoned these early experiences encouraged Thomas Coutts's naturally cautious nature and gave him a readiness to hedge his bets.

At fifteen he was sent to London with his eldest brother, Patrick, and for ten years worked in his father's import and export business in Jeffreys Square, where he gained valuable commercial experience. In 1761, he joined his elder brother James at a banking house in the Strand, founded in 1692 by John Campbell, a goldsmith-banker under the patronage of the Duke of Argyll. By 1775, James Coutts had married John Campbell's granddaughter, and after the death of her father in 1760, he inherited the bank, which in 1761 was styled James and Thomas Coutts.

When James became MP for Edinburgh (1762-7), Thomas took most of the responsibility at the bank. Later his brother had a mental breakdown, and he died in 1778, after which Thomas took sole charge. He displayed a masterly ability to delegate and made some shrewd choices in new partners at the bank, helping to turn the failing business of 1761, into a highly profitable and prestigious bank by the time Thomas Coutts died in 1822.

Coutts had other indispensable qualities which made him a top-drawer banker. He was the soul of discretion and he understood human nature well, inspiring trust and lasting affection among his clients. Allied to this, he ran the bank with clockwork efficiency, devising a daily routine for every clerk. He was of course operating in turbulent times at home and particularly abroad with the Napoleonic War occupying the energies of the government and populace. Coutts kept closely in touch with public affairs at home and throughout the world, through leading politicians such as Chatham and by maintaining a close network of Scottish friends and relatives abroad. Lord Macartney brought him wallpaper from China and Lord Minto news from India. He knew Paris well and followed the French Revolution with a personal interest, establishing a lasting link between his bank and the French royal family: Louis Philippe kept in touch with him during his years of exile. Many refugees left their valuables with him.

Some of the most influential aristocrats were Coutts's customers, but his greatest coup came when George III became a patron at the beginning of his reign, through the influence of his Prime Minister and Keeper of the Privy Purse, the Earl of Bute, who had known their father, Provost Coutts. So began the lasting connection between Coutts & Co. and the royal family. The king trusted the discretion of his banker and in November 1787, admitted him to the Privy Chamber. Royal customers brought prestige to Coutts & Co., but the accounts of the king's spendthrift sons caused Thomas Coutts more headaches than profit.

In spite of the huge wealth that Coutts built up, he lived relatively modestly. The simplicity, even shabbiness, of his dress led strangers to mistake him for a poor man. Unlike other great bankers, Thomas Coutts built no great country house, and he was happier in London in his modest villa and lovely garden on Highgate Hill than in his large house, 1 Stratton Street, Piccadilly. He preferred, he claimed, to keep his fortune liquid so that he could help his friends. Modestly, Coutts always referred to his prestigious bank as 'my shop'.

Outside of business he had a genuine love of the arts, and always carried a volume of Shakespeare in his pocket. A supporter of Drury Lane and Covent Garden theatres, he was a friend of Garrick and other actors. Coutts married twice. His first wife, a nursemaid to his brother's daughter, produced three daughters, all of whom married well. She died in 1815, and Coutts remarried soon after. His new bride was Harriot Mellon, an actress, and she made Coutts a happy man in his remaining years. To show his respect for Harriot's good judgement he bequeathed to her the bulk of his property, and his half share in the bank. After his death in 1822, William Cobbett wrote in his *Political Register* that:

A million or more of money got together during a marriage with one wife has been made to pass to a second.

That £1m fortune would be worth £3.5bn in today's money.

Sir Richard Radcliffe

(d 1485)
Land
Wealth: £15,000
Net National Income: £4.6m
% of NNI: 0.32%

£3.551 billion

A close ally of Richard III, Richard Radcliffe showed his loyalty in 1483, when he summarily executed four of the king's enemies with no form of trial. For this grisly deed, Radcliffe was made a Knight of the Garter and high sheriff of Westmoreland. He also received the lucrative stewardship of Wakefield and had estates conferred on him which produced an annual income of over £650 a year. But Radcliffe, who became one of Richard's most confidential counsellors, did not live long to enjoy his wealth. He fought with Richard at the Battle of Bosworth where he was killed while attempting to escape.

His wealth would have been around £15,000 or over £3.5bn in today's terms.

David & Simon Reuben

(dob 14/09/1939 and 20/05/1941)
Property

Wealth: £3.49 billion

Retirement homes and racecourses are interesting the Reuben brothers these days. In August 2006, the brothers were part of a consortium that spent £1.1bn buying retirement home builder McCarthy & Stone while in April 2007, they agreed a £65.9m agreed takeover of Northern Racing, owner of racecourses throughout Britain. But the brothers are able to spot value and make a profit by buying and selling on assets. In 2006, they made a 25% return on the sale of Shell Mex House in London and a £30m profit on the sale of their stake in the Stratford City development.

The Reubens, David and Simon, have been active in the British property market for the last decade after making their fortune in Russia in the 1990s, where they were dubbed the 'metal tsars' for their role in restructuring the aluminium industry there. But their origins were anything but regal. Born in Bombay, the Reubens made their way to London, where Simon went into property and David started trading in scrap metal.

Their foray into Russia, which ended in 1999, earned them at least £1.3bn according to a detailed analysis by *Fortune* magazine. Our sources suggest that following astute deals in the British property market, their property assets are now at least £1.8bn (mostly in the UK) with a further £1.6bn in liquid assets such as cash, bonds and their growing investment portfolio. Personal assets easily take them to £3.49bn.

The Duke Of Albany

(c 1340-1420)
Land
Wealth: £10,000
Net National Income: £3.2m
% of NNI: 0.31%

£3.44 billion

The Duke of Albany was the second surviving son of Robert II, King of Scotland, and in 1398, he became one of the only two Scottish dukes thus far created. His nephew, who became the Duke of Rothesay, was the other, and the two became bitter rivals in the struggle for power. Rothesay's abuse of power gave Albany the opportunity to strike. He persuaded the king (by then Robert III, his elder brother) to approve the arrest of Rothesay, his own son. Rothesay died in suspicious circumstances in his castle at Falkirk in 1402, but Albany's power was such that the Scottish general council ruled that the death was 'by divine providence and not otherwise'.

After Rothesay's death, only the younger son of Robert III, a seven-year-old boy called James, stood between Albany and the throne. Robert III, fearing for his son's life, ordered him to be sent to France for his own safety, but he was captured at sea by the English and taken to London. The news was enough to hasten Robert's death. James could not take the coronation oath or be crowned, so the general council made Albany governor of Scotland, with powers exceeding those which had been wielded by kings. He proceeded to loot the royal treasury and customs revenues, and made no effort to secure the release of James from the hands of the English. Albany's cornering of the royal perks lasted for around sixteen years until his death in 1420, at the ripe old age of 80, and by natural causes, which was also remarkable given the enemies he must have created.

His plundering of royal revenues etc. would have given him a £10,000 fortune, or about £3.4bn in today's terms.

John Colet

(c 1466-1519)
Land
Wealth: £15,000
Net National Income: £4.7m
% of NNI: 0.31%

£3.44 billion

It helped that John Colet's father had twice been Lord Mayor of London and was a member of the Mercers' Company, while his mother had connections to two very wealthy aristocratic families. Colet was the only one of twenty-two children to survive infancy. Colet showed formidable academic prowess and took his Oxford MA in 1490, at the age of 23. After a spell travelling on the Continent, he was ordained as a priest at 31. He later went to lecture at Oxford where, by all accounts, he was a breath of fresh air with lectures which seemed to bring the scriptures alive to his audience.

Colet's greatest role in life came when he was appointed as Dean of St Paul's Cathedral in 1504, a post he held until his death in 1519. He became something of a radical, living a simple life, wearing plain dress and delivering lectures and sermons from the pulpit in English.

When his father died, Colet became a very wealthy man, but typically, he decided to devote his fortune to education. In 1510, the building of St Paul's (now London's top public school) was finished, financed by Colet.

His unconventional views – and particularly his sermons against the riches of bishops made him powerful enemies. The Bishop of London had him charged with heresy; the Archbishop of Canterbury dismissed the charges as frivolous, but the persecution which Colet felt was kept up. He decided to retire but after three attacks of the sweating sickness, died in 1519. His £15,000 fortune would have been worth over £3.4bn today.

Rich list members born in the 14th century

Rich list member	Lifespan
Montagu, William Earl of Salisbury	1301-1344
Arundel and Warenne, The Earl of	c1307-1376
Knollys, Sir Robert	c1317-1407
Langton, Bishop Walter	d 1321
Menthermer, Ralph Earl of Gloucester	d 1325
Despencer, Hugh the Younger	d 1326
Black Prince, Edward The	1330-1376
Latimer, Lord William	1330-1381
De La Pole, Michael Earl of Suffolk	c1330-1389
Gloucester, The Duke of	1335-1397
Gaunt, John of The Duke of Lancaster	1340-1399
Albany, The Duke of	c1340-1420
Melton, Archbishop William	d 1340
Despencer, Henry	c1341-1406
Percy, Henry The 1st Earl of Northumberland	1341-1408
Courtenay, Archbishop William	1342-1396
Beauchamp, William	1343-1411
Arundel and Surrey, The Earl of	1346-1397
Exeter, The Duke of	1352-1400
Grey, Baron of Ruthin	d 1353
Westmoreland, The Earl of	1354-1425
Moleyns, Sir John	d 1361
Mowbray, Thomas	1366-1399
De La Pole, Sir William	d 1366
Chaucer, Thomas	c1367-1434
Mauny, Lord Walter	d 1372
Beaufort, Cardinal Henry	1375-1447
Sevenoak, Sir William	c1378-1433
Hungerford, Lord	c1378-1449
Fastolf, Sir John	c1378-1459
Arundel, The Earl of	1381-1415
Lyons, Richard	d 1381
Warwick, The Earl of	1382-1439
Philipot, Sir John	d 1384
Brembre, Sir Nicholas	d 1388
Burley, Sir Simon	d 1388
Cromwell, Ralph 3rd Lord	c1394-1456
Suffolk, The Duke of	1396-1450

Baron De Stern

(1815-1887)
Banker
Wealth: £3.544m
Net National Income: £1.195bn
% of NNI: 0.3%

£3.44 billion

Baron de Stern, the son of a Frankfurt wine merchant, was related by marriage on his father's side to the Rothschild family. He came to Britain in the 1830s as a young man with his brother and they set up the banking house of Stern Brothers, which by dint of hard work, they had built up into a large business with capital of £5m by 1887. Stern Brothers specialised in loans to foreign governments for railways and other capital works. For his services to Portugal, Hermann Stern was made a baron in 1864, and added the prefix 'de' to his name. He died in 1887, leaving £3.5m in his will, or £3.4bn in today's terms.

After his death, and that of his brother, the bank went downhill in an almost unprecedented way. The next generations seem to have been more interested in politics and society. Stern's son and nephew were created peers for doing nothing more than giving large sums of money to the Liberal Party.

Richard Fermor

(d 1552)
Merchant
Wealth: £25,000
Net National Income: £8m
% of NNI: 0.31%

£3.44 billion

A merchant of Welsh descent, Richard Fermor engaged in commerce in the Calais area, where for example, he was recorded as exporting large quantities of wheat and wool. Though he was described as a grocer, Fermor would turn his hand to anything where he could make a profit. He invested his profits in property and in July 1512, was granted several East Anglian manors which had belonged to the Earl of Suffolk. Subsequently, Fermor lived in a Northamptonshire manor and bought up estates in neighbouring counties.

But his zeal as a Catholic nearly proved his undoing. When Fermor's priest was imprisoned by Thomas Cromwell, Fermor visited him and gave him money and clothes. This act of generosity cost Fermor dear. He was imprisoned himself and after a trial at Westminster Hall, was stripped of all his property. He retired to a parsonage where he would no doubt have died quietly and impoverished but for the action of his jester, Will Somers, who had been transferred to the royal household. He mentioned Fermor's plight to Henry VIII, who expressed regret and directed that some reparation be made. In 1550, two years after Henry's death, Fermor had his property restored, but he only lived another two years to enjoy it.

His wealth in land and a result of the trading business he had built was around £25,000 or £3.4bn in today's money.

The Duke Of Newcastle

(1693-1768)
Land
Wealth: £500,000
Net National Income: £160m
% of NNI: 0.31%

£3.44 billion

Thomas Pelham-Holles, the 1st Duke of Newcastle, was derided by fellow ministers, and regarded by George II as unfit even to be a chamberlain at a minor German court. Nevertheless he was secretary of state for thirty years from 1724 to 1754, with a break of only two days, and later was First Lord of the Treasury for much of the period 1754-1762. He used his huge wealth to pursue political power and mined the various sources of government patronage to secure government majorities.

Newcastle also had a talent for management and delighted in electioneering, taking a prominent part in every election from 1715 to 1761 in his own counties of Sussex, Nottinghamshire, Lincolnshire and Yorkshire. He also ran elections for the government. In the riotous election of 1734, as one biographer noted:

The opposition had a good cry in "No excise" while bad harvests and trade were damaging government prospects; the ministers yet secured a comfortable majority.

That election was regarded as Newcastle's 'masterpiece'. He resigned from government in 1762, after an uneasy alliance with Pitt the Elder during the war with France, where Newcastle took the blame for a string of early disasters and for leaving the navy so unprepared.

He died in 1768, with a fortune of perhaps £500,000 from his land, around £3.4bn in today's terms.

Sir Dudley North

(1641-1691)
Merchant
Wealth: £150,000
Net National Income: £48m
% of NNI: 0.31%

£3.44 billion

The experience of being stolen as a child by a beggar woman who simply wanted his clothes did nothing to dampen the commercial acumen of Dudley North, a younger son of a London baronet. Sent to boarding school, North showed little interest in learning. Apprenticed to a London merchant, North was sent at the age of twenty to Smyrna where he took up the post of agent for his master's firm. North's talent for commerce meant that he was able to build up some capital of his own as well as his employer's trade. He fell out with his employer but received an offer to run an important business house in Constantinople, and rapidly became the leading merchant in the Turkey Company. At one stage, it seemed he might be appointed British ambassador to Constantinople, such was his influence locally.

Instead he returned to England in 1680, after nearly 20 years in the Near East and having realised a large fortune. He took a large house in the City where he became a sheriff. North's fortune was further augmented when he married the widow of a Gloucestershire landowner who was also the only child of a wealthy Bristol merchant. North supported Charles II and his brother, James II, but did not flee the country when William of Orange took the throne and James fled to France. Under the new regime, North confined himself to commerce on a grand scale. He was also something of an economist, and a few months before his death in 1691, he produced a tract on

'Currency', advocating free trade and anticipating many of the views of Adam Smith.

North's fortune at his death would have been around £150,000 or about £3.4bn at today's prices.

Sir William Sevenoak

(c 1378-1433)
Merchant
Wealth: £10,000
Net National Income: £3.2m
% of NNI: 0.31%

£3.44 billion

Said to have been found as an abandoned child in Sevenoaks, Sir William Sevenoak was fostered by an official of the town and named after his presumed birthplace. In 1393, at the age of fifteen, he was apprenticed to an ironmonger in London and later to a grocer. After his apprenticeship, he appears to have sought adventure in the war with France, and served Henry V so well that he was given a bag of crowns for his prowess. He returned to London where he became a leading figure in the city, serving as a warden for London Bridge, and later an alderman and Lord Mayor of London. Sevenoak built up a property portfolio and attained great wealth as a merchant.

When he died in 1433, he left some of his fortune of around £10,000 (£3.4bn in today's money) to establish a school in his native town. Today, the Queen Elizabeth Grammar School is one of the top grammar schools in the country.

Sir Charles Abney

(1640-1722)
Merchant
Wealth: £250,000
Net National Income: £82m
% of NNI: 0.3%

£3.329 billion

Raised in the East Midlands, Charles Abney was the youngest son of a local knight. He went to London presumably seeking his fortune and married in 1668. His wife produced seven children of whom six died in infancy or early youth. She died in 1698, by which time Abney was heavily involved in finance, as one of the promoters of the Bank of England in 1694, and later as a founding director. His services here resulted in a knighthood conferred on him by William III.

Abney re-married in 1700. His second wife was co-heir to considerable London property, and with the death of her brother three months after her marriage to Abney, she inherited the entire estate.

Abney lived on until the then ripe old age of 83. His family fortune would have been worth around £250,000 we estimate, or about £3.3bn in today's terms.

The 4th Marquess Of Anglesey

(1835-1898)
Land
Wealth: £3.317m
Net National Income: £1.075bn
% of NNI: 0.3%

£3.329 billion

The grandson of Wellington's famous cavalry commander at Waterloo, the 4th Marquess had largish estates in Wales and England – covering nearly 30,000 acres in 1882, at the time Bateman did his survey, 'Great Landowners of Great Britain'. The largest holding – some 17,441 acres in Staffordshire – produced a handsome income of £91,304 a year out of a total income of £110,598, which was presumably related to coal revenues.

On the back of that, the total family wealth at the time was around £3.3m, representing 0.3% of the then £1.075bn net national income. Today's equivalent would be over £3.3bn.

Richard De Lucy

(d 1179)
Land
Wealth: £3,000
Net National Income: £1m
% of NNI: 0.3%

£3.329 billion

One of the most prominent royal administrators in the twelfth century, Richard De Lucy came from minor nobility with land in Kent and East Anglia. He made his mark in the reign of Stephen, where he was castellan of the Tower of London and Windsor Castle. Henry II, on his accession to the throne in 1154, was careful not to alienate Stephen's supporters. With his frequent absences abroad, Henry needed trustworthy subordinates who could administer the country for him effectively. De Lucy proved just such a man. With Robert of Leicester, he ran the country for the king, with Robert (a powerful baron) concentrating on politics and De Lucy on administration.

With no vast land holdings of his own to inherit, De Lucy depended for his wealth and advancement on the king, who rewarded him with a growing landed fortune. He was an effective administrator in both financial and judicial matters. By 1166, he was regarded as a landowner of some consequence with estates being assessed at thirty knights' fees. His power and influence grew after the death of Robert of Leicester in 1168.

A rebellion in 1173, by the new Earl of Leicester and military activity by the King of Scotland threatened Henry's hold on the throne, but De Lucy's energy and loyalty held the country for the king. His reward was more land and power. But in

1178-79, De Lucy retired and went to live in an Augustinian monastery which he had founded in Kent.

He died in 1179, by which time his fortune would have been around £3,000 or over £3.3bn in today's money.

Rich list members born in the 15th century

Rich list member	Lifespan
Rivers, Earl (1st)	1410-1469
Cook, Sir Thomas	c1410-1478
Neville, Cecily, Duchess of York	1415-1495
Hende, John	d 1418
Wiltshire, The Earl of	1420-1461
Kent, The 1st Earl of	c1420-1489
Tiptoft, John, The Earl of Worcester	c1427-1470
Warwick, The Earl of	1428-1471
Howard, John 1st Duke of Norfolk	c1430-1485
Neville, Archbishop George	c1432-1476
Catesby, William	c1440-1483
Brampton, Sir Edward	c1440-1508
Rivers, Earl	c1442-1483
Percy, Henry, The 4th Earl of Northumberland	c1449-1489
Dorset, Marquess of	1451-1501
Lovell, Viscount	1454-c1487
Buckingham, The Duke of	c1457-1483
Boleyn, Sir Geoffrey	d 1463
Colet, John	c1466-1519
Wolsey, Cardinal Thomas	c1473-1530
Gresham, Sir Richard	c1485-1549
Radcliffe, Sir Richard	d 1485
Warren, Sir Ralph	c1486-1553
Spring, Thomas	d 1486
Clopton, Sir Hugh	d 1496

The 4th Marquess Of Londonderry

(1805-1884)
Land
Wealth: £3.303m
Net National Income: £1.075bn
% of NNI: 0.3%

£3.329 billion

The Londonderry family were the hated coal owners of the north-east. They met strikes and agitation with a hard-nosed determination to preserve their lot. Lock-outs and wage cuts would be the order of the day, backed up by the use of state force where necessary. It all helped to make the Londonderry family rich and their workforce bitter.

The 4th Marquess was born in 1805, and after his Eton education, sat as a Tory MP for Co. Down from 1826-52. He succeeded his father to the family estates in 1854. These ran to around 50,232 acres, which had a handsome annual income of over £100,000 in 1882. Over half of this (£56,825) came from the mines in Durham.

When he died in 1884, Londonderry left £385,348 in his will. But the value of his land and other assets in 1882, was over £3.3m, representing 0.3% of the then net national income. Today's equivalent would be over £3.3bn.

James Ratcliffe

(dob 18/10/1952)
Industry

Wealth: £3.3 billion

Chemical giant Ineos plans to build a £125m world-scale phenol and acetone plant in China by the end of 2008. It shows that James Ratcliffe's ambitions to build a world-beating chemicals operation are on track following its £5bn acquisition of BP's Innovene division in 2005.

From his base in the New Forest, the low-key Ratcliffe runs Ineos Group, which has become the world's third largest chemicals company, and the world's largest producer of a range of chemicals such as acetone, phenol and car air-conditioning fluids. The BP deal was a stunning coup, as he beat off the private equity industry to pull off the deal. But he knows the private equity boys well, having worked as a director of Advent International (Boston) from 1987 to 1992. Before that, however, he spent 15 years in accounting, marketing, and business management at Esso Petroleum and Courtaulds.

In 1992, he left Advent International and, together with Dr John Hollowood, led the management buyout of an earlier offshoot of BP – its speciality chemicals division – which became Inspec. It floated on the stock market in 1994, and four years later was taken over in a £611m deal by Laporte. Ratcliffe had left the operation by then, but his remaining shares and options were worth £28m at the time. The beach had no allure though as Ratcliffe was not yet finished with chemicals. Armed with his windfall, he headed a buyout team that acquired Ineos Group from Inspec in a £90.5m deal in 1998.

A series of bold takeovers followed and he went on to buy chunks of chemical giants ICI, Dow and Degussa. Ineos has purchased most of its assets in auctions where it was often competing against private equity capital companies.

'We've found greater receptiveness from sellers because we're not a private equity capital company,' says Ratcliffe. 'Chemical companies are more comfortable dealing with us than with accountants from the private equity capital sector, who are a different breed of people.'

The 2005 accounts for Ineos Group show that the combined Ineos and Innovene operation made over £414m profit on £15.2bn in sales in 2005. The net assets of the combined group stand at around £6.5bn. While we would normally value the group near these net assets, we are more cautious in the volatile markets and settle for £4.8bn, which implies a £3.2bn valuation on Ratcliffe's stake. He has a £100m stake in the separate Ineos Chlor operation. In all, Ratcliffe should easily be worth £3.3bn.

Baron Caledon

(1730-1802)
Merchant and landowner
Wealth: £700,000
Net National Income: £235m
% of NNI: 0.29%

£3.218 billion

Born James Alexander, the younger son of a Londonderry alderman in 1730, Caledon went to India to make his fortune in Bengal. Both at Patna and Murshidabad, the young Alexander took what has been called 'a rich harvest out of the early revenue administration'.

When he left Bengal in 1772, Caledon reckoned he was worth about £150,000. In fact he was a lot richer. He returned home to purchase estates in Ireland for around £600,000. He became an MP for Londonderry from 1775 to 1790 and was rich enough to derive £7,000 income from his 9,000 Irish acres.

He was created Baron Caledon in 1790, and was a strenuous supporter of the union with Britain until his death in 1802. In all, we rate him at about £700,000, or just over £3.2bn in today's terms.

Sir Geoffrey Boleyn

(d 1463)
Land
Wealth: £10,000
Net National Income: £3.5m
% of NNI: 0.28%

£3.107 billion

Grandfather of Anne Boleyn, one of Henry VIII's six wives, who was executed after failing to deliver a surviving male heir, Sir Geoffrey Boleyn was a wealthy London merchant. He purchased the manor of Blickling in Norfolk from Sir John Fastolf and was Lord Mayor of London in 1457.

He died six years later 'a great rich man' with 'about 100 markes of land' according to Leland, a contemporary chronicler. But the official extent after his death showed that apart from his London property and Norfolk manor, he had other manors in Kent and Sussex, representing an investment of over £2,000.

He left £1,000 in money and plate to his children and as much again to his wife. In all, his wealth was probably around £10,000 or some £3.1bn in today's money.

Sir Christopher Clitherow

(d 1641)
Merchant
Wealth: £100,000
Net National Income: £35m
% of NNI: 0.28%

£3.107 billion

The way to make money in the seventeenth century was simple: become involved in the East India Company. Sir Christopher Clitherow, who followed his father into the trade of ironmongery and rose to become master of the Ironmongers' Company, seems to have made his real fortune from East Indies trade. He subscribed to early voyages of the company where the profit margin was a healthy 95%. He built up great wealth as a result with property in London and estates in Essex and Hertfordshire.

Clitherow became Lord Mayor in 1635, and was knighted by Charles I. But he was no uncritical royalist as was demonstrated three years later when as governor of another company, the Eastland Merchants, he refused to admit a man who had been recommended by the king. Charles had promised a good turn if his candidate was accepted, to which Clitherow replied: 'They all knew what the king's good turns were when they came to seek them.' But he was also not in sympathy with the puritans. In the parliament of 1627-28, Clitherow was chosen as a representative of the City, but it was said his principles made him unacceptable to the puritans. Fortunately perhaps, he died before the Civil War which would have required him to choose sides.

At his death his wealth was around £100,000, equivalent to 0.28% of the £35m net national income. Today that would be £3.1bn.

Sir Richard Gurney

(1577-1647)
Merchant
Wealth: £100,000
Net National Income: £35m
% of NNI: 0.28%

£3.107 billion

If Clitherow missed the Civil War, poor Sir Richard Gurney was pitched right into the middle of the crisis which led to the fatal breach between Charles I and parliament.

Apprenticed to a London silkman, Gurney had the good fortune to be left the shop of his late master. This legacy was worth £6,000, but Gurney greatly increased his fortune by trade with France and Italy, which he visited. His first marriage was also advantageous and he worked his way up London politics through the Clothworkers' Company, and was Lord Mayor in 1641 – not a good time to be in such a post.

A staunch royalist who was knighted by the king, Gurney sought to halt the City's drift towards parliament in the growing crisis. Gurney became more embroiled in efforts by Charles to restore his authority in an increasingly hostile London. As the political temperature rose with riots and threats to call out troops, Gurney lost control. He was impeached by parliament and flung into the Tower, where he remained almost until his death in 1647. His loyalty to the king had cost him his life and losses of around £40,000. He could have paid £5,000 to be released but refused to pay.

At his peak, Gurney would have been worth perhaps £100,000, equivalent to 0.28% of the net national income of £35m. Today that would be £3.1bn.

John Scott

(1725-1775)
Gambler
Wealth: £500,000
Net National Income: £175m
% of NNI: 0.28%

£3.107 billion

'As rich as Scott,' was a popular proverb of eighteenth century polite society. A celebrated gambler, Scott's skill and phenomenal luck gained him a £500,000 fortune according to Horace Walpole, the diarist of the day. Giving the appearance of a bluff soldier, 'Pawkey' Scott, as his friends called him, simply fleeced them.

Scott rose rapidly in the Guards. In fourteen years he was a major-general at 45. But it was gaming and politics which seemed to have attracted him. He entered parliament in 1754, for Caithness, where his mother's relations had considerable interests. Scott's outright bribery in electioneering was condemned by a court of session in 1759, but it had no effect. Scott was still wheeling and dealing in parliament up until his death in 1775. By then, his gaming skill had allowed him to buy a large Scottish estate. A friend wrote at Scott's death:

General Scott is dead...The waiters are to have crepes round their arms and the dice to be black and the spots white, during the time of wearing weepers, and the dice box muffled.

Scott's £500,000 fortune was the equivalent of about 0.28% of the £175m net national income. Today that would be around £3.1bn.

Giles Strangways

(1615-1675)
Land
Wealth: £120,000
Net National Income: £42m
% of NNI: 0.28%

£3.107 billion

Giles Strangways, the son of a prominent Dorset landowner and MP, married the daughter of a London mercer who came with a £10,000 dowry. He served in parliament with his father in the run-up to the Civil War. During the war, he raised a cavalry regiment for the king, but was taken prisoner with his brother-in-law when Sherborne Castle fell in 1645. He spent nearly three years in the Tower with other leading cavaliers until his father paid the maximum £10,000 fine to secure his release.

During Cromwell's Protectorate, Strangways was careful to limit his role in royalist conspiracy, but sat in parliament on the restoration of the monarchy. He inherited his father's estate with an annual income of around £5,000 in 1666, and purchased further land.

When he died in 1675, Strangways was worth around £120,000, equivalent to 0.28% of the then £42m net national income. Today that would be £3.1bn.

Sir Richard Branson

(dob 18/07/1950)
Transport and media

Wealth: £3.1 billion

Sir Richard Branson is taking on a green hue. His Virgin Earth Challenge, announced in February 2007, offers a $25m reward for a winning plan to remove greenhouse gases from the atmosphere. Branson has also established Virgin Fuels, which will channel £200m into bio-fuel investments during the next three years, with a heavy emphasis on developing cellulosic ethanol, derived from agricultural waste and fast-growing crops such as switchgrass. This followed his announcement in September 2006, pledging to invest ten years of profits from Virgin Atlantic and Virgin Trains (£1.5bn) to finance research into environmentally-friendly fuels.

Aside from the environment, Branson is also locked in a battle over the future of the digital and pay television market. Virgin Mobile has teamed up with NTL, the cable operator, to form Virgin Media and it is challenging BSkyB for dominance in Britain's pay television market. It is early days yet but Branson has always loved a scrap and being seen as a plucky underdog from his earliest days of empire-building, which began in 1969, when he launched Virgin Mail Order to be followed by the first Virgin record shop in 1971, and the Virgin Records label in 1973.

Today, the empire embraces trains, planes, mobile phones, the internet, music, wine sales, and holidays to name but a few. In all, there are over 285 Virgin companies, either controlled by Branson or in which he has a significant stake, and they made a combined profit of around £265m on £5.8bn sales in 2005.

Virgin Holdings, the main parent company for the Virgin Atlantic airline and Virgin Trains, made an exceptional £878.2m profit on £3bn sales in 2005-06. Nearly £750m of this profit came from the sale of shares in Virgin Mobile, but the airline and train service are still making decent returns.

Some critics wonder whether Branson has spread himself too thin and claim the whole edifice will come crashing down. But Branson has thus far proved them wrong, though businesses have closed: the latest being Virgin Cars, which was sold to a partner early in 2006. While there are some hefty loss-makers, Branson has been able to sell stakes or entire businesses, raising around £1bn in recent years to invest elsewhere or to cover loss-making operations. He is now looking at floating the American mobile operation. This could crystallise another £500m stake for Virgin.

In Australia, Branson set up Virgin Blue in 2001, with a £4m investment and made £387m from share sales at its float two years later. He has been locked in battles with partners there and retains a 25% stake now worth £266m. Branson plans to replicate Virgin Blue's success in America and he has also taken over the national airline in Nigeria.

Branson is not one to flash his cash much on personal trinkets. A £5.3m yacht bought one Christmas was a rare indulgence. His wealth is carefully tied up in the company via overseas trusts. We reckon the total Virgin business empire should be worth at least £2.75bn on its current performance. We add another £300m for cash in the bank from disposals and windfalls plus another £50m for personal assets, homes and islands. Together, he is worth in the region of £3.1bn.

Michel & Charlene De Carvalho

(dob 21/07/1944 and 30/06/1954)
Brewing

Wealth: £3.05 billion

Dutch brewer Heineken had a good 2006, with profits up 10.7% at £828m, which delighted investors. Its premium brews sold well and it managed to cut its costs, with the new chief executive shaking up the brewer, promising £136m a year cost savings by 2008, and the company expects its profits growth to continue.

Heineken may be Dutch, but the biggest shareholder lives in Britain and is represented on the board. Charlene de Carvalho is the daughter of Freddy Heineken, the former boss of Heineken NV, the Dutch brewer. He died in January 2002, leaving his fortune to his only daughter who lives in London, with her banker husband, Michel de Carvalho. He started out as a child actor, reaching a career pinnacle when he appeared in 'Lawrence of Arabia', David Lean's Oscar-winning epic, starring Peter O'Toole. De Carvalho, under his acting name Michel Ray, played the Arab boy Farraj who befriends Lawrence. He also appeared in 'The Tin Star', with Henry Fonda, for which he won *Film Daily's* Critics Award. He gave up acting at the age of 17, a decision he claimed to regret later because he passed up the chance to earn a lot of money.

The de Carvalho family control exactly a quarter of Heineken shares but because of the complex voting structure, have control of the company. The family stake is now worth £2.9bn. Dividends and other assets should easily add another £150m, taking the total to £3.05bn.

Sean Quinn & Family

(dob 06/09/1946)
Property & construction equipment

Wealth: £3.05 billion

Serial Irish border entrepreneur Sean Quinn, and his family, join Ireland's elite sterling billionaire ranks, having built the Quinn Group from scratch over the past thirty-four years into a huge conglomerate.

A farmer's son, Quinn left school at fifteen to work on his family's twenty-three acre dairy farm in Derrylin, Co. Fermanagh. His breakthrough came in 1973, when at the age of twenty-six he realised the family was sitting on huge reserves of sand, gravel and shale. Buying a truck for £600 and borrowing money for a mechanical shovel, Quinn went into the quarrying business. One half of the quarry was in Northern Ireland and the other half in the Republic. The Troubles in the North meant a healthy demand for building products in construction and repair work. In 1975, Quinn started making concrete blocks, he followed that with cement, and in the early 1980s with roof and floor tiles.

By the mid 1980s, the Quinn Group had become Ireland's second largest cement manufacturer. Quinn diversified and bought nine Dublin pubs and a string of Irish hotels in the mid 1990s. The Irish property boom that followed increased their value six-fold. Quinn-direct Insurance, which now writes premiums of £350m a year, has also taken him into a new and lucrative market.

In 2006, the Quinn Group made £264m profit on £1bn. The family has amassed over £600m in assets, including building a 5%, £368m stake in Anglo Irish, a quoted Dublin business bank, hotels, wind farms, pubs and other investments.

Quinn has given much of the company to his five children – Brenda, Ciara, Sean Junior, Colette and Aoife – three of whom work for it. Right now we value the Quinn Group and the other assets at around £3bn, adding another £50m for other assets.

Rich list members born in the 16th century

Rich list member	Lifespan
Pembroke, The Earl of	c1501-1570
Derby, The Earl of	1508-1572
Sutton, Thomas	1532-1611
Howard, Thomas, 4th Duke of Norfolk	1536-1572
Palavicino, Sir Horatrio	c1540-1600
Craven, Sir William	c1545-1618
Campden, Viscount	1551-1629
Eldred, John	1552-1632
Fermor, Richard	d 1552
Wyche, Richard	1554-1621
Delaune, Gideon	c1561-1659
Cecil, Robert, Earl of Salisbury	1563-1612
Percy, Henry, 9th Earl of Northumberland	1564-1632
Clare, The Earl of	1564-1637
Abbot, Sir Maurice	1565-1642
Pindar, Sir Paul	c1565-1650
Cork, The 1st Earl of	1566-1643
Hewett, Sir William	d 1567
Campbell, Sir James	1570-1642
Garraway, Sir Henry	1575-1646
Gurney, Sir Richard	1577-1647
Audley, Hugh	1577-1662
Viner, Sir Thomas	1588-1665
Reynardson, Sir Abraham	1590-1661
Cavendish, William, 1st Duke of Newcastle	1592-1676
Stafford, The Earl of	1593-1641

Simon Halabi

(dob 02/08/1958)
Property

Wealth: £3.0 billion

The recent collapse of the Esporta health club operator will have caused some pain to Simon Halabi. He bought it just nine months previously in a deal reckoned to be worth £476m including debt. His losses on the venture could run as high as £150m according to authoritative press reports. He is also threatening legal action against the former owners.

The Esporta difficulty comes as Halabi's latest venture, 'The PM Club', is nearing completion. It aims to be one of the world's most exclusive and glamorous private members' clubs aimed at the global elite. The invitation only club will utilise his family trust's existing assets – the old In and Out Club in Piccadilly and Mentmore Towers, the former Rothschild estate in Buckinghamshire. These historic buildings are being painstakingly restored to their former glory.

The Halabi family trust, advised by Buckingham Securities, the family property group, has grown in value by at least £1bn on further trophy property assets in London, where Halabi has lived since he was a teenager. These include the King's Reach office development in the City, Alban Gate, The Bankside Estate, Millennium Bridge House and 60 Victoria Embankment. Before the recent Esporta problems, a recent revaluation of the property portfolio and his shareholding in "The Shard of Glass" tower project took the Halabi family trust's gross investment and development portfolio to around £5bn. Stripping out £2bn of debt leaves the Halabi family at £3bn. It was reported in March 2007 that Halabi is planning to float a real estate investment trust which could have up to £2.5bn of assets.

William Catesby

(c 1440-1483)
Land
Wealth: £10,000
Net National Income: £3.6m
% of NNI: 0.27%

£2.996 billion

William Catesby was an early example of a high-flying lawyer – a sort of fifteenth century George Carmen. His father was one of the leading gentry of Northamptonshire and left Catesby fourteen manors worth £250 a year. Catesby also married the daughter of a local landowner and went to the Inner Temple to study the law. By 1474-75, in his mid thirties, Catesby was lecturing on Magna Carta and had built up a lucrative legal practice advising barons and clergy alike.

He also involved himself in political intrigue, and was a political protégé of both the Duke of Buckingham and Sir Ralph Hastings, who confided their inner thoughts to him. Catesby promptly betrayed Hastings who went to the block as a result. Richard III heaped honours and rewards on Catesby including lands, which gave him a £323 a year income. He was also given lucrative offices, but this did not prevent him ultimately sharing the fate of Hastings after the Battle of Bosworth when Richard fell.

Catesby's £10,000 wealth was equivalent to about 0.27% of the £3.6m net national income at the time. That would be around £2.9bn today.

Aaron Franks

(d 1777)
Merchant
Wealth: £500,000
Net National Income: £180m
% of NNI: 0.27%

£2.996 billion

Aaron Franks's father founded the Jewish Ashkenazi community in the late seventeenth century. He was admitted to the Royal Exchange in 1697, which will have given his son a decent inheritance.

Aaron Franks was a highly successful jeweller in London for much of the eighteenth century. He attained enough wealth to be in a position to donate upwards of £5,000 a year to charity. In his country home in Isleworth on the banks of the Thames, he entertained the aristocracy. Despite the prejudice prevalent against Jews at the time, Franks sought the help of the British court in 1745, on behalf of Jews expelled from Prague.

When he died in 1777, he was worth around £500,000 representing about 0.27% of the then £180m net national income. Today's equivalent would be around £2.9bn.

The 6th Duke Of Rutland

(1815-1888)
Land
Wealth: £2.924m
Net National Income: £1.075bn
% of NNI: 0.27%

£2.996 billion

The 1st Duke of Rutland had been raised to a dukedom for the support he gave William of Orange in the 1688 Revolution. The family were (and remain) big landowners, particularly in the East Midlands. The 6th Duke, who was born in 1815, succeeded his father to the title in 1857, after serving as a Tory MP for fifteen years.

In 1882, Bateman calculated in 'Great Landowners of Great Britain' that he had over 70,000 acres producing an annual income of £97,486. Though when he died in 1888, he only left £104,136 in his will, the 1882 figure puts a £2.92m value on his asset wealth. That represented around 0.27% of the then £1.075bn net national income. In today's terms that would be over £2.9bn.

Sir Joshua Vam Neck

(1702-1777)
Merchant
Wealth: £500,000
Net National Income: £180m
% of NNI: 0.27%

£2.996 billion

Joshua van Neck and his brother Gerard were born in Holland, sons of the paymaster-general of the Dutch army. They came to London in the early eighteenth century to trade as merchants. The brothers built up a lucrative business as brokers and financiers to Dutch investors seeking a slice of the British market for government loans and company shares. They helped underwrite government loans in the wars against France in the 1740s and 1750s, and also acted as paymasters to the military in the war. They had valuable trade with the French, particularly the contract to supply the French tobacco monopoly. This was so valuable to all parties that the van Necks persuaded both the French and British governments that it should continue through the wars of 1744-48 and 1756-63. Gerard van Neck died in 1750, leaving nearly £150,000 of his £240,000 fortune to his brother. Van Neck was created a baronet in 1751, for his financial help to the government.

Joshua died in 1777, described by *The Gentleman's Magazine* as 'one of the richest merchants in Europe'. He was worth around £500,000, representing about 0.27% of the then £180m net national income. Today's equivalent would be around £2.9bn.

Sir Ralph Warren

(c 1486-1553)
Merchant
Wealth: £25,000
Net National Income: £9m
% of NNI: 0.27%

£2.996 billion

The great-grandfather of Oliver Cromwell, Ralph Warren was the son of a fuller. Born in about 1486, he joined the Mercers' Company in 1507, after serving his apprenticeship. By 1530, he was master of the Mercers' Company, and also belonged to two other mercantile bodies: Merchants of the Staple and Merchant Adventurers.

By this time, Warren's wealth was huge. His early tax demand of £3,000 was a third larger than any other leading merchant. He served as Lord Mayor twice and was knighted by Henry VIII. At the same time he was busy extending his landholdings in Cambridgeshire and Suffolk. He seemed to have spent considerable time trying various aristocrats on treason charges. He was also able to supplement his mercantile activities by large financial deals with the monarch.

When he died in 1553, Warren was worth perhaps £25,000, representing 0.27% of the then £9m net national income. Today's equivalent would be over £2.9bn.

James Williamson, Baron Ashton

(1842-1930)
Industry
Wealth: £10.5m
Net National Income: £3.957bn
% of NNI: 0.27%

£2.996 billion

The son of a Lancaster painter and decorator, Williamson received a good education at Lancaster's Royal Grammar School and at a private school in Cheshire. When his father died in 1879, he took over the firm with his elder brother, but within four years, Williamson had bought him out.

By 1887, he was making linoleum for floors, building his Lune Mills factory into a huge operation employing 4,000 people at its peak before the First World War. A paternalistic employer, Williamson was reluctant to sack his staff in a downturn. But equally he paid low wages and repeatedly resisted efforts to unionise his workforce. Independent Labour Party members sacked from his works for their agitation would find it difficult to obtain work elsewhere. From 1886 to 1895, Williamson was a Liberal MP, and bought a peerage with a £10,000 donation to party funds. Generous to his native Lancaster, he built the local town hall and gave £500,000 to the town. He was still running the firm to within a week of his death in 1930. At the time, it was facing serious competition from America and needed extensive modernisation.

Williamson left £10.5m in his estate though he died intestate, then a record in intestacy. That was equivalent to about 0.27% of the then £3.9bn net national income. In today's terms, the wealth figure would be £2.9bn.

The 5th Marquess Of Downshire

(1844-1874)
Land
Wealth: £2.9m
Net National Income: £1.075bn
% of NNI: 0.26%

£2.885 billion

A low-key Northern Ireland landowner, Downshire was born in London in 1844. After serving in the Life Guards, he succeeded his father to the title in 1868. But he did not live long to enjoy his huge inheritance.

John Bateman's book, 'Great Landowners of Great Britain', published in 1884, put the Downshire total acreage at 120,000 acres, with about 65% being in Co. Down. Bateman's calculations for land value are based on 1882 figures, which are conveniently near to Downshire's death in 1874 at the age of twenty-nine.

His £2.9m wealth would have represented about 0.26% of the £1.075bn net national income of the time. Today's equivalent would be over £2.8bn.

Thomas Foley

(1617-1677)
Ironmaster
Wealth: £120,000
Net National Income: £45m
% of NNI: 0.26%

£2.885 billion

Thomas Foley's father was one of the early pioneers of the Industrial Revolution. An ironmaster based in West Bromwich, he had five furnaces in operation by 1636. A supporter of Charles I in the Civil War, he cast cannon for the royalist forces. He did not seem to suffer any persecution from the victorious parliamentary forces and died a rich man in 1657. Thomas Foley, his second son, took over the ironworks with a younger brother and became very wealthy as a result.

Foley had an income of £5,000 a year, which suggested a fortune of about £120,000 when he died in 1677. That represented about 0.26% of the then £45m net national income. In today's terms the equivalent figure would be over £2.8bn.

Rich list members born in the 17th century

Rich list member	Lifespan
Cutler, Sir John	c1608-1693
Spencer, Sir John	d 1610
Smith, Erasmus	1611-1691
Strangways, Giles	1615-1675
Foley, Thomas	1617-1677
Western, Thomas	1624-1707
Cokayne, Sir William	d 1626
Banks, Sir John	1627-1699
Fox, Sir Stephen	1627-1716
Spencer, Robert	d 1627
Clayton, Sir Robert	1629-1707
Child, Sir Josiah	1630-1699
Viner, Sir Robert	1631-1688
Halifax, The Marquess of	1633-1695
Herne, Sir Joseph	c1639-1699
Abney, Sir Charles	1640-1722
North, Sir Dudley	1641-1691
Clitherow, Sir Christopher	d 1641
Edwin, Sir Humphrey	1642-1707
Child, Sir Francis	1642-1713
Guy, Thomas	1644-1724
Wharton, The Marquess of	1648-1715
Hoare, Sir Richard	1648-1718
Shepheard, Samuel	c1648-1719
Churchill, John, 1st Duke of Marlborough	1650-1722
Heathcote, Sir Gilbert	c1651-1733
Craggs, James	c1657-1721
Janssen, Sir Theodore	c1658-1748
Page, Sir Gregory	1668-1720
Chandos, The Duke of	1673-1744
Lowther, Sir James	1673-1755
Backwell, Edward	d 1683
Pulteney, William, Earl of Bath	1684-1764
Bowles, Phineas	1690-1749
Newcastle, The Duke of	1693-1768
Gideon, Sampson	1699-1762

Hugh McCalmont

(c 1810-1887)
Finance
Wealth: £3.121m
Net National Income: £1.195bn
% of NNI: 0.26%

£2.885 billion

An Ulsterman by birth, McCalmont made his money in nineteenth century London as a stockbroker and foreign merchant. He died unmarried in 1887, leaving £3.121m in his will to his great-nephew, who had to wait seven years before getting his hands on the money.

McCalmont's fortune represented 0.26% of the then £1.195bn net national income. Today's equivalent would be over £2.8bn.

Elijah Of Menahem

(c 1232-1284)
Finance
Wealth: £10,000
Net National Income: £3.8m
% of NNI: 0.26%

£2.885 billion

Elijah was one of the leading moneylenders in the Jewish community of the thirteenth century. Born in London not later than 1232, of a rabbi and businessman, Elijah followed his father into business. Aside from lending money, he was a corn and wool wholesaler. He was also active as a physician, helping treat nobles or their relatives. With anti-semitism rife at the time, his healing powers may explain how Elijah had surprisingly good relations with successive monarchs and even with the papal legate in England.

He died in 1284, worth around £10,000. That represented about 0.26% of the then £3.8m net national income. Today's equivalent would be over £2.8bn.

Bishop Walter Merton

(c 1205-1277)
Church
Wealth: £10,000
Net National Income: £3.8m
% of NNI: 0.26%

£2.885 billion

Born in Basingstoke of prosperous parents, Walter Merton was the only son in seven children. From 1233, he was a rector of a Surrey church but rose through his administrative abilities to the chancellorship of England from 1272 to 1274. He was virtually Regent while Edward I was abroad. Merton became Bishop of Rochester in 1274, by which time he had accumulated several church livings and been rewarded for his administrative skills by patrons.

A skilled conveyancer of land, Merton dealt in estates before inheriting his parents' Basingstoke estates. He was able to purchase a large estate for his foundation and bequeathed £5,000 in his will. He founded Merton College, first in Surrey, before its transfer to Oxford in 1274.

Merton died in 1274, with a £10,000 fortune, representing 0.26% of the then net national income. Today's equivalent would be over £2.8bn.

Sir Abraham Reynardson

(1590-1661)
Merchant
Wealth: £100,000
Net National Income: £38m
% of NNI: 0.26%

£2.885 billion

Another Lord Mayor of London whose loyalty to the monarchy led to conflict with parliament during the Civil Way, Reynardson, the son of a Plymouth merchant, was born in 1590, and came to London to serve his apprenticeship. He became a leading member of the Merchant Taylors' Company and was also prominent in the Turkey and East India companies. Becoming master of the Merchant Taylors in 1640, he helped Charles I raise loans from the company.

During 1642-43, Reynardson refused to raise loans for parliament except under compulsion, and he became Lord Mayor in 1648-49, where he did all in his power and beyond to support the king and obstruct parliament. After the king's execution in 1649, Reynardson became even more alienated from parliament and was virtually thrown out of office and threatened with imprisonment in the Tower. He refused to pay a fine of £2,000 and an order was issued in 1651 for all his estate to be seized until the fine was paid. There is no record that it was but Reynardson later maintained that his tenure as mayor had cost him £20,000.

Little is known about Reynardson's role during the Protectorate, though his loyalty to the king was recognised on the restoration. Charles II knighted Reynardson in 1661, and he was restored to City offices, though he declined the Lord Mayorship for 1660-61, on grounds of ill-health.

Reynardson died in 1661, still a rich man. He had estates in Essex and Sussex as well as extensive London property. He had also made large loans through his life to the Merchant Taylors. In all, he was worth around £100,000, representing 0.26% of the then net national income. Today's equivalent would be over £2.8bn.

Sir Henry St John Mildmay

(1764-1808)
Land
Wealth: £750,000
Net National Income: £280m
% of NNI: 0.26%

£2.885 billion

'A capricious, vain, ill-tempered man, with some minor talents and insufferable pretensions,' wrote one of his contemporaries of St John Mildmay.

The son of a Hampshire landowner and baronet, he was born in 1764, and succeeded his father to his title and estate in 1784. He had a good marriage to an heiress who was left land in Essex and Somerset by a great uncle. St John Mildmay became MP for Westbury in 1796, and remained in the Commons until his death from liver disease in 1808. During that time, he was putting forward bills, moving from one faction to another, wheeling and dealing but with a singular lack of success in advancing his political career and gaining a peerage. His fortune proved useful and he spent £2,500 in the election of 1806 to secure one seat without success, but he had taken the precaution of having another in reserve.

The Gentleman Magazine put his income at £25,000 a year in 1808, which implies wealth of around £750,000. That would represent 0.26% of the then £280m net national income. Today's equivalent would be over £2.8bn.

William Barwell

(d 1769)
Merchant
Wealth: £400,000
Net National Income: £150m
% of NNI: 0.26%

£2.880 billion

William Barwell was a leading agent of the East India Company and was chief of its operation in Dacca in the mid eighteenth century. He had the opportunity there to dip into the company's revenue stream and to farm its salt, making a £400,000 fortune by the time he died in 1769.

Among his assets were a house and estate in Surrey valued at £10,500 and he had £106,000 in Bank stock and annuities, South Sea stock and East India stock. His fortune would represent 0.26% of the then £150m net national income. Today's equivalent would be over £2.8bn.

Sir Richard Hoare

(1648-1718)
Banker
Wealth: £200,000
Net National Income: £75m
% of NNI: 0.26%

£2.880 billion

Sir Richard Hoare, the son of a London horse dealer and grandson of a Buckinghamshire farmer, was born in 1648. He served his apprenticeship as a goldsmith and joined the Goldsmiths' Company in 1672. His business prospered and around 1693, he moved his business to Fleet Street and added banking to his goldsmith's trade. Today, over three hundred years later, the Hoares' banking firm is still based on the same site.

Hoare was heavily involved in funding government spending by loans. In 1710, for example, he joined with three other merchants to supply the treasury with £350,000 for the use of the army in Flanders. Hoare also refuted charges that he had been an early George Soros speculating against the pound in 1707, when there were fears of a Jacobite invasion.

At his death in 1718, Hoare was worth perhaps £200,000, representing 0.26% of the then £75m net national income. Today's equivalent would be over £2.8bn.

Adam De Basing

(1240s)
Merchant
Wealth: £10,000
Net National Income: £3m
% of NNI: 0.33%

£2.854 billion

Adam De Basing came from one of the leading merchant families of London. His grandfather had been one of the great mayors of an earlier generation and de Basing established himself in a lucrative position as Household merchant to the court, supplying a range of goods from cloth of gold, chasubles, mitres, copes, vestments, banners and occasionally precious metals. His payments for this work over a twenty-two year period totalled some £1,733. But he was also paid in other ways as well. In 1244, for example, he was granted the entire wool production of the bishopric of Winchester. He also paid some royal wages and made loans to the king.

De Basing was also an early investor in property. In 1247, for example, he bought six shops in the City and later built a mansion in Aldermanbury. His family gives its name to several of the choicest addresses in the City today, including Basinghall Street. The family property interests extended to at least eight parishes as far as Hendon and Kentishtown.

De Basing's total wealth would have been in the order of £10,000 when he died, or about £2.8bn today.

Kirsten & Jorn Rausing

(dob 06/09/1946 and 12/02/1960)
Industry

Wealth: £2.825 billion

Sales are booming at Tetra Laval, the Swiss-based packaging group. In 2005, they rose 7.5% and even higher in 2006, when they rose above £6bn. The group is also expanding its operations in the fast-growing Chinese market with a near £20m investment to double the size of an existing plant. This is good news for the brother and sister team of Jorn and Kirsten Rausing, who are both on the board of Tetra Laval. The pair live and work in Britain and are two of the three children of the late Gad Rausing, co-founder of the Swedish Tetra Pak packaging group which merged with Alfa-Laval to form Tetra Laval in 1993.

Aside from his role in Tetra Laval where he heads its mergers and acquisitions operation, Jorn Rausing is a shrewd investor in his own right. He has a 7% stake in Ocado, the online retailer. Ocado's flotation has been postponed while the group concentrates on building its business. Sales in 2005, soared 70% to £153m, which will be welcomed by the low-key Jorn. His stake costs him £15m but will be worth a multiple of that when a float takes place possibly in 2007.

Kirsten owns two Suffolk stud farms and is a passionate horse racing enthusiast. But despite her inheritance, Rausing did not use any of her family money to set up the stud operation. She did it all herself, with a perfectly balanced mix of knowledge of horses, and pure chutzpah. In 1994, she became a non-executive director of the British Bloodstock Agency, which buys and sells racehorses on behalf of wealthy clients. She bought a near 10% stake in February 1991. Kirsten also owns the Staffordstown Stud in County Meath, Ireland.

On the basis of the growth in Tetra Laval sales, *Forbes* valued the combined stake of the Rausing family at £5.65bn in its list of world billionaires in March 2007. We ascribe half of that to Kirsten and Jorn, putting them at £2.825bn.

Rich list members born in the 18th century

Rich list member	Lifespan
Bowes, George	1701-1760
Van Neck, Sir Joshua	1702-1777
Warren, Sir Peter	1703-1752
Fludyer, Sir Samuel	c1705-1768
Beckford, William	1709-1770
Dundas, Sir Lawrence	c1710-1781
Duncombe, Sir Charles	d 1711
Denison, William	1713-1782
Tufnell, John	1720-1794
Queensberry, The Duke of	1724-1810
Clive, Robert 1st Baron Clive of Plassey	1725-1774
Scott, John	1725-1775
Pulteney, Sir William	1729-1805
Rockingham, The Marquess of	1730-1782
Wedgwood, Josiah	1730-1795
Caledon, Baron	1730-1802
Cavendish, The Hon. Henry	1731-1810
Coutts, Thomas	1735-1822
Bridgewater, The 3rd Duke of	1736-1803
Thellusson, Peter	1737-1797
Crawshay, Richard	1739-1810
Rundell, Philip	1746-1827
Peel, Sir Robert	1750-1830
Hollond, William	c1750-1836
Farquhar, John	1751-1826
Arkwright, Richard	1755-1843
Sutherland, The Duke of	1758-1833
Lambton, William	1764-1797
St John Mildmay, Sir Henry	1764-1808
Cleveland, The Duke of	1766-1842
Barwell, William	d 1769
Denison, William	1770-1849
Miles, Philip	1773-1845
Thornton, Richard	1776-1865
Rothschild, Nathan Meyer	1777-1836
Franks, Aaron	d 1777
Goldsmid, Sir Isaac	1778-1859
Loder, Giles	1786-1871
Morrison, James	1790-1857
Overstone, Lord	1796-1883
Portman, The 1st Viscount	1799-1888

Joseph Lewis

(dob 05/02/1937)
Finance and property

Wealth: £2.8 billion

A new, very exclusive golf resort is taking shape in the Bahamas as Joseph Lewis and his friends Tiger Woods and Ernie Els develop the Albany Golf & Beach Club. Lewis is also planning a 2,200 acre casino resort destination on Jamaica's northern coast in partnership with the government.

It's a far cry from Lewis's early roots in his family's restaurants in London and running his own tourist shops in European capitals. Lewis saw the huge potential from foreign exchange dealing and moved to the Bahamas in the 1970s. He remains an extremely active foreign exchange trader and has shrewdly invested his profits through The Tavistock Group, his key investment vehicle. It has interests in 100 companies in areas including property, financial services, life sciences, energy, industry and consumer goods. It also has significant holdings in Russian oil and gas positions.

Among Lewis's property holdings are 3,600 acres in the Bahamas and 8,000 acres in Florida. He also has a 50,000 acre ranch in Argentina. Lewis also backed Dr Mike Lynch's Autonomy Corporation in its early days, making a substantial return on his investment. His stake in auctioneer Christie's was sold to a French tycoon in 1998 for £200m.

Lewis is a leading if low-key donor to charities, channelling over $75m to spur the growth of a 'medical city' at a 6,900 acre master planned community at Lake Nona in Central Florida, which will open a new medical school, hospitals, and numerous biotech research institutions in 2009-11. The project is unusual in that Lewis has made his gift public to encourage further outside gifts.

With other assets such as stakes in Tottenham Hotspur and Glasgow Rangers football clubs, Lewis is easily worth £2.8bn.

Rich list members born in the 19th century

Rich list member	Lifespan
Portland, The 5th Duke of	1800-1879
Brassey, Thomas	1805-1870
Londonderry, The 4th Marquess of	1805-1884
Buccleuch and Queensbury, The 5th Duke of	1806-1884
McCalmont, Hugh	c1810-1887
Cadogan, The 4th Earl	1812-1873
De Stern, Baron	1815-1887
Rutland, The 6th Duke of	1815-1888
Fitzwilliam, Earl	1815-1902
Dudley, 1st Earl of	1817-1885
Bedford, The 9th Duke of	1819-1891
Westminster, The Duke of	1825-1899
Anglesey, The 4th Marquess of	1835-1898
Williamson, James, Baron Ashton	1842-1930
Downshire, The 5th Marquess of	1844-1874
Bute, 3rd Marquess of	1847-1900
Iveagh, The Earl of	1847-1927
Wernher, Sir Julius	1850-1912
Beit, Alfred	1853-1906
Wills, Sir George	1854-1928
Yule, Sir David	1858-1928
Vestey, Lord	1859-1940
Ellerman, Sir John	1862-1933

Erasmus Smith

(1611-1691)
Merchant
Wealth: £120,000
Net National Income: £48m
% of NNI: 0.25%

£2.774 billion

Born into minor Leicestershire nobility in 1611, Erasmus Smith went to London to make his fortune. He became a Turkey merchant and member of the Grocers' Company. By 1650, he was an army contractor supplying provisions to troops in Ireland and Scotland. He soon profited from Cromwell's campaign in Ireland, acquiring land in Tipperary. Even after the restoration, he continued to extend his Irish estates and by 1684, had over 46,000 acres in nine counties. He used his growing wealth to further education in Ireland, establishing grammar schools and endowing Trinity College, Dublin.

Smith died in 1691. At its peak, his fortune would have been £120,000, representing 0.25% of the then £48m net national income. Today's equivalent would be over £2.7bn.

Richard Arkwright

(1755-1843)
Industry
Wealth: £1.2m
Net National Income: £466m
% of NNI: 0.25%

£2.774 billion

Arkwright's father, Sir Richard Arkwright, was one of the early pioneers of the Industrial Revolution. Born of poor parents in Preston, Sir Richard invented a spinning machine which he installed in his factory in Lancashire.

In 1771, he moved to his famous site at Cromford in Derbyshire, where he had ample water power from the River Derwent to power his machines. Sir Richard died in 1792, worth around £500,000. His son, born in 1755, lived until he was 88 and carried on the business after his father's death. He had a good business brain and the business prospered. The care of his workforce was also important to Arkwright and he improved the ventilation and warmth of the mill.

At his death he was regarded as the richest commoner in Britain, worth £1.2m. This represented 0.25% of the then £466m net national income. Today's equivalent would be over £2.7bn.

Gregory De Rokesle

(d 1291)
Merchant
Wealth: £10,000
Net National Income: £4m
% of NNI: 0.25%

£2.774 billion

A goldsmith by trade, de Rokesle seems to have had his fingers in several pies in the late thirteenth century. He sold wax to the royal household, and traded in wool, corn and fish. By 1285, he was regarded as the leading wine merchant in Britain, perhaps borne out by one contract in 1281, where he bought 100 tuns of Bordeaux wine for £150 cash. He also dealt in wines for the court and became royal butler in 1275, a post he held for three years.

But possibly his most lucrative trade came in 1278, when he was made Master of Exchange. De Rokesle was heavily involved in the royal fiscal service and in 1280, for example, he administered thirty-one loans totalling over £30,000. He served until his death in 1291, and that would have presumably given him ample opportunity for profitable trades and speculation.

De Rokesle's wealth at his death would have been around £10,000, representing around 0.25% of the then £4m net national income. Today's equivalent would be over £2.7bn.

Sir Humphrey Edwin

(1642-1707)
Merchant
Wealth: £150,000
Net National Income: £60m
% of NNI: 0.25%

£2.774 billion

Born in 1642, the son of a mayor of Hereford, the young Humphrey Edwin came to London to make his fortune. He married the daughter of a wealthy London merchant, and started in business himself, probably as a wool merchant. He amassed considerable wealth and joined the Skinners' Company.

A strong nonconformist, Edwin was nonetheless courted by James II who was keen to win over dissenters and secure their help in relaxing laws which discriminated against Catholics. In 1687, Edwin was appointed a City alderman by the king, and a month later, James knighted him. It didn't do him much good or harm Edwin. When James fell and William of Orange took the throne a year later, Edwin remained in royal favour. He was a commissioner of excise, drawing a £1,000 salary. He owned extensive London property and also had estates in Wales, which he added to. In 1697, he became Lord Mayor, but caused some controversy by attending nonconformist services in his full mayoral attire, which roused the wrath of high churchmen. Apart from this minor fracas, he did well from his term of office, making £4,000 by filling many City posts which fell vacant during his term of office.

Edwin died in 1707, worth perhaps £150,000. This represented 0.25% of the then £60m net national income. Today's equivalent would be over £2.7bn.

William Hollond

(c 1750-1836)
Merchant
Wealth: £1m
Net National Income: £395m
% of NNI: 0.25%

£2.774 billion

An obscure official of the Bengal Civil Service in the late eighteenth and early nineteenth, centuries, Hollond was the son of a major in the East India Company's private army. Little is known about Hollond's activities, but he must have been able to dip into revenue funds or accept 'commissions' to have accumulated the £1m fortune he had built up by the time of his death in 1836. That would represent around 0.25% of the then £395m net national income. Today's equivalent would be over £2.7bn.

Philip Miles

(1773-1845)
Merchant
Wealth: £1.2m
Net National Income: £480m
% of NNI: 0.25%

£2.774 billion

Philip Miles, a little-known Jamaica plantation-owner and merchant, had strong connections with Bristol. His father had been a merchant and banker in the city. Miles also became a local banker and served in his later years as a Tory MP from 1820-1837, for various Bristol and West Country seats.

He died in 1845, leaving a £1.2m fortune, representing around 0.25% of the then £480m net national income. Today's equivalent would be over £2.7bn.

Sir Thomas Viner

(1588-1665)
Merchant
Wealth: £100,000
Net National Income: £39m
% of NNI: 0.25%

£2.774 billion

Sir Thomas Viner was an object lesson in how to remain prosperous in difficult times. A Gloucestershire lad, he came to London soon after his father's death in 1600, when he was just twelve. He lived with his half-sister's family and joined their profession as a goldsmith.

By 1624, he was a leading member of the Goldsmiths' Company, serving James I as comptroller of the mint. Later, under Cromwell, he supplied large quantities of bullion and plate to the state and the East India Company for use in minting coinage. He also undertook large loans to the government of the day. With the restoration of the monarchy in 1660, Viner kept his offices despite the gains he had made during Cromwell's rule. Indeed, Charles II gave him a baronetcy.

He died in 1665, worth perhaps £100,000, representing 0.25% of the then net national income of £39m. In today's terms that would be over £2.7bn.

Phinease Bowles

(1690-1749)
Land
Wealth: £200,000
Net National Income: £82m
% of NNI: 0.243%

£2.721 billion

Coming from a family of London glass makers, Phineas Bowles went on to have a career in the army. In 1710, aged just twenty, he was commissioned a captain in the 27th (Inniskilling) Regiment of Foot, initially stationed in Spain. In 1713, Bowles transferred to the 3rd Foot Guards (later the Scots Guards), as captain and lieutenant-colonel. In 1715, he helped in suppressing the Jacobite rising, and in March 1719, he succeeded his cousin as colonel of the 12th Lancers, stationed in Ireland.

Bowles settled in Ireland for the remainder of his life. His marriage in 1724 to heiress Alethea Maria brought with it a large Irish estate: portions of the estate were settled absolutely on Bowles and the rest was entailed strictly on the male issue of the marriage, an arrangement which was to cause much family argument and a long-running lawsuit after Bowles's death.

Between 1735 and 1741, Bowles was MP for Bewdly. His loyalty to the government of the day ensured rapid military promotion. In December 1735, he was raised to brigadier general, and in 1739, he was promoted major general and appointed governor of Limerick. Bowles lived at his town house in Dublin and his county seat, Beaulieu, near Drogheda, and died in his sixtieth year in 1749.

By his will of 11 September 1749, he left an estate valued at £200,000. In today's money that would be around £2.7bn.

Sir George Wills

(1854-1928)
Tobacco
Wealth: £10m
Net National Income: £4.154bn
% of NNI: 0.24%

£2.663 billion

Sir George Wills was born into the Bristol tobacco dynasty in 1854. His role was crucial in transforming what was a prosperous, if parochial, Bristol tobacco manufacturer into a global multinational, making the Wills family enormously rich in the process.

He joined the business at eighteen and three years later was appointed factory manager. Wills was instrumental in persuading older and more conservative family members to buy a patent in 1883, for the Bonsack cigarette-making machine in Paris. The £4,000 cost of an exclusive patent was one of the bargains of industrial history. It enabled Wills to launch the cheap Woodbine label at 1 d for five cigarettes, which helped create a mass market. He later played a leading role in the creation of Imperial Tobacco, which was a response by the British tobacco industry at the turn of the century to an aggressive push into the British market by the American Tobacco Company.

In 1911, Wills took over the chairmanship of Imperial, a post he held until 1924. He died four years later, leaving £10m in his will. Before his death, he had lavished large endowments on Bristol University.

His wealth represented around 0.24% of the then £4.15bn net national income. Today's equivalent would be over £2.6bn.

Earl Cadogan & Family

(dob 06/09/1946)
Property

Wealth: £2.61 billion

Soaring central London property values and the completion of new developments in the Sloane Square area of Chelsea have helped to raise the net asset value of the Cadogan Group to £2.36bn at the end of 2006. There has of course been a remarkable transformation of Chelsea in the last few years by Earl Cadogan into one of the most fashionable areas of London, indeed Europe.

Having inherited the title from his late father in 1997, Cadogan has presided over a hefty investment programme covering the 90 acre estate. The crowing glory is the new £150m redevelopment of the old barracks and sports ground at Duke of York Square on fashionable Kings Road. Estates, past dividends, quoted investments and personal property add £250m, taking the Cadogan family to around £2.61bn.

Sir Geoffrey Scrope

(c 1285-1340)
Judiciary
Wealth: £15,000
Net National Income: £5m
% of NNI: 0.3%

£2.595 billion

The younger son of minor Yorkshire nobility, Sir Geoffrey Scrope followed his elder brother into the legal profession, rising to become Chief Justice of the king's bench in 1324. His legal connections enabled him to build up substantial land holdings in thirteen counties.

Royal bounty and his fees from office do not explain his total wealth. He made money from legal retainers (some illegally), and other legal fees from third parties. He lent money to neighbours and on at least two occasions seized land and used his position to prevent any inquiry into his high-handedness.

Despite this shadow of corruption, Scrope served the Crown with distinction; in the military, financial and diplomatic fields. He served on twenty missions abroad and died in 1340, while on a mission with Edward III to Ghent in what is now Belgium.

His £15,000 fortune would be worth over £2.5bn in today's money.

Nadhmi Auchi

(dob 11/06/1937)
Property and hotels

Wealth: £2.575 billion

One of Surrey's more colourful entrepreneurs, Nadhmi Auchi has been in Britain for more than two decades. In that time, he has turned a small company into a multinational conglomerate with 120 firms worldwide spanning luxury hotels to telecom companies in the Middle East. Among his recent deals are a £740m Chicago property development, new hotels in Egypt and a £71m investment in telecoms. The Kingston-based tycoon has still found time to invest in the Lebanon team participating in the new A1 Grand Prix racing series that is a rival to Bernie Ecclestone's F1 series.

Baghdad-born Auchi, the son of an accountant, studied economics and politics at university as befitting a middle class Iraqi. He joined the Ba'ath party which, at the time, was fighting for democracy in Iraq and was not in power. But he left the Ba'ath party in 1962, only to be jailed out of spite a year later when his erstwhile comrades came to power. He left the country in 1980, after the Iran-Iraq War broke out.

Auchi had set his heart on business not politics. In 1997, three years before he left Iraq, he had founded his main company, General Mediterranean Holdings, which was three years old and expanding. GMH, which is registered in Luxembourg, made £145m profit in 2005.

Auchi's total portfolio is worth £2.575bn, split 45% in investments, 25.9% in property and 28.9% in hotels, including the luxurious Le Royal hotel complexes in Beirut, Amman and Tunisia. We value Auchi on this figure.

Thomas Spring

(d 1486)
Clothier
Wealth: £8,200
Net National Income: £3.6m
% of NNI: 0.228%

£2.553 billion

Lavenham in Suffolk was the centre of the fifteenth century cloth trade and that made it a very prosperous town. At the top of the trade were the Spring family, notable at the time for their generous donations to the local church.

Thomas Spring inherited the business from his father (also Thomas) who died in 1440. The younger Thomas continued his father's good work in helping the church and paying for repairs of local roads. He died in 1486, and was buried in some style at Lavenham Church. He left £8,200 in his will and passed on the business to his son (yet another Thomas) who became known locally as the "rich clothier".

At the time the cloth trade prospered – particularly in Lavenham – on the back of a strong export trade. But the details of the rich clothier's fortune remain a mystery. His father's estate would have been worth around £2.5bn in today's money.

Gideon Delaune

(c 1561-1659)
Merchant
Wealth: £90,000
Net National Income: £38m
% of NNI: 0.23%

£2.552 billion

Gideon Delaune, the son of a French Protestant pastor, was born in Rheims in the mid sixteenth century. He accompanied his father to Britain and became apothecary to Anne of Denmark, queen of James I. Delaune must have impressed James, as he played a leading role in the incorporation of the Society of Apothecaries in 1617, and became master in 1637. Delaune was highly regarded for his pills and potions, which made him immensely rich. He had a Bedfordshire estate, a Kent manor, a London house and extensive property in Bermuda and Virginia.

When he died in 1659, after a pious life, he was in his mid-to-late nineties. A contemporary account at his death wrote that Delaune was 'worth (notwithstanding his many acts of public and private charity) near as many thousand pounds as he was years'. The author reckoned that Delaune was 97 at his death, which is disputed, but he was certainly worth at least £90,000, representing 0.23% of the then £38m net national income. Today's equivalent would be nearly £2.5bn.

Josiah Wedgwood

(1730-1795)
Industrialist
Wealth: £500,000
Net National Income: £220m
% of NNI: 0.27%

£2.518 billion

Wedgwood pottery is of course regarded as some of the finest in the world, and the emphasis on quality came from the founder of the business. Josiah Wedgwood was born in 1730, the thirteenth and youngest child of a Staffordshire potter. With little formal education beyond the age of nine, when his father died, Wedgwood was taken on by his elder brother, also a potter. Here he learnt all the various aspects of the pottery trade, despite a virulent attack of smallpox when he was eleven. His love of experimenting did not go down well with his brother who declined to take him into partnership when Wedgwood's apprenticeship finished.

Through the 1750s Wedgwood worked for a variety of potters until 1759, when he started out on his own at a small pot works in Burslem. Wedgwood's pottery was so much better than any rival ware that the business grew fast and became very profitable. But Wedgwood realised that a purpose built factory was needed to achieve the quality work that he aspired to. In 1766, he acquired for £3,000 a site between Burslem and Stoke where he built the famed Etruria works, which were finally occupied in 1773. From here, armed with bold designs from teams of skilled craftsmen and artists, he conquered the world. He was also regarded as a model of the paternalistic employer, building a village for his workers and instituting an insurance scheme.

Wedgwood also saw the value of the canal system for carrying his raw materials and finished products. He played a leading role in the building of the Trent and Mersey Canal, which passed through Etruria when it opened in 1777.

Wedgwood died of overwork in 1795, worth around £500,000 including his factory assets. That represented about 0.27% of the then net national income of £220m. Today's equivalent would be over £2.5bn.

Rich list members born in the 20th century

Rich list member	Year of birth
Rausing, Hans (& family)	1926
Ecclestone, Bernie	1930
Lewis, Joseph	1937
Auchi, Nadhmi	1937
Reuben, David & Simon	1939
Hinduja, Gopi & Sri	1940
Sainsbury, Lord (& family)	1940
de Carvalho, Michel & Charlene	1944
Cadogan, Earl (& family)	1946
Quinn, Sean & Family	1946
Branson, Sir Richard	1950
Mittal, Lakshmi	1950
Westminster, The Duke of	1951
Ratcliffe, James	1952
Green, Sir Philip & Lady	1952
Halabi, Simon	1958
Rausing, Kirsten & Jorn	1960
Abramovich, Roman	1966

John Tufnell

(1720-1794)
Land
Wealth: £650,000
Net National Income: £220m
% of NNI: 0.29%

£2.508 billion

John Tufnell, the son of an MP, was educated at Cambridge before following in his father's footsteps and becoming MP for Beverley in Yorkshire in 1754. He remained in the Commons until 1761, when he did not stand again. Regarded as a country gentleman, he lived a fairly uneventful life until his death in 1794. Burke's 'Landed Gentry' put his wealth into perspective:

He was one of the most wealthy commoners in England; the rental of his landed property in Essex and the north amounted to £18,000 per annum, and his ready money and stock in funds is expected to amount to near £150,000.

Add in the value of the land and a £650,000 wealth figure is appropriate, or about £2.5bn today.

Lord Sainsbury & Family

(dob 24/10/1940)
Food
Wealth: £2.5bn
Net National Income: £1,065bn
% of NNI: 0.22%

Wealth: £2.5 billion

Lord Sainsbury took control of his shares in the family supermarket firm in February 2007. For eight years, while he was science minister in Tony Blair's government, they were in a blind trust, run by trustees and out of his control. Sainsbury has regained control of his 7.73% stake just as the group is at the centre of takeover speculation that have driven the shares to all-time highs, valuing J Sainsbury at over £9.9bn. Sainsbury has backed the company's management, which has turned J Sainsbury round, with sales and profits moving up sharply over the crucial Christmas period.

Ennobled by Tony Blair, Sainsbury has given £11.5m to Labour over seven years. After his period in government, Sainsbury is keen to become involved in his charity work and said in 2005, that he wanted to be the first Briton to give £1bn to charity in his lifetime. The main beneficiaries of Lord Sainsbury's largesse will be neuroscience research, plant biology and African development. He has already put £400m into his Gatsby Charitable Foundation.

Sainsbury himself heads the family and spent thirty-five years in the business, founded by his great-grandparents in 1869. The wider Sainsbury family's stake (excluding charitable stakes) is now around 19% of the company, worth around £1.9bn. Other assets, share sales and huge dividends totalling £450m from 1999-2005 take the family to £2.5bn after tax and charitable donations.

Bernie Ecclestone

(dob 28/10/1930)
Motor racing
Wealth: £2.5bn
Net National Income: £1,065bn
% of NNI: 0.22%

Wealth: £2.5 billion

He may be nearly 77, but Bernie Ecclestone is as passionate about the future of Formula One motor racing as ever. He wants to expand the sport into Asia with new F1 races there. Before the 2007 season started he said:

I'm speaking to Singapore and in talks with South Korea with a view to staging a grand prix there very soon. An Indian Grand Prix will definitely happen, it's just a question of where.

The 2006 season showed a business in fine fettle with £2bn in broadcast and licensing revenues and a worldwide TV audience of approximately 580m. Abu Dhabi will host its first F1 race in 2009.

Ecclestone may no longer have financial control of F1, but it is his vision and drive that keeps the show on the road, making huge amounts of money. It was in November 2005, that five years of wrangling over the future of F1 ended when CVC, the private equity giant, bought F1. Ecclestone is now a minority shareholder in the new company, Alpha Prema, that owns F1 but he remains as chief executive.

The November deal was a triumph for the Suffolk trawler skipper's son, who began racing in 1949. An accident two years later ended his driving career but he went into team management and eventually took over the whole of F1. The modern sport is virtually Ecclestones creation, and he has made his fortune from the television rights and spin-offs from F1 being second only to football as an international spectator sport.

A bond issue in 1999, and the sale of 75% of the business a year later to Kirch netted Ecclestone £1.9bn. That money was transferred to Jersey-based trusts controlled by his wife, Slavica, 48, a Croatian model. He has some choice assets to enjoy including a new £75m, 85 metre yacht being built in Turkey, a £12m Falcon jet and his own hotel and chalet at Gstaad.

Despite this wealth, Ecclestone never carries a credit card and pays by cash. He is also a generous donor to charity, always anonymously, to the tune of around £50m a year. To his £1.9bn of earlier proceeds, we add at least £300m for his stake in Alpha Prema, and another £300m for other assets, taking Ecclestone to £2.5bn.

APPENDICES

The Rich List in alphabetical order

Name	Lifespan	Wealth £bn
Abbot, Sir Maurice	1565-1642	6.326
Abney, Sir Charles	1640-1722	3.329
Abramovich, Roman	1966	10.800
Albany, The Duke of	c1340-1420	3.440
Anglesey, The 4th Marquess of	1835-1898	3.329
Aquitaine, Eleanor of	c1122-1204	9.989
Arkwright, Richard	1755-1843	2.774
Arundel and Surrey, The Earl of	1346-1397	55.498
Arundel and Warenne, The Earl of	c1307-1376	59.382
Arundel, The Earl of	1381-1415	29.520
Auchi, Nadhmi	1937	2.575
Audley, Hugh	1577-1662	11.679
Backwell, Edward	d1683	7.325
Banks, Sir John	1627-1699	3.661
Barwell, William	d1769	2.880
Bayeux, Odo of	c1030-1097	55.498
Beauchamp, William, 1st Baron Bergavenny	1343-1411	9.329
Beaufort, Cardinal Henry	1375-1447	16.968
Becket, Archbishop Thomas	c1120-1170	24.641
Beckford, William	1709-1770	6.659
Bedford, The 9th Duke of	1819-1891	11.321
Beit, Alfred	1853-1906	4.816
Belleme, Robert of, The Earl of Shrewsbury	c1052-1130	17.759
Bishop of Salisbury, Roger	c1065-1139	7.878
Boleyn, Sir Geoffrey	d1463	3.107
Bowes, George	1701-1760	4.661
Bowles, Phineas	1690-1749	2.721
Brampton, Sir Edward	c1440-1508	3.884
Branson, Sir Richard	1950	3.100
Brassey, Thomas	1805-1870	3.884
Brembre, Sir Nicholas	d1388	3.884
Bridgewater, The 3rd Duke of	1736-1803	12.725
Buccleuch and Queensbury, The 5th Duke of	1806-1884	8.102
Buckingham, The Duke of	c1457-1483	18.425
Burley, Sir Simon	d1388	3.884
Bute, The 3rd Marquess of	1847-1900	4.661
Cade, William	d1166	7.325

Name	Lifespan	Wealth £bn
Cadogan, The 4th Earl	1812-1873	4.883
Cadogan, Earl & family	1946	2.610
Caledon, Baron	1730-1802	3.218
Campbell, Sir James	1570-1642	4.661
Campden, Viscount	1551-1629	9.212
Catesby, William	c1440-1483	2.996
Cavendish, The Hon. Henry	1731-1810	4.328
Cavendish, William, The 1st Duke of Newcastle	1592-1676	7.880
Cecil, Robert, Earl of Salisbury	1563-1612	4.883
Chandos, The Duke of	1673-1744	16.649
Chaucer, Thomas	c1367-1434	6.881
Child, Sir Francis	1642-1713	3.884
Child, Sir Josiah	1630-1699	6.659
Churchill, John, The 1st Duke of Marlborough	1650-1722	13.644
Clare, Elizabeth Lady of	c1294-1360	8.879
Clayton, Sir Robert	1629-1707	5.549
Cleveland, The Duke of	1766-1842	10.877
Clitherow, Sir Christopher	d1641	3.107
Clive, Robert 1st Baron Clive of Plassey	1725-1774	4.491
Clopton, Sir Hugh	d1496	4.106
Cokayne, Sir William	d1626	11.876
Colet, John	c1466-1519	3.440
Cook, Sir Thomas	c1410-1478	6.104
Cork, The 1st Earl of	1566-1643	15.761
Cornwall, Richard The Earl of	1209-1272	14.370
Courtenay, Archbishop William	1342-1396	3.662
Coutts, Thomas	1735-1822	3.583
Craggs, James	c1657-1721	20.804
Craven, Sir William	c1545-1618	5.337
Crawshay, Richard	1739-1810	5.517
Cromwell, Ralph The 3rd Lord	c1394-1456	12.980
Cutler, Sir John	c1608-1693	7.214
De Basing, Adam	1240s	2.854
De Carvalho, Michel & Charlene	1944 & 1954	3.050
De la Pole, Michael The Earl of Suffolk	c1330-1389	7.881
De la Pole, Sir William	d1366	12.760

Name	Lifespan	Wealth £bn
De Lucy, Richard	d1179	3.329
De Mandeville, Geoffrey	d1144	5.549
De Rokesle, Gregory	d1291	2.774
De Stern, Baron	1815-1887	3.440
Delaune, Gideon	c1561-1659	2.552
Denison, William	1770-1849	4.994
Denison, William	1713-1782	4.515
Derby, The Earl of	1508-1572	7.325
Des Rivaux, Peter	c1190-1262	6.659
Des Roches, Peter	d1238	5.882
Despencer, Henry	c1341-1406	3.662
Despencer, Hugh the Younger	d1326	17.759
Dorset, Marquess of	1451-1501	5.549
Downshire, The 5th Marquess of	1844-1874	2.885
Du Puiset, Bishop Hugh	c1120-1195	5.543
Dudley, The 1st Earl of	1817-1885	4.772
Duncombe, Sir Charles	d1711	5.882
Dundas, Sir Lawrence	c1710-1781	5.216
Ecclestone, Bernie	1930	2.500
Edwin, Sir Humphrey	1642-1707	2.774
Eldred, John	1552-1632	3.662
Ellerman, Sir John	1862-1933	10.877
Espec, Walter	d1158	3.662
Farquhar, John	1751-1826	3.861
Fastolf, Sir John	c1378-1459	11.321
Fermor, Richard	d1552	3.440
Fitzpeter, Geoffrey	d1213	9.989
Fitzwilliam, Earl	1815-1902	4.217
Flambard, Bishop Ranulf	1060-1128	22.190
Fludyer, Sir Samuel	c1705-1768	6.215
Foley, Thomas	1617-1677	2.885
Fox, Sir Stephen	1627-1716	3.884
Franks, Aaron	d1777	2.996
Garraway, Sir Henry	1575-1646	3.774
Gaunt, John of, The Duke of Lancaster	1340-1399	55.498
Gaveston, Piers	c1284-1312	5.549

Name	Lifespan	Wealth £bn
Gideon, Sampson	1699-1762	4.661
Glanvill, Ranulf	c1120-1190	11.099
Gloucester, The Duke of	1335-1397	22.190
Gloucester, The Earl of	1291-1347	4.440
Goldsmid, Sir Isaac	1778-1859	4.328
Green, Sir Philip & Lady	1952 & 1949	4.900
Gresham, Sir Richard	c1485-1549	7.325
Grey, Baron of Ruthin	d1353	4.439
Gurney, Sir Richard	1577-1647	3.107
Guy, Thomas	1644-1724	3.916
Halabi, Simon	1958	3.000
Halifax, The Marquess of	1633-1695	7.767
Heathcote, Sir Gilbert	c1651-1733	7.769
Hende, John	d1418	3.662
Hereford & Essex, The Earl of	1276-1322	6.659
Herne, Sir Joseph	c1639-1699	4.438
Hewett, Sir William	d1567	3.884
Hinduja, Gopi & Sri	1940 & 1935	6.200
Hoare, Sir Richard	1648-1718	2.880
Holland, John, The Duke of Exeter	1352-1400	18.420
Holland, Sir Robert	c1270-1329	4.106
Holles, John, The Earl of Clare	1564-1637	5.105
Hollond, William	c1750-1836	2.774
Howard, John, The 1st Duke of Norfolk	c1430-1485	9.212
Howard, Thomas, The 4th Duke of Norfolk	1536-1572	9.212
Hungerford, Lord	c1378-1449	8.102
Iveagh, The Earl of	1847-1927	3.662
Janssen, Sir Theodore	c1658-1748	13.874
Kent, The 1st Earl of	c1420-1489	6.104
Knollys, Sir Robert	c1317-1407	22.190
Lambton, William	1764-1797	4.994
Lancaster, Henry Earl of	c1281-1345	11.030
Lancaster, The Duke of	1299-1361	42.622
Lancaster, The Earl of	1245-1296	12.209
Langton, Bishop Walter	d1321	11.099
Latimer, Lord William	1330-1381	5.882
Lewis, Joseph	1937	2.800

Name	Lifespan	Wealth £bn
Lincoln, Aaron of	d1186	27.749
Loder, Giles	1786-1871	3.773
Londonderry, the 4th Marquess of	1805-1884	3.329
Lovell, Viscount	1454-c1487	5.993
Lowther, Sir James	1673-1755	16.427
Lyons, Richard	d1381	3.884
Mansel, John	d1265	4.994
Marshall, William	1147-1219	12.750
Mauny, Lord Walter	d1372	6.104
McCalmont, Hugh	c1810-1887	2.885
Melton, Archbishop William	d1340	4.217
Menahem, Elijah of	c1232-1284	2.885
Menthermer, Ralph Earl of Gloucester	d1325	8.324
Merton, Bishop Walter	c1205-1277	2.885
Meulan, Robert of, Lord of Beaumont and Earl of Leicester	1046-1118	12.653
Miles, Philip	1773-1845	2.774
Mittal, Lakshmi	1950	19.250
Moleyns, Sir John	d1361	6.104
Montagu, William The Earl of Salisbury	1301-1344	5.549
Morrison, James	1790-1857	7.214
Mortain, Robert of	c1031-1090	59.155
Mortimer, Roger Earl of March	1286-1330	10.605
Mowbray, Thomas, 1st Duke of Norfolk	1366-1399	9.296
Neville, Archbishop George	c1432-1476	7.880
Neville, Cecily, The Duchess of York	1415-1495	5.993
Newcastle, The Duke of	1693-1768	3.440
North, Sir Dudley	1641-1691	3.440
Norwich, Jurnet of	c1130-1197	7.981
Overstone, Lord	1796-1883	7.120
Page, Sir Gregory	1668-1720	8.324
Palavicino, Sir Horatrio	c1540-1600	4.994
Peel, Sir Robert	1750-1830	4.883
Pembroke, The Earl of	c1501-1570	7.325
Percy, Henry The 4th Earl of Northumberland	c1449-1489	9.212
Percy, Henry The 9th Earl of Northumberland	1564-1632	12.875
Percy, Henry The 1st Earl of Nortumberland	1341-1408	11.090

Name	Lifespan	Wealth £bn
Philipot, Sir John	d1384	7.880
Pindar, Sir Paul	c1565-1650	7.436
Portland, The 5th Duke of	1800-1879	8.768
Portman, The 1st Viscount	1799-1888	8.435
Pulteney, Sir John	c1290-1349	13.873
Pulteney, Sir William	1729-1805	12.133
Pulteney, William, Earl of Bath	1684-1764	14.896
Queensberry, The Duke of	1724-1810	5.549
Quinn, Sean & Family	1946	3.050
Radcliffe, Sir Richard	d1485	3.551
Ratcliffe, James	1952	3.300
Rausing, Hans & family	1926	5.400
Rausing, Kirsten & Jorn	1946 & 1960	2.825
Renger, Richard	d1239	3.884
Reuben, David & Simon	1939 & 1941	3.490
Reynardson, Sir Abraham	1590-1661	2.885
Rhys, The Lord	d1197	5.549
Rivers, Earl (1st)	1410-1469	12.653
Rivers, Earl (2nd)	c1442-1483	12.320
Rockingham, The Marquess of	1730-1782	4.217
Rothschild, Nathan Meyer	1777-1836	10.100
Rufus, Alan	d1093	81.331
Rundell, Philip	1746-1827	4.106
Rutland, The 6th Duke of	1815-1888	2.996
Sainsbury, Lord & Family	1940	2.500
Scott, John	1725-1775	3.107
Scrope, Sir Geoffrey	c1285-1340	2.595
Sevenoke, Sir William	c1378-1433	3.440
Shepheard, Samuel	c1648-1719	11.528
Smith, Erasmus	1611-1691	2.774
Spencer, Robert	d1627	19.091
Spencer, Sir John	d1610	21.311
Spring, Thomas	d1486	2.553
St John Mildmay, Sir Henry	1764-1808	2.885
Stafford, The Earl of	1593-1641	7.880
Strangways, Giles	1615-1675	3.107

Name	Lifespan	Wealth £bn
Stratton, Adam	d1294	8.324
Suffolk, The Duke of	1396-1450	16.747
Sutherland, The Duke of	1758-1833	21.421
Sutton, Thomas	1532-1611	6.548
The Black Prince, Edward	1330-1376	34.852
Thellusson, Peter	1737-1797	3.884
Thornton, Richard	1776-1865	3.995
Tiptoft, John, The Earl of Worcester	c1427-1470	7.880
Tufnell, John	1720-1794	2.508
Van Neck, Sir Joshua	1702-1777	2.996
Vestey, Lord	1859-1940	7.145
Viner, Sir Robert	1631-1688	7.325
Viner, Sir Thomas	1588-1665	2.774
Walter, Archbishop Hubert	1140-1205	9.989
Warenne, William of	d1088	73.923
Warren, Sir Peter	1703-1752	4.439
Warren, Sir Ralph	c1486-1553	2.996
Warwick, The Earl of	1382-1439	33.631
Warwick, The Earl of	1428-1471	15.761
Wedgwood, Josiah	1730-1795	2.518
Wernher, Sir Julius	1850-1912	5.902
Western, Thomas	c1624-1707	3.661
Westminster, The Duke of	1825-1899	9.656
Westminster, The 6th Duke of	1951	7.000
Westmoreland, The Earl of	1354-1425	8.648
Wharton, The Marquess of	1648-1715	3.662
Williamson, James, Baron Ashton	1842-1930	2.996
Wills, Sir George	1854-1928	2.663
Wiltshire, The Earl of	c1420-1461	6.326
Wolsey, Cardinal Thomas	c1473-1530	11.099
Wyche, Richard	1554-1621	3.662
Yule, Sir David	1858-1928	4.005

Key dates in the growth of private wealth

Date	Event
1066-90	William I conquered England and rewarded his followers with large but scattered estates throughout the country, augmented by later conquests in the north of England and in Wales.
c1193	The City of London was already a flourishing commercial centre by the time of the election of the first Mayor, Henry Fitzailwin, and, indeed, London had semi-independent status.
By 1216-63	Eight intermarried mercantile families produced 45 aldermen.
1327	After a long period of turmoil, the City of London ceased to be subject to direct royal interference.
1361	First fortune of £100,000 or more – The Duke of Lancaster
1397	Richard Whittington established the London Cloth Fair.
1610	First business fortune of £500,000 – Sir John Spencer
1720	First British millionaire – James Brydges, Duke of Chandos, briefly during this year at the height of the South Sea Bubble.
1833	First British business fortune of £5m or more – The 1st Duke of Sutherland. He was followed in 1883 by Baron Overstone (£5.331m).

1872-75	The Return of Owners of Land: An official parliamentary listing of all landowners and their annual incomes from land (outside of London, which was excluded from the Return), revealed that the largest landowner in terms of acreage was the Duke of Sutherland (1,358,545 acres, chiefly in Sutherlandshire), while the richest in terms of landed income was the Duke of Buccleuch, £217,163. However, if London land had been included, the Duke of Westminster would have been worth £300,000 or more at that time.
1899	Death of the 1st Duke of Westminster, generally reputed to be worth £14m, and the richest man in Britain.
1909	Charles Morrison (1817-1909), son of James Morrison, left the first probated estate of £10m or more (actually £10,939,000).
1916	Sir John Ellerman (1862-1933), shipowner and financier, stated that he is worth £55m, by far the largest fortune in current terms ever known (though earlier wealth-holders left larger ones as a percentage of NNI). Ellerman left £37m when he died.
1963	The death of William Morris, Lord Nuffield (1877-1963), automobile manufacturer, who left £3.5m but reputedly gave away £36m to charities and educational causes.
1969	The *New York Times* claimed that Viscount Cowdray was worth £100m.
Mid 1970s	The wealthiest property developers like Harry Hyams were reputed to be worth over £100m.
1980s onwards	Development of the annual *Sunday Times* Rich Lists, edited by Philip Beresford, which greatly increased data about and visibility for the very rich in Britain. The richest persons in Britain topped the billion pound mark.
2005	The first £10bn plus fortune when steel tycoon Lakshmi Mittal headed *The Sunday Times* Rich List worth £14.8bn.
2007	Mittal's fortune near to £20bn.

The Rules of Engagement

1.	The 250 richest people in Britain of all time have been selected from the time of William the Conqueror until the present day. Figures were virtually non-existent before the Conquest. After William took the throne, figures for wealth and land ownership gradually improve. But the further we go back over the last millennium, information becomes less reliable and scant.
2.	It must be emphasised that the pre-1800 sources do not provide comprehensive lists of the names of the wealthiest people in Britain at that time. It is possible, even likely, that some persons have been omitted who should have been included in this list, especially if they attracted no attention from contemporaries or from later historians, but we have hopefully included every person who was hugely wealthy. From around 1800 onwards, we are reasonably confident about the accuracy of the figures because of the comprehensive nature of the probate records and other sources.
3.	In order to put the 250 in a ranking order by wealth at today's prices, we took each individual's wealth at their death or his/her estimated peak value, whichever was higher. This figure was then compared to the estimated Net National Income (NNI) at the time. All pre-1800 figures for NNI are subject to significant margins of error, with medieval figures obviously being merely estimates by today's economic historians, based upon such sources as have survived and assumptions about the British economy at the time. The NNI figures did not rise at a uniform rate as Britain became more prosperous. War, Plague (particularly the Black Death of the fourteenth century) and economic crisis took its toll, but generally there was a gradual increase over time.
4.	We then took that percentage share of NNI for each individual and multiplied the figure by the current, estimated gross domestic product for Britain at the start of 2007. This figure was £1,065bn. This then gave us each individual's wealth at prevailing prices. As the list shows, this gives some enormous figures for some of the very early wealthy nobility who commanded large percentages of the NNI at the time. We did not try to adjust the figures for smaller economies or different economic or social conditions at the time. It was simply impossible to determine what sort of adjustments to make and where to draw the line. The uniformity of the calculation does provide for consistency and shows just how powerful – and wealthy – some of the very early Britons were, albeit in much smaller and more primitive economies. No one in the nineteenth or twentieth centuries makes it near the top of the list. The reason is simple: as the economy grew much faster in the nineteenth and twentieth centuries, the NNI figure grew and the percentage shares commanded by one individual fell as the growth in the personal wealth of multimillionaires did not keep pace. We might term this the democratisation of wealth.

5.	Our valuations were always made on the low side of any reasonable range of estimates, unless there was clear evidence for a higher figure, and should be regarded as possible underestimates in some cases. For instance, contemporary estimates of the wealth of Sir John Spencer (d 1610), who was known as 'Rich Spencer' and was the wealthiest merchant of his time, ranged from £500,000 to £800,000. We have taken the lower of these figures, and Spencer's wealth could have been far higher. We have done this for all the entries.
6.	Landed aristocrats who were rich over several generations were a particular problem. We could have swamped the list with several Earls of Shrewsbury or Earls of Arundel, to name but two families. Instead we chose either the richest or most influential and tried to mention other later or earlier generations for the same family in one entry. Where a dukedom has ended in one family and later been granted by the monarch to another family, then the same title may appear twice. The two Dukes of Newcastle are an example of this.
7.	Prior to the nineteenth century, no comprehensive lists of wealthy people were produced. We gathered names from a wide variety of sources, especially: The on-line edition of the *Oxford Dictionary of National Biography*, The Complete Peerage, *The History of Parliament*, Alfred Beaven's *Alderman of the City of London*, and Geoffrey Treasure's *Who's Who in British History: Beginnings to 1901*. A wide variety of monographs were used. For the medieval period these included: KB MacFarlane's 'The Nobility of Medieval England', S. Thrupp's 'The Merchant Class of Medieval London', and GA Holmes' 'The Estates of the Higher Nobility in the Fourteenth Century'. For the early modern period down to 1800 these included: Lawrence Stone's 'The Crisis in The Aristocracy', PJ Marshall's 'East India Fortunes', Valerie Pearl's 'London at the Outbreak of the English Civil War', FF Foster's 'The Politics of Stability', JR Woodhead's 'The Rulers of London', Garry Stuart DeKrey's 'A Fractured Society', Peter Throrold's 'The London Rich', as well as scholarly articles by Richard Grassby, Nicholas Rogers and David Joslin. For the nineteenth century, the previous research by WD Rubinstein was the chief source, especially 'British Millionaires, 1809-1949' in 'The Bulletin of the Institute of Historical Research' (1974) and 'Men of Property: The Very Wealthy in Britain Since the Industrial Revolution'. These were supplemented by *The Dictionary of Business Biography, History of Parliament, Ancestral Houses, Great Houses of Britain*, and John Bateman's *Great Landowners of Great Britain and Ireland* (1884). The post-1980s research was based on the work of Philip Beresford in successive *Sunday Times* Rich Lists. *The Oxford Dictionary of National Biography* (ODNB), published in sixty-five volumes in 2004, gives a figure for the wealth at death of many of its entries. By using its superb on-line edition, it was possible to construct a list of many of the richest persons in the past. We should stress that the ODNB merely supplemented our previous research, and that the great majority of the richest Britons noted in this work were identified by us before the ODNB was published. Nevertheless, it was an invaluable aid.

8.	Figures for NNI were taken from NJ Mayhew's 'Population, Money Supply and the Velocity of Circulation in England, 1300-1700' (*Economic History Review* 1995); Graeme Donald Snooks' 'The Dynamic Role of the Market in the Anglo-Norman Economy and Beyond 1086-1300' in Richard H. Britnell and Bruce M. Campbell, eds, *A Commercialising Economy* (1995); B.R. Mitchell and Phyllis Deane's *Abstract of British Historical Statistics* (1971) and David Butler and Gareth Butler's *British Political Facts 1900-1994*. We are grateful to Dr. Phillipp (sic) Schofield (University of Wales, Aberystwyth) and Professor John Hatcher (Corpus Christi College, Cambridge) for information on sources.
9.	Land valuation figures prior to the nineteenth century are a multiple of the estimated net annual landed income. Prior to c1350, this is taken as ten years' purchase (i.e. the net landed income is multiplied by ten to arrive at its capital value); from c1350-c1500 at twenty years' purchase; since c1500 at thirty years' purchase. These multiples are commonly used by economic historians.
10.	Non-landed wealth, where this was not known from contemporary estimates was derived from an estimated retained portion of maximum income, generally about one-third for the highest five years. For many merchants and others, however, estimates of peak wealth or wealth at death does exist and this figure was used if it appeared accurate.
11.	From 1809, figures are generally taken from the probate valuation of wealth left at death, with an addition for the capitalised value of any land owned (land was not included in the probate valuation figures in the nineteenth century, only personalty) derived from Bateman's *Great Landowners* (the 1884 edition where the figures relate to 1882), and from a scholarly article with estimates for the landed incomes of the major London landowners in the early 1890s by Professor Peter Lindert. London was not included in Bateman's impressive work. Some supplementation was made to these figures when they were known to be incomplete. Post-1980 figures were taken from *The Sunday Times* Rich Lists.
12.	Reigning monarchs are not included in these figures, although their close relatives are. It is virtually impossible, and almost meaningless, to attempt to estimate the wealth of, say, William the Conqueror, who may be said to have 'owned' the whole of England.

INDEX